Cloud Attack Vectors

Building Effective Cyber-Defense Strategies to Protect Cloud Resources

Morey J. Haber
Brian Chappell
Christopher Hills

Apress®

Cloud Attack Vectors: Building Effective Cyber-Defense Strategies to Protect Cloud Resources

Morey J. Haber
Lake Mary, FL, USA

Brian Chappell
Basingstoke, Hampshire, UK

Christopher Hills
Gilbert, AZ, USA

ISBN-13 (pbk): 978-1-4842-8235-9
https://doi.org/10.1007/978-1-4842-8236-6

ISBN-13 (electronic): 978-1-4842-8236-6

Managing Director, Apress Media LLC: Welmoed Spahr
Acquisitions Editor: Susan McDermott
Development Editor: Laura Berendson
Coordinating Editor: Jessica Vakili

Distributed to the book trade worldwide by Springer Science+Business Media New York, 233 Spring Street, 6th Floor, New York, NY 10013. Phone 1-800-SPRINGER, fax (201) 348-4505, e-mail orders-ny@springer-sbm.com, or visit www.springeronline.com. Apress Media, LLC is a California LLC and the sole member (owner) is Springer Science + Business Media Finance Inc (SSBM Finance Inc). SSBM Finance Inc is a **Delaware** corporation.

For information on translations, please e-mail booktranslations@springernature.com; for reprint, paperback, or audio rights, please e-mail bookpermissions@springernature.com.

Apress titles may be purchased in bulk for academic, corporate, or promotional use. eBook versions and licenses are also available for most titles. For more information, reference our Print and eBook Bulk Sales web page at http://www.apress.com/bulk-sales.

Any source code or other supplementary material referenced by the author in this book is available to readers on the Github repository: https://github.com/Apress/Cloud-Attack-Vectors. For more detailed information, please visit http://www.apress.com/source-code.

Printed on acid-free paper

This book is unsecure. It contains unencrypted data at rest and in transmission.

—Morey

To Ruth, my parents, my friends, and colleagues for all the support and love over the years.

—Brian

---

*You merely adopted the dark; I was born in it.
– To my wife Heidi, for all the years it took to pull me to the dark side. Thank you.*

—Chris

Table of Contents

About the Authors

Morey J. Haber

BeyondTrust, Chief Security Officer

Morey J. Haber is the Chief Security Officer at BeyondTrust. He has more than 25 years of IT industry experience and has authored four related books: *Privileged Attack Vectors, Asset Attack Vectors, Identity Attack Vectors*, and this one – *Cloud Attack Vectors*. He is a founding member of the industry group Transparency in Cyber and in 2020 was elected to the Identity Defined Security Alliance (IDSA) Executive Advisory Board.

Morey currently oversees BeyondTrust security and governance for corporate and cloud-based solutions and regularly consults for global periodicals and media. He originally joined BeyondTrust in 2012 as a part of the acquisition of eEye Digital Security, where he served as a Product Owner and Solutions Engineer since 2004. Prior to eEye, he was Beta Development Manager for Computer Associates, Inc. He began his career as Reliability and Maintainability Engineer for a government contractor that built flight and training simulators. He earned a Bachelor of Science degree in Electrical Engineering from the State University of New York at Stony Brook.

If you ever meet Morey in person and want to strike up a conversation, just lead in with science fiction or Star Trek. That is an instant hook and the source for many of the corny jokes throughout this book.

Brian Chappell

BeyondTrust, Chief Security Strategist

Brian Chappell is Chief Security Strategist at BeyondTrust. During over 35 years of IT experience, he has held senior positions in both the vendor and the customer spaces including organizations such as Amstrad plc, BBC Television, GlaxoSmithKline, and, of course, BeyondTrust. Through over 10 years at BeyondTrust, Brian has been a Sales Engineer, Director of Sales Engineering, Senior Director of Solutions Architecture, Director of Product Management, and now focuses on security strategies and new technologies within the Office of the CSO. Brian can also be found speaking at conferences, authoring articles and blog posts, and commenting on cybersecurity in the media. Outside of work, Brian can be found horse riding, developing software, gaming (loving VR racing currently), and learning obscure facts.

By the way, if you ever meet Brian and want to learn more about him, this book, or anything in any way related to cybersecurity, he likes whisky or gin and particularly people who buy them for him (shamelessly paraphrased from the late great Terry Pratchett [X-Clacks-Overhead: GNU Terry Pratchett] – if you know, you know). It's still worth a try.

Christopher Hills
BeyondTrust, Chief Security Strategist

Christopher Hills is Chief Security Strategist at BeyondTrust. He has more than 18 years of IT experience, which started when he was in the navy. Following his nine-year naval career, he moved to Arizona, where he finished his degree in Network Engineering Technology and graduated with honors as valedictorian. Following graduation, Chris went from working with the State of Arizona on their Bioterrorism network as a Systems Administrator to consulting on state contracts as a jack-of-all-trades.

Prior to joining BeyondTrust, Chris was a customer at a large financial institution as a Technical Director, leading everything related to PAM security, maturity, architecture, and operations. During the last two and a half years of his nine-year tenure, he had the opportunity to work with BeyondTrust, implementing several security solutions in Microsoft ESAE Architecture. Chris' transition to BeyondTrust landed him as a Senior Solutions Architect while the Office of the CTO was built. He transitioned to Deputy CTO and then acquired the Deputy CISO title a year later. Chris finds himself most comfortable in front of people. Teaching and sharing knowledge are two of his passions. He finds himself at home bridging the gaps between sales, technology, and customers.

When you meet Chris, start a conversation about speedboats, time on the water, and off-road racing. If he is not playing in the dirt or water, you'll find him supporting his youngest son's football passion.

Darran Rolls

Darran Rolls has a long history in Identity Management and Security at IBM Tivoli Systems, Waveset Technologies, Sun Microsystems, and SailPoint. Over the past 20 plus years, Darran has helped design, build, and deliver groundbreaking technology solutions that have shaped the Identity and Access Management industry. Darran served as SailPoint's Chief Technology Officer for 12 years, and he spent 4 years as the company's Chief Information Security Officer. Darran oversaw SailPoint's internal security and compliance. He also led SailPoint's successful IPO in late 2017.

Today, Darran is an investor, advisor, and industry specialist, working with vendors, customers, and financial institutions to help them understand and take full advantage of the latest identity and security technologies. He works closely with a portfolio of growth companies to design and deliver the next generation of IAM solutions worldwide. In 2020, Darran was awarded the title of Research Fellow with the leading identity and security analyst firm, KuppingerCole, where he now assists the team with directed research projects.

Darran has been a frequent contributor to IAM standards at OASIS, the W3C, and the IETF for many years. He frequently speaks at industry events and to customers about IAM technologies and security solutions. Organizations and industry peers alike appreciate his unique vendor in/out perspective on designing, delivering, and deploying an identity-centric enterprise security architecture.

Greg Francendese
BeyondTrust, Graphics Designer

Greg Francendese is the brand graphic designer at BeyondTrust. Originally from Atlanta, GA, Greg now calls Chicago, IL, home. After graduating from the University of South Carolina, he has gained around 10 years of design experience, from print illustration to digital design and animation. His clientele ranges from retail companies like Sears and Walgreens to athletic companies like Varsity Spirit to local Chicago restaurants and shops. Greg joined BeyondTrust in 2019 as a junior graphic designer. He now is leading creative initiatives in the tech industry, amplifying customer events, and developing video content for cybersecurity issues. As a creative side hobby, he illustrates Chicago neighborhoods to sell at local gift shops.

About the Technical Reviewer

Derek Smith is available for training services for cybersecurity-, leadership-, and project management-related subjects. He teaches CISSP, Security+, CASP, and CySA+ as well as leadership-related courses.

Derek is also a Certified Financial Education Instructor^{SM}, has his Financial Literacy Certification (CFEI®), and is a Certified Personal Finance Consultant (CPFC) and Financial Coach.

Acknowledgments

Contributing Editor
Mathew Miller, Director, Content Marketing & SEO

A sincere thank you to:
Laura Bohnert, Content Marketing Manager
Greg Francendese, Graphics Designer
Joshua Miller, Customer Trust Manager
Anna Forman, Compliance Analyst
Justin Sparks, Director, IT Governance, Risk and Compliance
Amy Feldman, Compliance Analyst
John Titor, Faux CEO and Time Traveler
...for your technical knowledge, insight, and skills in helping to edit this book.

And a special thank you to:
Darran Rolls, for his opinion in the Foreword on the cloud and its future.

Foreword

(By Darran Rolls)

Collaboration

I've had the great pleasure of collaborating with Morey Haber for more years than we both probably care to mention. Over those years, our professional paths have crossed and intersected on several fronts. As CTOs at our respective identity management companies, we partnered and collaborated on client engagements, market events, and industry initiatives. Coming from separate "legs" of the now changing "three-legged stool of IAM," we have always shared a brotherhood of IAM orientation and a distinct passion for the delicate intricacies that surround the topics of privilege, access, and security controls. During my time at SailPoint, we counted BeyondTrust as a trusted partner, and I considered Morey a good friend.

Morey and I also shared the unique alignment of transitioning into formal CSO/CISO roles within those same companies. For us both, taking on responsibility for product and corporate security was a logical career progression and something of great value to our companies. We have since shared many stories on the significant challenges and unique opportunities that come from being responsible for security inside a security company.

Every CSO has a tough job, but being inside the "security chain" itself is a whole different story. As more recent security supply-chain vulnerabilities have shown, being a link in that chain drives a certain focus and concern for yourself and hundreds of others. *Under Attack* may not have been the rock band Abba's best-known single, but the title pretty much sums up the experience of being a CSO in today's increasingly complex and interdependent security supply chain.

Morey asked me to write the Foreword for this book because of another prior successful and rewarding joint collaboration. As I hope the reader will already know, in 2019, we co-authored the third book in this series, *Identity Attack Vectors: Implementing an Effective Identity and Access Management Solution.*[1] That book was both interesting to write and intellectually rewarding to work on with Morey. Our conversations during that book's writing were always a source of inspiration and motivation.

I've always found that when technical specialists from opposite corners of the same InfoSec "camp" come together in the center to "warm their hands" around the embers of a good IAM campfire, interesting things happen. Our unique perspectives, kept on track through the common thread of privileged access and entitlements, lead to what has been referred to as one of the industry's leading texts[2] on using IAM technologies to enhance the prevention, detection, and mitigation of cyberattacks.

Cloud Attack Vectors

In name or in concept, the cloud may seem like a distant, faraway place, both above and apart. But today, even though most significant cloud providers run separate hordes of servers in isolated server farms, in every sense, "the cloud" has become endlessly entwined with itself (from one cloud to another) and with the existing on-premise information technology (IT) operations. The cloud and "traditional on-premise

---

[1] https://link.springer.com/book/10.1007/978-1-4842-5165-2
[2] https://solutionsreview.com/identity-management/the-highest-rated-books-for-identity-management-engineers/

compute" are common bedfellows, as comfortable as Grandpa Joe and Grandma Georgina in *Charlie and the Chocolate Factory* by Roald Dahl. They are now so interrelated that they can only really be thought of as a single, end-to-end system.

The average enterprise data center is a complex mix of on-premise "legacy" systems, virtualized servers, and containerized complex web applications – all connected to and integrated with shared cloud infrastructure and cloud delivered Software as a Service (SaaS) applications (more on this later). As every IT practitioner knows only too well, today's innovation is tomorrow's legacy – so that mix of new and old goes on. Just like the books in this series, one builds upon the next until they make a stack. Our legacy systems support a hybrid cloud stack that employs a complex combination of on-premise and public cloud service elements.

All new and old systems contain data, privilege, and access that must be secured and managed throughout their life cycle. Quite literally, the "web of complexity" now spans cloud and enterprise. Ubiquitously adopted new-school CI/CD pipelines, DevOps, microservices, and an API-first economy have introduced an exponential level of complexity. This new, complex reality is littered with identities, user accounts, passwords, proxy access, keys, secrets, privileges, and fine-grained authentication and authorization access policies.

New cloud infrastructure entitlement models are shockingly complicated to understand and manage. They inevitably have data, access, and privileges bouncing back and forth across what can accurately be described as the IT blood-brain barrier. This security configuration and resulting IAM stuff, spanning cloud and on-premise, must all be accounted for, tracked, and managed, if we have any hope of retaining control.

In this, the latest book in what can only be referred to as "Morey's Attack Vector Series," the authors look across that cloud stack, with an IAM-centric eye, and carefully consider the people, the process, and the technology required to mitigate a myriad of potential issues.

Cloud Attack Vectors adds to the series of asset, privilege, and identity texts to focus on the essential cloud elements that live under, over, and inside everything we now do in enterprise computing. As you will observe, the more things change, the more they stay the same. This theme undeniably links the disciples from on-premise to the cloud, but breaks away from traditional best practices to resolve the same threats we have struggled with for years.

DevOps and DevSecOps (SecDevOps)

Today, most development organizations follow core DevOps principles and best practices in their application and software development processes, especially when creating applications for the cloud. In a DevOps approach, the overall application context is not delivered as a single whole. Instead, it is developed and delivered iteratively based on "modules and dependencies" that come together on a cadence that often goes down to the hourly level. Finding security vulnerabilities in such a complex, dynamic, and modular process requires focus. It is, therefore, no wonder that security is one of the core tenets of any DevOps process or system.

Each part of the application development, test, and operations life cycle is, by convention, responsible for understanding and managing the necessary security measures that ensure minimum vulnerability, while maximizing protection, detection, and mitigation. DevSecOps logically becomes the overarching methodology that unifies and coordinates the various security tools required during the DevOps life cycle.

Any high school–level cybersecurity textbook will quote the mantra, "application development starts and finishes with security." DevOps people, processes, and technology are intended as the unification of that directive. Hopefully, removing the potential "security silos" that inevitably develop within a dynamic, independent, but highly interdependent application delivery process results in the inclusion of security in the same model. Hence, DevSecOps is now responsible in every sense. DevSecOps teams choose the tools that track and monitor their usage. DevSecOps engineers must understand the nuances of asset, privilege, access, and identity in their "new stacks" and their "existing legacy."

In the cloud, DevSecOps is an attack vector – every part of the application development life cycle is poised to protect against cyber threats. This leads me to some "truisms" for consideration.

Perpetual Truths

One of the greatest things about writing the Foreword to this book is that I don't have to hunker down and cook the full course meal – only the appetizer! I get the privilege and convenience of creating an abstract.

Having been in systems administration and, more specifically, security delivery for most of my 30-plus-year career in IT, I find great significance and considerable discomfort in the fact that nothing really seems to change that much. Of course, everything changes on the ground, in practice, in tools, and in approach, but somehow, it always stays the same.

So many of the lessons I learned from the "old mainframe guys" when I first started doing system administrative work have remained true. As I myself have worked through the coming and going of client–server, everyone gets a desktop (PC), Web 2.0, and now cloud and SaaS, so much has changed, but so much of what needs to be done to create good identity and good security has changed very little.

The cyclic nature of the underlying elements of IT is fascinating. The repeating cycle of distribution and re-centralization of systems design has already played out many times. The perpetual balance of homogeneity and heterogeneity has played out time and time again over the years. And, sadly, this perpetual cycle of innovation introduces complexity that is the ultimate enemy of all security systems.

These ever-repeating "trends" and their resulting costs are a source of career stability and, ultimately, intellectual frustration for many in IT. The fact that "everything is new, but nothing ever changes" personally drives me just a little crazy! As a programmer at heart, I hate repetition without automation. I can live with "Groundhog Day" if all I do is press the "replay" button without having to do it all from scratch every time.

Unfortunately, all too often, security program design and spending learn little from their past experiences. I never like to use the sour words of recent breach reporting as a proof point, but you've read the tech press lately, right? The phrase "shit happens" is a universal truth, and "here but for the grace of God go I..." is a secular truism. But that said, we should always look for the "perpetual truths," the repeating memes, or "rules to live by" that sit above the changing drivers of security program spending. Some things do stay the same.

Visibility Is a Quintessential Control

Someone early in my career, probably at Tivoli Systems before it was merged into IBM (and, as I recently learned, a competitor to Morey when he was at Computer Associates managing teams with Unicenter), once said to me, "always remember you can't manage what you can't see." This has remained true for me throughout my time at Waveset, Sun Microsystems, and at SailPoint.

Visibility is the baseline for any security control. An extensive, stable, and dependable discovery and inventory process is, therefore, the cornerstone of any asset, privilege, identity, or cloud security program. Any person, process, or technology in the IT security space should always start with asset management. Understand the scope, assess the weaknesses, and plan the mitigation. *Cloud Attack Vectors* follows this same principle, and Chapter 6 highlights the tools and techniques that help you get there from the weakest point – the people.

Doors and Corners

If you're a science fiction fan, as I am (if you haven't read "The Expanse"[3] series of novels by James Corey), the term "Doors and Corners" will conjure up images of the crusty old Belter cop "Miller" as his ghostly figure laments the best approach to entering a dangerous room. That reference neatly codifies the perpetual truth that security weakness is always in the forgotten corners of complex systems design and, therefore, an unexplored attack vector until it is exploited.

In today's complex, cloud-delivered systems, the vulnerability is often exposed and exploited via something simple that was overlooked or forgotten. All too often, post-breach forensic analysis highlights a misconfiguration or an untracked dependency at fault lurking in that dark corner, ready to jump out and eat you up!

As we perpetually expand the footprint and integrated scope of cloud-based and cloud-integrated systems, we continually add new corners and new doorways that must be documented, assessed, and, ultimately, protected. The universal truth in this statement is simply knowing where the doors and corners are and taking the time (and the project scope) to "threat-model" their potential vulnerability (even if it can't be fully mitigated). Taking the time to play out the possibilities, model the threat scenarios, and walk through at least "a plan for a plan" is one of the most proactive and essential elements of a cloud security program.

---

[3] www.amazon.com/Expanse-Hardcover-Boxed-Set-Leviathan/dp/0316536466/ ref=asc_df_0316536466/?tag=hyprod-20&linkCode=df0&hvadi d=385629070985&hvpos=&hvnetw=g&hvrand=14559134387710751485&hvpon e=&hvptwo=&hvqmt=&hvdev=c&hvdvcmdl=&hvlocint=&hvlocphy=9011759&h vtargid=pla-841586555466&psc=1&tag=&ref=&adgrpid=78303888146&hv pone=&hvptwo=&hvadid=385629070985&hvpos=&hvnetw=g&hvrand=-14559134387710751485&hvqmt=&hvdev=c&hvdvcmdl=&hvlocint=&hvlocphy=9011 759&hvtargid=pla-841586555466

Complexity: The Sworn Enemy of Security

A podcast I highly recommend tuning into is Steven Gibson's *Security Now*.[4] Steve is a long-time programmer, hacker, technologist, and security practitioner who's been a regular on my subscription list for many years. Steve has a repeating meme that has been a mantra for me in my time designing, delivering, and securing systems: Gibson always says, and I quote, "complexity is the enemy of security." Oh boy, that is never more true than when deploying cloud and SaaS at scale. Remember, complexity creates the doors and corners where vulnerabilities lurk. Complexity in composition, configuration, and deployment is a likely cause in most attack vectors – cloud or otherwise.

To continue the somewhat curmudgeonly theme of this Foreword, I'm horrified and perpetually amazed by the level of complexity that I see in modern systems and infrastructure design. Any application that merges on-premise, private cloud, and SaaS is an Eddie Krueger[1] poster child for complex configuration. Of course, I fully understand and appreciate the need for that configuration capability, especially in an infrastructure-to-application "as code" model like today's cloud.

But have we now gone hog wild? Just take a look at the manual pages for a K8 (Kubernetes) control verb, read through the security model settings for a Salesforce application, or worse, crack open the complexity of the end-to-end authorization model in AWS. It's nothing short of mind blowing.

The IAM model that spans these systems is cut from the same complex hyper-weave cloth. One would have thought that, in the post-SAML and OAuth2 world, newer applications would, at least, have a unified authentication. Sadly, this unified, seamless experience rarely exists.

For example, I recently reviewed the IAM model deployed at a major retail bank. In just one of their complex systems, I counted five different

---

[4] Security Now (Audio) itunesu_sunset - Apple Podcastshttps://podcasts.apple.com › podcast › security-now-au...

forms of authentication spanning account passwords, keys, tokens, scopes, and attribute policies. Ouch – and let the pain sink in. The picture for authorization in these systems is often worse, with profiles, groups, roles, ABAC, PBAC, and OAuth scopes all hard-coded into an end-to-end system busting at the seams with rich complexity. These IAM "crimes" are not crimes of end-user convenience; they are simply the innocent result of a multitiered cloud system that strives for flexibility and functional supremacy in architecture and implementation.

Trade-offs

The cloud is not all complexity and risk. Far from it. In many ways, it is also a unique and exceptionally powerful inflection point, a time to review, redesign, and re-implement when considering the transition.

Consolidation and simplification themes reign on the field marketing banners of just about every cloud and SaaS offering these days. I wholeheartedly subscribe to that philosophy. I will always trade reduced cost, simplification, and better security to live "inside the box" with less customization and more shared intelligence. This is where the application's use case stays the same, but the implementation can change for the better.

During my time as the CISO at a public company (yes, I could have said "when I was in the barrel"), like everyone, I had to make trade-offs. Trade-offs between vendors and applications, infrastructure and code, and cost and complexity. For me, the most powerful tool in that selection process was always the careful consideration of risk as a direct result of measured complexity. I've always come back to those memes or mantras that "you can't manage what you can't see" and balancing functionality with simplicity and security. Hopefully, this concept will remain true and valuable to you; it always has for me.

Have fun learning from the rest of the book.

—Darran

CHAPTER 1

Introduction

Imagine a cool, sunny spring day: an adult and a child are strolling through the park. The sky is blue and filled with puffy, white cumulus clouds. The child turns to the adult and asks, "What are clouds made of?" The adult, with a keen sense of subtle technical humor, replies, "My dear, mostly Linux servers; mostly…"

Here is where our book begins because even clouds in the sky are not always as benign as they might appear. They can be dangerous, proffering lightning, wind, and heavy rain when environmental conditions are ripe for a storm. Clouds used for computing can be just as dangerous. This is often the case when we do not understand associated attack vectors (excessive privileges, vulnerabilities, etc.) and how they can be exploited.

Today, as social distancing initiatives fade, a more flexible hybrid work environment is taking root (pun intended), primarily in the cloud – the "new normal" is here. Strolls in the park are more frequent as we begin to embrace a work-from-anywhere (WFA) world. While a lingering uncertainty remains over the ultimate course of the pandemic, one thing is clear: we will need new information technology, security, and processes to accommodate the health and well-being of employees while enabling diverse use cases.

The *Wall Street Journal* article, "Why the Hybrid Workplace Is a Cybersecurity Nightmare," articulated pervasive IT security fears about the hybrid workplace. It also briefly called out how organizations can address these fears – with strong, identity-centric security and zero trust.

© Morey J. Haber, Brian Chappell, Christopher Hills 2022
M. J. Haber et al., *Cloud Attack Vectors*, https://doi.org/10.1007/978-1-4842-8236-6_1

Both zero trust and identity-centric security will loom large in our ensuing cloud attack vectors discussions throughout this book. In addition, a McKinsey study[1] reported that organizations responded to the pandemic by reprioritizing digitization of their customer and supply-chain interactions, and their internal operations, by three to four years. McKinsey also found that the share of digitally enabled products in an organization's portfolio has been accelerated by a remarkable seven years (against a baseline of growth seen in 2017–2018). As McKinsey summed up, "Digital adoption has taken a quantum leap at both the organizational and industry levels."

In today's world, remote workers regularly connect from unsecure home or public Wi-Fi networks. Those workers are using personal devices for a number of reasons, including convenience, to keep business costs down or simply due to supply-chain shortages. Many users have self-provisioned various apps (often referred to as "Shadow IT") to be productive at home or as they work from anywhere. Remote access technologies, like virtual private networks (VPN) and remote desktop protocol (RDP), are routinely (and frighteningly) being stretched for use cases far beyond what is secure and are often implemented hurriedly in insecure ways. It is easier than ever for attackers to find the gaps and deliver malicious payloads, including ransomware, via the Internet to the cloud and to assets operating remotely.

During this period of accelerated digital transformation, the cloud attack surface has grown exponentially. Today, most organizations are not merely in "a" cloud – they are in many clouds using many services (PaaS, IaaS), and their end users consume ever more SaaS applications, many of which are occurring as Shadow IT. Information technology (IT) teams struggle to manage and control security across complex multiple cloud

---

[1] www.mckinsey.com/business-functions/strategy-and-corporate-finance/ our-insights/how-covid-19-has-pushed-companies-over-the-technology-tipping-point-and-transformed-business-forever

environments. Each cloud has its own shared responsibility model and native toolsets. Additionally, most companies are not 100% cloud; they work within a hybrid model that includes an on-premise infrastructure, often including legacy technology that cannot be secured with modern best practices.

Yet, while digital transformation has experienced an evolutionary quantum leap (including quantum computing services in the cloud), so too has the cyber threat landscape. The problem is that cybersecurity controls and strategies have not experienced similar growth in their maturity, like the move to the cloud itself.

Security exposures, gaps, and vulnerabilities are increasing exponentially. Without question, this is playing a pivotal role in the spectacular scope and number of cybersecurity incidents and breaches since late 2020. SolarWinds, Verkada, Colonial Pipeline, JBS, Kaseya, and a relentless scourge of crippling ransomware attacks are recent examples of threats endangering supply chains. These attacks affect the daily lives of millions of people. All of these breaches were made possible by attacks executed through the Internet that targeted cloud resources.

The rapid acceleration of digital transformation has tipped the scales of the perpetual cyber arm's race decidedly favoring cybercriminals and adversarial foreign nations. The United States' Federal Bureau of Investigation (FBI) received a record-breaking 791,790 cybercrime complaints in 2020, according to the Bureau's 2020 Internet Crime Report (ICR).[2] The number of cybercrime complaints made by victims surged 69% year over year.

Over the years, organizations have increasingly been forced to buy cyber insurance to help protect against the financial costs of cyberattacks, most notably, ransomware. Sometimes, the purchase of cyber insurance is contractually obligated. However, the blistering pace and expanding scope of cyber threats and ransomware attacks have prompted cyber insurance providers to steeply increase their premiums, mandate specific security

---

[2] https://www.ic3.gov/Media/PDF/AnnualReport/2020_IC3Report.pdf

controls, demand greater proof of security maturity from their customers, and even drop coverage entirely for high-risk organizations. Some cyber insurance providers are exiting the industry altogether.

The era of multicloud environments and WFA (work from anywhere) has also become the era of "assume breach" and "it will happen to us." Clearly, we need to rethink security and recalibrate for what and where it is being offered.

Threat actors no longer need to be sophisticated to conduct malicious activity. Attackers can leverage powerful, free tools, such as Shodan, to find unprotected cloud assets and associated accounts. Control planes, which govern the entire cloud infrastructure, are often inadequately locked down or exposed to the Internet, leaving them vulnerable to brute-forcing attacks and other emerging exploits. Lack of proper controls also results in misconfigurations that can cause outages or expose buckets of data to anyone looking for them. All of these will be defined, explored, and have mitigation strategies presented later in this book.

As proof, threat activities waged on cloud services by external actors surged 630% in early 2020, according to McAfee's Cloud Adoption and Risk Report.[3] McAfee also reported that the average organization used 1,935 cloud services, which helps explain the expanding risk surface problem.

In the cloud, the following attack vectors form the basis for almost all attacks:

- Insecure remote access (RDP, VPN, Secure Shell [SSH], FTP, Telnet, etc.)

- Unpatched vulnerabilities (including ones like Log4J that affect almost everyone)

- Stolen, default, or compromised credentials and secrets used for authentication

---

[3] https://www.mcafee.com/enterprise/en-gb/lp/cloud/cloud-adoption-risk-report-business-edition.html

- Improperly managed, overly provisioned, or compromised privileged accounts and insecure privileged credentials

- Improper resource, asset, or application hardening

- Exposed data (insufficient encryption or improper storage)

- Social engineering of resources responsible for cloud resources

- Infiltration of malware causing ransomware or other attack vectors (file, fileless, or living off the land using native operating systems and commands)

- Insider threats, insiders that have gone rogue, insider execution or configuration errors, or insiders that have become unknowing cyber mules for third-party threat actors

- Supply-chain attacks serving as a beachhead into organizations based on their usage of a third-party solution

As we focus on the challenges of securing the cloud, we can correlate long-standing problems on-premise with problems in the cloud. In a study BeyondTrust conducted with Forrester Consulting,[4] surveyed organizations overwhelmingly predicted that the primary cause of future breaches would be the compromise of privileged accounts and their associated identities over the next two years. A follow-up question shed light on the "why" for this increase, digital transformation to the cloud. Figure 1-1 shows the results from a survey for the expected increase in privileged accounts.

---

[4] https://www.beyondtrust.com/resources/whitepapers/evolving-pim-forrester

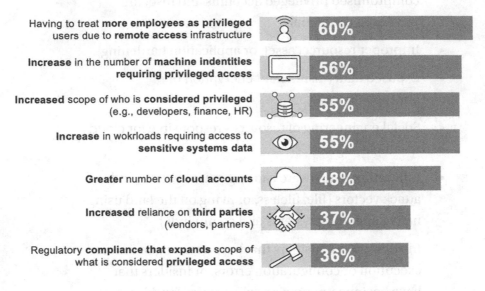

"Why do you except the number of privileged sessions (human or machine) within your organization to incresase in the next two years?"

Having to treat **more employees as privileged** users due to **remote access** infrastructure — **60%**

Increase in the number of **machine indentities requiring privileged access** — **56%**

Increased scope of who is **considered privileged** (e.g., developers, finance, HR) — **55%**

Increase in wokrloads requiring access to **sensitive systems data** — **55%**

Greater number of **cloud accounts** — **48%**

Increased reliance on **third parties** (vendors, partners) — **37%**

Regulatory **compliance that expands** scope of what is considered **privileged access** — **36%**

Base: 241 IT security & operations professionals in NA, EU, or APAC
Source: A commissioned study conducted by Forrester Consulting on behalf of BeyondTrust, June 2020

Figure 1-1. *Surveyed results on privileged accounts on behalf of BeyondTrust and Forrester Consulting*

This illuminates a pattern in current cloud attack vectors. It also shows where the technology community believes the next biggest failure will be. While we may be able to secure cloud technology and make it more resilient to cyberattacks, the interaction with humans, and from machine to machine, will continue to be the predominant attack vector for the foreseeable future.

The motivation behind these attacks is critical to understanding them. It has become big business for cybercriminals. According to Deloitte,[5] some common cybercrime businesses can be run for as little as $34 per month and could return $25,000 in the same time period. Put simply,

---

[5] https://www2.deloitte.com/us/en/pages/about-deloitte/articles/ press-releases/deloitte-announces-new-cyber-threat-study-on-criminal- operational-cost.html

cybercrime has a low barrier to entry, coupled with a potentially lucrative Return on Investment (ROI) – and it's generally all tax-free. Depending on where the cybercriminal organization is based, and whom they are targeting in their attacks, there is a great likelihood of avoiding government intervention.

In 2021, the average ransomware payout soared to $541,010 from $115,000 in 2019, according to a study by Palo Alto Networks[6]. We also saw numerous ransomware victims and their cyber insurers make eyepopping multimillion dollar payouts, including $4.4 million by Colonial Pipeline (some of which has since been recovered, thanks to the United States government) and $11 million by meat supplier JBS.

A report from the Identity-Defined Security Alliance (IDSA)[7] found that regular reviews of privileged access were the security control most cited (50% of respondents) to prevent or mitigate the breaches that the respondents experienced. Often, too much access is provisioned by default in the cloud, or the access is open ended (standing privileges), when it should only be provisioned just in time, when certain contextual parameters are met, and then revoked when the task or duration for acceptable access is complete.

This is the fourth book in the Attack Vector series.[8] The first book in this series, *Privileged Attack Vectors*,[9] started with the statement that most cyberattacks originate from outside the organization. As we see the ever-accelerating move to the cloud, more organizations are starting to build mitigation plans for cloud attack vectors. This is encouraging and

---

[6] https://unit42.paloaltonetworks.com/ransomware-threat-report-highlights/

[7] www.beyondtrust.com/resources/whitepapers/2021-trends-in-securing-digital-identities

[8] https://smile.amazon.com/s?k=Haber+attack+vectors&crid=123MDGYIA11DI&sprefix=haber+attack+vectors%2Caps%2C119&ref=nb_sb_noss

[9] https://link.springer.com/book/10.1007/978-1-4842-5914-6

disappointing in equal measure since both the origin of the threat and the attack surface being targeted lie outside the corporate environment, both of which should have raised alarm bells from day one.

Applications, data, and infrastructure are all being run outside of the perimeter on systems that are not owned, or even managed, by the organizations that own them. And as we jokingly said at the beginning of this chapter, the vast majority of cloud systems are based on Linux – limiting the variety of targets. As you can imagine, this has not gone unnoticed by the cybersecurity community (good guys and bad actors).

In reality, critical systems are now outside of the typical perimeter defenses – designed to stop the bad actor from gaining initial access to the corporate network. Teams trained to manage non-Windows resources are in high demand and, as such, constitute a significant staffing challenge when it comes to properly securing these Linux-based environments. These systems are also now accessible on the Internet and can allow logical connections from anyone, anywhere in the world. These systems are exposed once the cloud has been embraced as remote access is the only way to manage them.

What's more, given the critical nature of many of these assets and the volume of sensitive data within them, they present an irresistible honeypot (with real data) to anyone who can compromise them for their own nefarious mission.

CHAPTER 2

Cloud Computing

The move to cloud computing has accelerated rapidly in recent years, and there's no slowdown on the horizon. Organizations are moving their infrastructure, including mission-critical systems, out of their direct control and onto platforms that are delivered and supported by cloud service providers (CSP). When we consider the value of the data that's being processed and stored in the cloud, this is a move that might have seemed impossible, or at least very improbable, not so long ago.

After decades of building walls around our infrastructure to prevent the unauthorized from gaining access to our crown jewels, our data, and our intellectual property, we now move it wholesale onto systems that we have little or no direct control over. What does cloud computing offer that is of such value that it outweighs so many of the risks? Well, it offers us flexibility, both in structure and in cost.

In the early days of the Internet, a television commercial featuring your company URL could result in the website breaking under the sheer volume of traffic it generated. This was before Internet access was as ubiquitous as it now is, when the traffic was directed to a company-hosted web server within their own organization's data center (or co-opted cupboard). Companies could arrange to stand up extra web servers in their farm ahead of time to address those peaks. However, the servers and traffic to host them were still the responsibility and ownership of the company. Those servers would be physical servers with physical costs, both for the hardware and for the people required to build and commission them.

© Morey J. Haber, Brian Chappell, Christopher Hills 2022
M. J. Haber et al., *Cloud Attack Vectors*, https://doi.org/10.1007/978-1-4842-8236-6_2

And, when loads were light, they sat idle, becoming a sinkhole for the cost of their software, hardware, power, and cooling.

Another area of benefit from the cloud approach emerged when users required access to critical computing services while they were away from the office. Historically, organizations implemented various remote access mechanisms enabling employees to have access to the systems inside the infrastructure. Initially, these were phone-based, dial-up connections directly wired into the company network, before later being moved onto virtual private networks (VPN). I'm sure many of us remember the challenges of commissioning a VPN across an early Internet router with dial up. This process multiplied in difficulty when network address translation (NAT) emerged and became ubiquitous for appropriately routing traffic. As well as being difficult to set up and complex to manage, these connections offered direct connectivity into our corporate networks long before many realized the risk behind them.

Today, we have a multitude of cloud-based service types delivered on-demand and typically on a pay-as-you-go or consumption model. This model eliminates much of the capital expenditure involved in earlier approaches to the problems of scale and flexibility. Many of these services can be delivered and controlled through application programming interfaces (APIs), allowing for a high degree of automation, for example, responding to excessive website traffic by spinning up extra instances of a web server and shutting them down again when the demand subsides.

Cloud-based services are also commonly hosted entirely outside of the company network, allowing core services to be accessed from anywhere in the world without the need for a VPN. This is a much-improved experience for the average end user and a significantly reduced cost (and risk) to the organization.

As you can surmise from the "Introduction," privileged access plays a pivotal role in all aspects of cloud computing, from the administrators who set up and manage the cloud computing services to the processes that use the APIs to adapt the environment to the needs of the moment. Every stage has privileged access that offers the malicious actors the opportunity to disrupt operations, steal valuable data, or both. This occurs on top of the ever-present race to patch vulnerabilities before they are exploited.

As we continue to move our operations into the cloud, it is increasingly important to be conscious of our responsibilities in securing these solutions. Yes, every provider has the responsibility to deliver a safe and secure platform that you will use, but there is no doubt that this is where their responsibility ends. How you use that platform and ensure your organization's use of it is secure is still entirely your responsibility. To that end, the different ways you can use the cloud will help you formulate strategies for securely defending it from threats. Let's take a high-level tour through some of the more common cloud-based services.

Software As a Service

For many of us, Software as a Service (SaaS) is where the cloud became something new, not just someone else's computer. It is a model in which a service provider hosts one or more applications and makes them available to users on a subscription basis, often from a cloud-hosted location (or locations). This is a paradigm shift from the older, commercial off-the-shelf (COTS) approach, where software is bought on a perpetual license, installed and run locally by the organization themselves. The only similarity of COTS with a cloud-based service is the support and maintenance contract that supplies ongoing updates, upgrades, and break/fix support for running the software.

SaaS should not be confused with software licensed on a subscription basis but hosted by the purchaser, whether within their own infrastructure or in a rented third-party infrastructure. The applications provided via SaaS are commonly, but not exclusively, accessed using web browsers, though they can also be service-based to host distributed technology, like agents on end-user assets without the need for VPN or similar technologies.

The breadth of application types offered today in the cloud is immense, with examples such as

- Office 365 (office applications)

- Sage Accounting (business accounting)

- Salesforce (customer relationship management)

- SAP S/4HANA Cloud (enterprise resource planning [ERP])

- ServiceNow (service desk management)

- Okta (identity management)

- BeyondTrust (privileged access management [PAM])

- SailPoint (identity governance)

- Tenable (vulnerability management)

- Autodesk AutoCAD (computer-aided design)

Plus many, many more (The services and organizations listed are examples and not in any way endorsed by the authors).

Nearly all enterprise-level companies use SaaS solutions, and most use more than one, with some using thousands. For example, a medium-sized company like our employer, BeyondTrust, who has fully embraced the cloud, uses hundreds of SaaS applications spread across the entire business. That sounds like a lot until you look at the McAfee 2019 Cloud Adoption and Risk Report,[1] which gives the average number of distinct cloud services used by organizations as 1,935. That's nearly 2,000 services, on average, in use by every organization surveyed – the average IT team believed the number was closer to 30.

---

[1] www.mcafee.com/enterprise/en-us/forms/gated-form.html?docID=59d987b2-5df5-4fa2-a6b3-f9f7c204140f

Selecting the right SaaS vendor to solve each business need has deep roots in cost and potential cloud attack vectors. A pretty user interface or cool, unique technology certainly shouldn't be primary considerations. The focus should be on providing solid foundations, creating reliable and resilient implementations, and solving real business needs, underpinned by good value for money and transparent cybersecurity practices.

Some definitions and business requirements for SaaS also include the notion that the solution is multitenant, that is, a single implementation of the solution is used to provide service for many customers, while maintaining segregation between each customer for operations and their data. This is illustrated in Figure 2-1. (Note: This will be explored in more detail later in the book.)

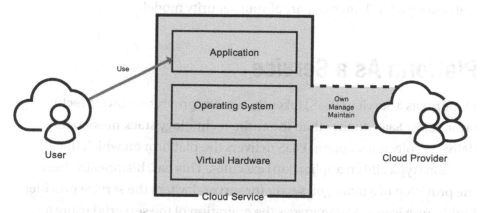

Figure 2-1. *Software as a Service responsibility scope*

Irrespective of tenancy model, licensing a SaaS application is arguably the most secure of the service provisions because the application (not necessarily the infrastructure) is entirely under the control of the SaaS provider. That said, poor password choices and misconfigured permissions can still lead to significant risks. The top attack vector for most SaaS-based solutions is a credential compromise, either at the user interface or an underlying API used for integrations or automation.

For example, APIs tend not to lock accounts when incorrect credentials or secrets are provided. Doing so would become a denial-of-service opportunity for threat actors to lock out services with multiple, deliberately incorrect, login attempts. This can be mitigated with ever-increasing delays in the response to bad credentials, offering some defense against brute-force and dictionary attacks, but such mechanisms shouldn't be relied upon as an exclusive defensive strategy. It does provide one illustration of why privileged accounts in this space should be managed with a commercial privileged account and session management (PASM) solution that automates the creation of long, random, complex passwords to mitigate this attack vector. This will be discussed in detail later in this book. For now, rest assured that password attacks and password management will remain a fundamental part of your security model.

Platform As a Service

Platform as a Service (PaaS) takes the service provision down a technology layer below SaaS. Rather than the entire technology stack needed to deliver a software solution, PaaS delivers the platform on which the solution (typically an application) executes. This has, historically, been the provision of a managed server (or servers) where the service provider builds, provisions, and manages the operation of the server(s) using a management and sustainment model. Users of the PaaS then build or install their applications on the platform and manage only the applications themselves, taking a significant portion of the effort and complexity involved off their shoulders and onto the PaaS service provider. More recently, PaaS has expanded to include container-based platforms and other serverless environments that host applications without excessive overhead. This is slightly different than Function as a Service, covered a little later.

Unfortunately, this is one of the scenarios where responsibility for security has become a potential source of contention. While the service provider manages the platform, the security of the platform, depending on application requirements, remains (unless explicitly indicated in the service contract) with the service user. Consider the two approaches in Figures 2-2 and 2-3.

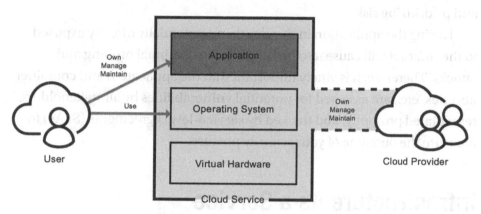

Figure 2-2. *End-user PaaS security responsibilities for operating systems*

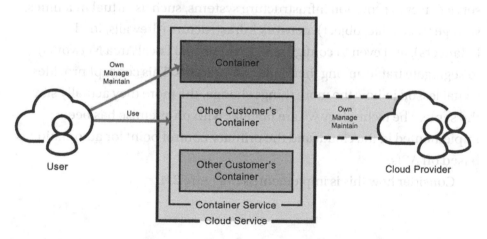

Figure 2-3. *End-user PaaS security responsibilities for containers*

15

Like SaaS solutions, PaaS is at risk from credential theft. Unlike SaaS, it is most at risk for un-remediated vulnerabilities or poor configuration management in the hosted application or the container management system. The risk for vulnerabilities in PaaS needs to be clearly defined when implementing a solution since multiple organizations and departments will ultimately share the responsibility of keeping it secure and prioritizing risk.

Having the application in the cloud and potentially directly exposed to the Internet will cause it to be subjected to continual probing and attacks. Therefore, it is vitally important that the application and container libraries, etc., are assessed for potential vulnerabilities by all stakeholders, remediated promptly, and tracked by service-level agreements (SLAs) to measure the outcome of your security posture.

Infrastructure As a Service

As we continue down the layers of services, we reach Infrastructure as a Service (IaaS). IaaS offers online services accessed via APIs that allow the service user to provision infrastructure systems, such as virtual machines, storage (block, file, object), network infrastructure (firewalls, load balancers), and even to configure VLANs (Virtual Local Area Networks) to segregate traffic among their IaaS components. This concept provides a vital lesson in how the more things change, the more they actually stay the same. The technology we are familiar with on-premise has been implemented in the cloud, and the primary control point for automation is based on APIs.

Consider how this is implemented in Figure 2-4.

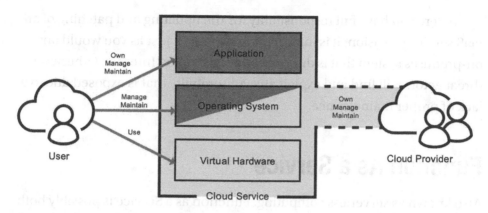

Figure 2-4. *IaaS implementation with end-user interaction*

In this service provision, the users don't manage the cloud infrastructure itself, but they do manage all the IaaS-provisioned systems that run on top of it.

It's important to be aware of the scope of responsibility you, as the user, have for each of the IaaS provisions you are using. If we start with what might commonly be called infrastructure, that is, network devices, you may have control over the configuration of those devices. You may be able to change the rules on a firewall or router, but you probably won't have control over the lowest levels of the devices themselves. This makes you more of a standard user than an administrator, in terms of privileges. Similarly, with virtual machines, you will probably have control over the entire operating system running on the VM and the maintenance of it, but no access to the underlying hypervisor or the virtual hardware configuration.

As you can see, for each IaaS provision, it's important to understand what you control and what the service provider is managing because this is the demarcation point for security responsibility. No one is going to take responsibility for the security of a system when the user can compromise that security through their legitimate access and controls. Don't assume the service provider is doing something; verify it and ensure it is documented that way – this will save a lot of time in the long run.

Where you have full responsibility for the updating and patching of an IaaS service provision, it is important to support it just as you would any on-premises system that is directly connected to the Internet. Otherwise, threat actors will find and exploit any vulnerability that is exposed due to a lack of proper maintenance.

Function As a Service

Also known as serverless computing, Function as a Service is possibly both the most abstract of the cloud computing models and the most "cloud" of them all. The service user writes code that runs either monolithically (one large application), as microservices interacting to supply a function or application, or somewhere in between using both concepts.

The code runs as needed, rather than persisting in memory between runs, by storing results or states to a persistent storage medium, that is, a database. This allows the resources for the execution to be given dynamically. When the code is not running, there are no compute resources used, and thus, there are minimal (if any) costs associated with the runtime. The application developers aren't concerned with the infrastructure at all, just the code, keeping the complexity of the execution environment hidden and managed.

As an example, serverless databases extend the serverless services model to applications eliminating the need to manage database server infrastructure and provide direct database access without all the overhead. This architecture is shown in Figure 2-5.

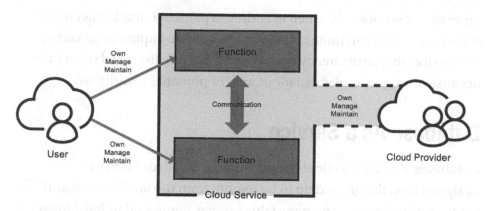

Figure 2-5. *Databases implemented as a Function as a Service (serverless)*

As with all cloud service provisions, there are risks. The predominant risk here is the security of the data passed between functions, but it's important to be aware of data held at rest between executions. This data is the lifeblood of the system, and any opportunity to poison that would lead to a catastrophic failure.

Typically, the usual suspects raise their heads once more with access controls (privileged by their very nature, even if not seen as such), configuration management, and vulnerability management being core among them. Even in this, the most cloud-like of cloud implementations, it's still the same basics that we struggle with on-premises that are most likely to trip us up in this "new world."

X As a Service

While SaaS, PaaS, and IaaS are the original trio of services offered as cloud computing, more variations of on-demand, centrally managed software services have emerged. There is now a plethora of "X As a Service" offerings that can be delivered, where X represents a technology substitution by asset or application. Many are specific instances of the more classic services, designed to address a particular market need. For convenience, you can think of them as less generic implementations of the services that have already been covered but are discussed separately because of unique implementations and/or potential security risks.

Database As a Service

Databases offer an excellent opportunity for a delivered service designed from the ground up to be remote from the applications and services using them. A nuance of this service, compared to full-blown database servers hosted in the cloud, is that the scope of the service is the database – not the underlying database server or supporting infrastructure. The server infrastructure is hosted and managed by the cloud service provider, hence being commonly referred to as a cloud database. The customer is instantiating databases through the service provision, and the provider is managing the scale, availability, and database maintenance support.

Hosting the database in the cloud offers a tempting target for many threat actors because the database infrastructure is necessarily accessible via the Internet. While your databases are only accessible to you, the database server itself may be providing service to 10s, 100s, or even 1000s of others. As a result, the database servers cannot be firewalled to only allow your IP addresses access. Every customer needs access to every database server (including redundant servers). This leaves the database servers open for indirect attacks if another component is compromised.

Although traditional mitigation controls, like access control lists (ACL), can prevent direct access for the unauthorized, this is far from perfect. This is a scenario where the layering of security measures can deliver significant value. While each layer may be relatively simple, breaching multiple layers increases the opportunity to detect and defend against an attack.

Desktop As a Service

Desktop as a Service (DaaS) provides a modern version of virtual desktop infrastructure (VDI) hosted in the cloud. While this concept has existed for decades, implemented using solutions from Citrix and Microsoft, the move to the cloud warrants further discussion on this subject. DaaS allows organizations to enable their users to have access to a virtual image of their corporate desktop, with all necessary applications and storage, from virtually anywhere and at any time. Access is often via a browser, extending the "anywhere" aspect and avoiding asset loss when hardware, like a laptop, is misplaced or stolen. DaaS is convenient and flexible, but as is common, those benefits are accompanied by risk. This is functionally illustrated in Figure 2-6.

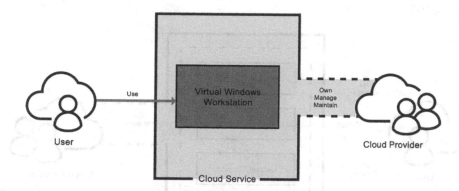

Figure 2-6. *Desktop as a Service implementation*

DaaS risks include everything from inappropriate access to stolen or shared credentials, to exposing an application with potentially sensitive information directly on the Internet – all threats that must be considered in your cloud security model. This is not to say that services like this are inherently unsecure, but rather that they need to be approached eyes wide open, with a full appreciation of the potential for misuse.

21

Data Center As a Service

Data Center as a Service (DCaaS) offers a service where a physical data center infrastructure and actual facility, or the virtual equivalents, are provisioned for users. This is conceptually similar to data center colocation (Colo), but it bundles the entire experience, the management, and the offering to the subscribing organization as a service. This concept is a layer down from IaaS, allowing companies to use the skills of the provider and capitalize on the best practices for data center management, all while operating the data center's services for their specific needs. The DCaaS provision can, like most cloud computing requirements, scale to the immediate needs of the user without requiring the infrastructure to be held at maximum capacity indefinitely. Functionally, this is illustrated in Figure 2-7.

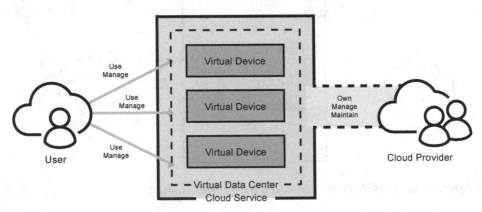

Figure 2-7. *Typical DCaaS implementation for virtual machines*

While the attack vectors for DCaaS may sound obtuse for this book, you need to consider the physical security controls that were implemented on-premises to protect your data center. If you consider relinquishing them to a third party and sharing them with other organizations that leverage DCaaS services, you begin to appreciate the complexity of the attack vectors that this service could be subject to, even if the entire environment is virtualized. This includes the physical access required to manage the assets and resources used to support your services.

Managed Software As a Service

Managed Software as a Service is a hosting model where an organization licenses (subscription or perpetual) a software solution, but uses an independent service provider to host and manage the software for their use cases. This offering provides a service that bridges the SaaS and PaaS provisions by providing the platform and the management without directly providing the software and actual solution. Figure 2-8 illustrates how only the software is delivered as a management component of the service.

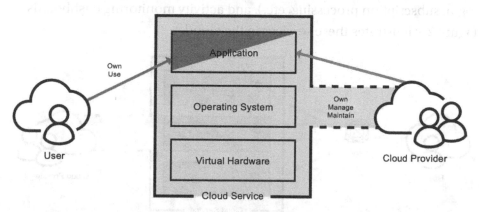

Figure 2-8. *Managed Software as a Service implementation*

While the hosting itself has its own security risks that should be managed by the hosting provider, the application (software) security has a shared responsibility model. The hosting provider typically manages application security patches for deployment, but the runtime of the application, which can be misconfigured or can have weak credential security, is managed by the end user. Both can open critical paths of exposure to the business and the managed software. Some service providers will undoubtedly offer services to cover the application runtime as well.

Backend As a Service

Backend as a Service delivers a mechanism for Internet (web) and mobile application developers to link their software to cloud storage and computing services through an abstraction layer interface, like an API. These services deliver capabilities, such as push notifications (sending notifications to a web browser or mobile application to alert the user to some change of state), centralized user management (registration, login, subscription processing, etc.), and activity monitoring dashboards. Figure 2-9 illustrates these services in the cloud.

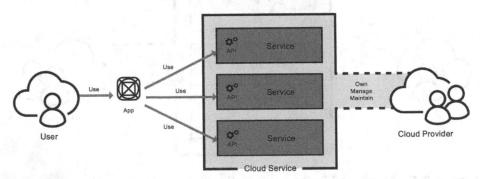

Figure 2-9. *Mobile application services via Backend as a Service implementation*

Attack vectors for Backend as a Service target operational runtime of data required by the back end to properly host applications. If the compromised data is shared via multiple applications, like the ability to deliver traffic or weather information, then all subscribers could potentially have incorrect, even potentially life-threatening, information.

As you may have begun to realize, there are many "As a Service" provisions and potential services on the market today. Not all of them are truly under the cloud computing "As a Service" model, and some providers are simply jumping on the messaging to differentiate with new offerings. This is where concepts like "cloud washing" (discussed later) become important in understanding cloud attack vectors. For solutions that are not cloud native, but which adhere to similar models as XaaS, you will find clear parallels to the concepts that follow in subsequent chapters.

CHAPTER 3

Cloud Service Providers

Before we embark on the attack vectors that make the cloud akin to the Wild West, we need to establish that the cloud is not a mysterious entity that operates in the vacuum of deep space (insert your favorite episode of Firefly here). In fact, while there are some companies that run their own clouds exclusively for their own solution, the vast majority of companies, application vendors, and third-party service providers use one of a handful of leading cloud computing providers for all their services and hosted solutions.

While the following list of functional capabilities is not exhaustive, it is important to document them since many of the boutique cloud computing providers will sublease their services, rebrand them, and may implement features that are unique to the offering, regardless of how they are hosted. In addition, some cloud vendors have customized these offerings based on geographical or political reasons, and they would not be able to provide services in that region otherwise. Regardless, in almost all conversations, these are the capabilities most businesses should consider to be available in the cloud. These capabilities should form the basic footprint of services, regardless of actual solution, for all cloud computing offerings.

- **Compute**: These services enable a licensed identity to deploy and manage VMs, containers, and other batch workloads, as well as to configure role-based access

© Morey J. Haber, Brian Chappell, Christopher Hills 2022
M. J. Haber et al., *Cloud Attack Vectors*, https://doi.org/10.1007/978-1-4842-8236-6_3

controls (RBAC) for application access. Compute resources can be configured with either public IP (IPv4 or IPv6) addresses or private IP addresses (RFC 1918)[1], depending on whether the resource needs to be Internet facing or available on a private network.

- **Mobile**: Cloud-based services offer a platform for organizations to develop cloud applications for mobile devices, providing notification and messaging services, support for back-end compute resources, tools for building application program interfaces (APIs), and the ability to link to other data sources, like geolocation.

- **Web Services**: These services support the development, deployment, maintenance, and reporting of web-based applications. They also offer features for search, content delivery, and security.

- **Storage**: This classification of services offers scalable cloud storage for structured and unstructured data. It also supports disaster recovery, backup, archival, and security for cloud-based storage. For some cloud computing providers, it also includes the storage for big data projects and data lakes. Storage is also a consideration for any cloud-based database services.

- **Analytics**: These services provide distributed analytics and accompanying storage. As a feature set, it includes real-time analytics, big data analytics, and support for data lakes, business intelligence, and data warehousing.

---

[1] https://datatracker.ietf.org/doc/html/rfc1918

- **Networking**: This group is based on virtual network technology in the cloud. This is often referred to as software-defined networks (SDN) and includes dedicated networks and access gateways, as well as services for traffic flow management, load balancing, domain name service (DNS) hosting, and network-based security from attacks like distributed denial of service (DDoS).

- **Content Delivery Network (CDN)**: CDN services include on-demand content streaming, delivery of popular web development libraries and resources, digital rights protection, and media content indexing for a rich end-user experience. CDN is often associated with the secure delivery of multimedia through the Internet.

- **Identity Management**: Identity management features ensure only authenticated and authorized users can access the cloud provider's services and manage sensitive data, settings, and runtime in the cloud. These services can include native identity management, integration into third-party identity stores, and security controls for authentication, like multi-factor authentication (MFA). As a subset of identity management, use cases for privileged access management (PAM) are also available to secure secrets and authentication in the cloud.

- **Internet of Things (IoT)**: These services are designed for workloads to capture, monitor, and analyze IoT data from deployed assets. IoT-specific services include notifications, analytics, monitoring, data storage, and specific technology support for IoT platforms.

- **SecDevOps**: This group provides project and collaboration tools for the software development process and the resources to secure the deployment and testing of code. This process operates from developers through quality assurance, deployment, and final production release of a solution. It also offers features for application diagnostics, automation tool integration, and test labs for build tests and experimentation.

- **Development**: These services help application developers share and develop code, test applications, and track potential security and quality assurance issues. Cloud computing providers typically support a wide range of application programming languages to accommodate and replace workloads and processes that were on-premise or optimized for the cloud.

- **Security**: These solutions provide capabilities to detect and respond to cloud security threats, as well as to manage secrets used for cloud access by human or machine identities, like encryption keys. Security as a cloud offering is a wide-ranging topic, with many solutions and use cases all implemented in the cloud and used for cloud security, on-premise, and in hybrid cloud and multicloud environments.

- **Artificial Intelligence (AI)/Machine Learning (ML)**: Cloud computing providers offer an expansive range of tools and solutions application developers can implement for artificial intelligence, machine learning, and cognitive computing. The goal is to provide security insights into applications and datasets that would not be available via traditional, statistical, or pattern-based modeling. These capabilities are typically used in threat hunting exercises or during advanced threat detection.

- **Containers**: These services help an organization create, register, orchestrate, and manage containers in the cloud using common platforms, such as Docker and Kubernetes (these technologies and definitions will be explored later). In many cases, there are dedicated tools and solutions to assist with the volume, ephemeral nature, and security of the containers being instantiated and destroyed to support an objective.

- **Databases**: This category is typically represented as Database as a Service (DBaaS) and includes cloud-based versions of solutions that were previously found on-premise and in cloud-native (e.g., blockchain) databases that take advantage of the computing power and storage capabilities in the cloud. Cloud-based databases can be plumbing for an application or provided as a service to host other applications.

- **Migration Services**: These are provided as a collection of tools and procedures to help an organization migrate resources, assets, and workloads from on-premise to the cloud or from one cloud computing provider to another. Entire businesses have been developed around this category to help with digital transformations or multicloud workload management, where migration of services between clouds can be optimized based on cost.

- **Management and Governance**: These services provide a range of tools for compliance, automation, scheduling, reporting, and monitoring to help an organization administer the cloud-based environment and report on asset and risk status for compliance initiatives.

To help compare these capabilities, Figure 3-1 illustrates how some of these services potentially link together in the cloud and support PaaS, IaaS, and SaaS, vs. on-premise.

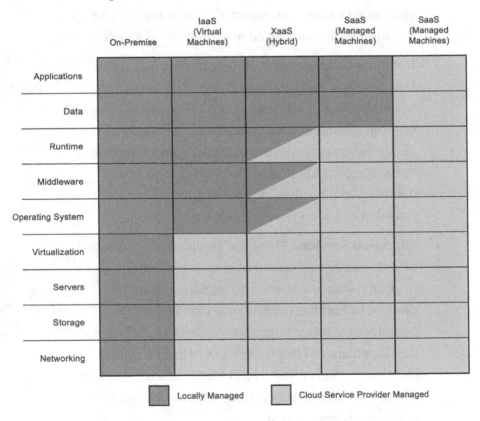

Figure 3-1. *Services rendered based on the type of cloud services*

Next, let's explore the leading cloud service providers (CSP) and their footprints in the market. This will expand our understanding of their capabilities as we begin to delineate the cloud attack vectors that are common to each and unique to others.

Amazon Web Services

Amazon Web Services (launched in 2006 and commonly referred to as AWS) is an innovative and mature cloud service provider (also called a cloud computing platform) that offers a wide variety of services for IaaS, PaaS, and SaaS. As a part of these services, AWS offers all the solutions and tools necessary for capacity computing power, storage, management, database services, etc.

This technology stack was originally based on the success of Amazon. com and later offered as a product for external users. This is whimsically illustrated in Figure 3-2 as a complete suite of solutions because it is nearly impossible to illustrate all potential offerings and capabilities AWS truly can offer. A goal of AWS is to make it a one-stop shop containing everything you could ever need to enable your business.

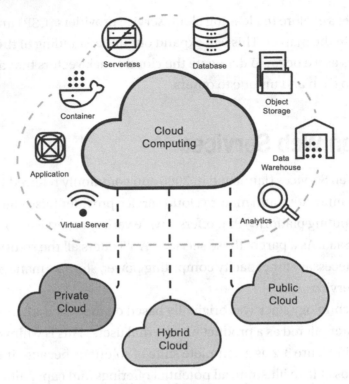

Figure 3-2. "Complete" offering of AWS service

Organizations worldwide utilize AWS Availability Zones (AZ) based on regional data centers to provide services for nearly every vertical, from financial organizations to nonprofits and even to highly secure government environments based on the Federal Risk and Authorization Management Program (FedRAMP). With hundreds of different services, attack vectors in the cloud can target any of them to compromise an individual client environment or AWS itself.

While many AWS services are public facing, many are designed to be plumbing, either of which can suffer from vulnerabilities that could be exploited as a part of an attack. Therefore, it is relevant that all aspects of an AWS deployment be considered for an organization's risk assessment.

This includes items offered as services and not under the end user's control, because monitoring how AWS mitigates risk could also impact your offering.

Microsoft Azure

Microsoft Azure provides a vast trove of computing technology in the cloud based on Microsoft's world-renowned Windows technology. Microsoft first unveiled its plans for a cloud computing platform called Windows Azure in 2008 and commercially launched the service in early 2010. While it is well known that early releases of Azure cloud services fell behind more established offerings like AWS, the offering continued to evolve and support a larger base of programming languages, service fabrics, and operating systems. In 2014, Microsoft rebranded its cloud service platform to Microsoft Azure to realize the full potential of their strategy and separate Windows as an operating system from a cloud computing platform.

To that end, Azure today provides IaaS, PaaS, SaaS, and serverless services for their own applications, like Office 365, as well as for vendors and clients to develop and build their own environments for internal use, hosting, or resale. Azure's services are designed to help businesses manage organizational goals via distinct services vs. AWS services, which are more of a building block approach to build whatever you need. Figure 3-3 illustrates the service-layered approach Microsoft has instrumented with Azure.

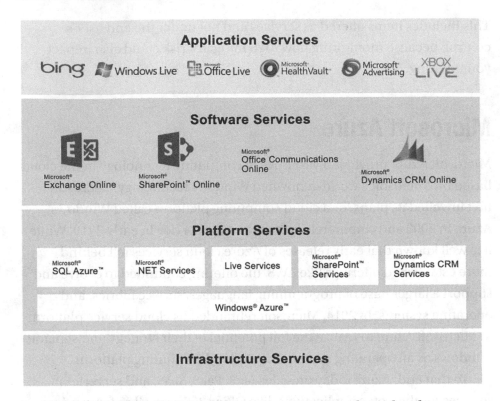

Figure 3-3. *Microsoft Azure service layer approach to cloud computing*

While Azure has more services at the application layer than the competition, threat actors typically attack vulnerabilities, misconfigurations, the authentication model, and the API to compromise the environment at this layer. This occurs via unsecure credentials, cloud-based entitlements, and unpatched security flaws that highlight how inadequate implementation of the security basics plague cloud environments just as with on-premise technology.

Google Cloud Platform

The Google Cloud Platform (commonly referred to as GCP) is a suite of cloud computing services that offers the same infrastructure and services that Google uses internally for its end-user products. In addition to platform unique management tools, GCP supplies a series of modular cloud services that highlight their perspective on cloud computing. For example, GCP includes specialty versions of data analytics and machine learning that excel compared to the competition's similar branded offerings. Like the other leading cloud computing providers, Google Cloud Platform provides IaaS, PaaS, and serverless computing environments with support for SaaS through vendors that develop their applications on Google's native platform. Therefore, GCP is not ideal for cloud washing or for a lift and shift of workloads to become SaaS applications.

In 2008, Google announced the first versions of its platform for developing and hosting web applications in Google-managed data centers. After three years of development, their services became generally available in November 2011. Since the original release, Google has added significant new services to compete with other providers, including G Suite and the geolocation and map services commonly found in many mobile applications.

While many in the industry would consider Google to be number three in the cloud computing space (with AWS at number one and Microsoft at number two), the solutions available on GCP should not be dismissed and offer strong competition to the leaders. This is true from the productivity applications hosted in the cloud all the way down to the end users who are deployed with Chrome OS in lieu of Microsoft Windows or Apple macOS.

To simplify the madness of what a cloud computing provider is offering for a given organization, Figure 3-4 provides an easy comparison of their technology stacks and the names each provider uses to market them.

Services	aws	▲ Azure	Google Cloud Platform
Virtual Servers	Instances	VMs	VM Instances
Platform-as-a-Service	Elastic Beanstalk	Cloud Services	App Engine
Serverless Computing	Lambda	Azure Functions	Cloud Functions
Docker Management	ECS	Container Service	Container Engine
Kubernetes Management	EKS	Kubernetes Service	Kubernetes Engine
Object Storage	S3	Block Blob	Cloud Storage
Archive Storage	Glacier	Archive Storage	Coldline
File Storage	EFS	Azure Files	ZFS / Avere
Global Content Delivery	CloudFront	Delivery Network	Cloud CDN
Managed Data Warehouse	Redshift	SQL Warehouse	Big Query

Figure 3-4. *Major cloud service providers compared with applicable services*

Having a clear understanding of equivalent offerings provides simplicity, standardization, and security for many organizations. Attack vectors against GCP are primarily around unpatched vulnerabilities, zero-day browser attacks, insecure credentials, and inappropriate hardening. The primary difference between GCP and other providers related to attack vectors is based on the open source foundation used to build GCP services. This contrasts the typically closed nature of services used in providers like Microsoft Azure. In fact, just because something is open source or closed source doesn't make it more secure; rather, the differences can lead to more complex attacks versus those that are trivial. Recent exploitation of Log4J can help explain this – it is widely used open source software and was easy to exploit.

Alibaba Cloud

While you may have read the brief descriptions of the leading three cloud computing providers, there is a fourth that is arguably number one, depending on which region of the world your organization is servicing. Alibaba Cloud (also known as Aliyun) is a subsidiary of the Alibaba Group. It delivers cloud computing services to China and the Asia Pacific. Alibaba Cloud is considered the largest cloud computing platform in the region and, by some accounts, in the world. Founded in 2019, they offer a wide range of cloud services for merchants and online businesses, as well as Alibaba's own ecommerce ecosystem. While Alibaba Cloud started in China, today, it operates in 24 data centers around the globe. Through partnerships with third-party organizations, Alibaba Cloud even has a presence in geographically sensitive areas, like Germany.

Alibaba's service offerings are mature and include IaaS, PaaS, DBaaS, and SaaS solutions, all of which can be managed natively through their platform. While many organizations may not consider them to be a viable platform, they are the best choice for businesses that want to provide services on their platform within the Asia Pacific and China. Of course, local laws prevail, and any solutions built upon Alibaba Cloud will need to adhere to the country's data privacy and government access requirements.

As for attack vectors, anything that is platform specific will be unique to Alibaba, and the open source code used as a foundation is the primary target, just like GCP. However, all the same credential attacks and misconfigurations that we have briefly discussed can also be leveraged, just as with any other provider.

Oracle Cloud

The Oracle Cloud is a cloud service and computing provider that delivers services through a global network of managed data centers, primarily focused on offering Oracle solutions in the cloud. While Oracle allows competing operating systems and databases to be hosted in their cloud environment, their primary offering best suits organizations looking to embrace Oracle technology (new) or to migrate legacy on-premise Oracle solutions to the cloud.

As a point of reference, the Oracle Cloud was one of the latest offerings to be made available in the market, and it only became generally available in 2016. Like the other cloud computing providers, they offer a variety of IaaS, PaaS, and SaaS solutions, primarily based on their own solutions. In addition, they are one of a few vendors that offers DaaS (Data as a Service) based on their infamous Oracle database and reporting technology.

While there have been relatively few publicized attacks against the Oracle Cloud, it does not mean that their environment is any more or less secure than other providers. In fact, almost all leading cloud computing vendors offer secure cloud offerings that meet FedRAMP specifications for the most sensitive government use cases.

Oracle Cloud does not rank as one of the top three CSPs as they have a much smaller share of clients. Consequently, they are just not a big focus for threat actors, despite being built on Oracle Linux and similar open source foundational technology. To that end, Oracle Cloud's commercial offerings tend to have risks associated with their cloud-enabled applications since they share many of the same components (code) as on-premise. Unfortunately, Oracle does not participate in full and prompt vulnerability disclosure like Microsoft and tends to shield these risks from the general public.

IBM

The IBM Cloud is an ecosystem of cloud computing services that primarily provides PaaS and IaaS. Notably, to date, SaaS is not a strength in their offerings. Using the IBM Cloud, organizations can deploy virtual information technology assets to supplement or replace existing data centers and create hybrid environments that span the entire globe. To make this easy for organizations, IBM uses an open source platform that developers can create, manage, maintain, execute, and deploy, both in the cloud and on-premise. This model creates a seamless offering that blurs the lines of on-premise and cloud for hybrid environments and delivers operational transparency regardless of where the assets and data reside.

In addition to the cloud computing basics, IBM Cloud includes specialty tools, like IBM Watson, for advanced artificial intelligence services, as well as serverless computing using native engines that support third-party vendors.

With these capabilities in mind, IBM offers three distinct cloud models for organizational deployment as part of their DCaaS strategy:

- **Public**: Internet facing with virtual servers that are hosted in a multitenant deployment

- **Dedicated**: A single tenant dedicated to an organization that is hosted in an IBM data center with connectivity provided by technology like VPN

- **Private**: A dedicated environment that is segmented, isolated, and managed behind a firewall within an IBM data center

IBM competes with AWS, Azure, Oracle, and GCP for market share. The IBM Cloud was initially offered as a service in 2013 after IBM acquired SoftLayer to build the foundation of their offerings.

Other Services

A small number of CSPs dominate the cloud computing space. At the beginning of 2021, AWS held almost a third of the market (32%), with Azure not far behind at 20%. The next three vendors (GCP, Aliyun, IBM) controlled another 20% of the market (9%, 6%, and 5%, respectively). Those five vendors account for 72% of all cloud service provision. That still leaves 28% to the remaining providers, offering a lot of space for bespoke and boutique services for just about every possible use.

Some of these vendors provide value-added services utilizing the platforms of the larger, more prominent players, while others use their own data centers and capacity as resalable services. It is also not uncommon to see telecommunications and other Internet service providers selling cloud computing services of their own using existing brick and mortar data centers. Other brands also address niche markets with specific services.

In fairness, there is nothing wrong with any of the smaller boutique cloud computing providers. In fact, many offer unique capabilities that you will not find in the big five. However, for any provider, you must always consider their business model, financial stability, security program, and disaster recovery capabilities against your organizational needs. Above all, your cloud provider must answer the security questionnaire in Appendix A to your satisfaction:

- What is the financial stability of the cloud computing provider?

- What is the service-level agreement for uptime and problem resolution? Note: If it is a boutique CSP hosted on another vendor's platform, like AWS, any SLAs cannot exceed the host's stated agreements unless it uses multicloud failover.

- How many data centers can host the services my organization is licensing?

- Which geolocations will support my organization, and what geographical boundaries are not acceptable to provide services?

- What is the cloud computing provider's backup and restoration plan?

- How does the cloud computing provider deliver high availability?

- What are their disclosure plans for a cybersecurity attack?

- Does the provider have adequate cybersecurity insurance?

While this is not an exhaustive list (Appendix A has more, and more detailed, questions), it should be clear that selecting a CSP is a serious business decision. For example, financial stability is critical when selecting a small cloud computing provider compared to a big six vendor. This is not something you would consider asking of Amazon or Microsoft, but if the smaller company went bankrupt the next day, what effect would it have on your business?

If you consider a small cloud computing provider, evaluate their business and services to ensure their stability is in line with your business risk appetite. Also consider vendor lock-in. If you need to change CSPs in the future, how hard would it be, what unique technology would you need to reengineer, and ultimately, how much time and money would it cost to switch off a proprietary implementation? These are all factors in your CSP selection.

CHAPTER 4

Cloud Definitions

Without a doubt, the cloud has changed the way we do business. The growth of the cloud has also given rise to many marketing buzzwords, such as "digital transformation" and "zero trust." However, while these terms push the use cases and architectures for cloud deployments to new levels, cloud deployments have pushed several industry standard terms to evolve to include the cloud in their definitions.

We can no longer think of an identity or account as being properties of Active Directory (AD) or LDAP; they can also belong to the services provided by a cloud service provider, hosted in Azure AD, or that even form a part of a vendor's proprietary identity services. The definitions have evolved. Therefore, we now must expand and rethink some basic terminology to understand the cloud and associated attack vectors. And remember, the more things change, the more they stay the same, definitions included.

Availability

While availability isn't exclusive to cloud services, it is essential when considering the impact that attack vectors might have on their operation. If your overall service has relatively low availability, any attack has a higher chance of success. This is simply a case of fewer points of resiliency resulting in greater impact when components are damaged or destroyed. Availability itself is an area that's often poorly understood as we are bombarded with the basic "nines," for example, 99.9%, in

© Morey J. Haber, Brian Chappell, Christopher Hills 2022
M. J. Haber et al., *Cloud Attack Vectors*, https://doi.org/10.1007/978-1-4842-8236-6_4

most documentation. High levels of availability, three nines (99.9%), four nines (99.99%), and five nines (99.999%), are regularly sought from vendors without consideration of what's actually needed by the business. Understanding the business needs is also vital when determining the risks to the cloud provisions you are using.

One key scope for availability that is often misunderstood is complex systems, something which you'll encounter even within a single CSP. Consider, for example, a web application running on a PaaS provision with DBaaS as the back-end storage. You will probably find yourself looking at two different availability values.

Let's imagine the PaaS provision is 99.9% available and the DBaaS is 95% available. This might lead you to assume that the system's combined availability, and thus your web application, is 95% as the lowest value. However, as the web application cannot operate without both elements, the actual availability of the system is 95%×99.9%, or 94.9%. This might not seem like an issue, but even in this scenario where we haven't considered all the systems involved, it has a significant impact on the overall availability figure. This can be a problem when chasing high availability, like 4 and 5 nines. The cost of each extra 9 is also going to increase geometrically. Achieving 5 nines is expensive, and you'll need deep pockets, but 100% is next to impossible, or at least very, very improbable, and is likely to have a cost that will make even highly successful accountants spit their tea across the room.

The one thing that improves availability is redundant components (even if they are all in use in a load balanced mechanism). If we could duplicate the DBaaS service, let's start with a simple mirror. We have two DBaaS provisions each available 95% of the time. The combined availability is not 95%×95% (90%), but rather 95%+((1-95%)×95%), or 99.75%, a significant improvement over the starting position. In English, the first instance is available 95% of the time, and even when that instance is down, the other is expected to be available for 95% of the time, or 95% of the 5% of time that the first instance might be down. That equates to an additional 4.75% availability across the pair. This is an improvement, but many of you will have noted that you got 95% availability for your first instance but only an additional 4.75% for the second instance. The third instance adds 95% of the 0.25% of time that both of the initial instances could be down. It's an example of the law of diminishing returns.

Three DBaaS instances get us almost to 3 nines (99.875%) *for the DBaaS*, but it's our PaaS that comes in and pulls our overall availability back to 99.77%. To get the two layers operating at 99.9% as a total service, each layer needs to be operating at 99.995%. Let's call it four instances of each layer – otherwise known as a lot of money! This complexity is also going to entail more monitoring.

Lastly, even in our simple example, we've missed some important aspects. The network on which these services are running will have an availability value. If we are accessing the solution from our office(s), our networks, our Internet connections, our firewalls, etc., all have independent availability measures. All of these should be factored into the service availability to our end users. The Internet itself can't really be factored into the calculation because it's beyond our control, although we are, however, aware of it.

All of this might seem a little doom and gloom, but I'm not looking to discourage you from availability planning or implementation. I am trying to encourage you to really understand how resilient your systems are and what that improvement means. It's hard work, albeit worth the effort to achieve and articulate.

If you understand where your systems are vulnerable to DDoS, to having elements being taken offline, or to being otherwise impacted, it'll be all that much easier to plan defenses to those attacks or at least to have plans for how to respond when it does happen.

One last point, and possibly the most important one: availability figures generally relate to unplanned downtime – not planned downtime. Planned downtime usually includes bringing services down for maintenance and updates/upgrades. While most services are resilient and can be upgraded in place, without downtime, the need to bring the whole thing down could arise. This isn't service providers trying to be clever with you; it's just making sure they can take the necessary time. Of course, planned downtime should be scheduled well ahead of time and communicated with the customers. Just make sure you are aware of the conditions of your services, so these things don't come as a surprise.

Identity

A digital identity (commonly shortened and referred to as just an identity, which is the same term used for a natural person or human being) is an object used by electronic systems to represent an entity with a function within the resource. That instantiation may be a person, organization, application, or device used for authentication, authorization, automation, and even impersonation during runtime.

Attributes about the identity itself help classify ownership for other processes. The attributes contained in an identity allow for attestations, authentication, and authorization of a corresponding account to interact with a resource in the cloud via entitlements, permissions, privileges, and rights. This could be interactive or automated.

The concept of an "identity" also denotes different aspects for business and personal use when owned by a human being. These two types of identities should typically never be mixed, especially when using cloud resources for one use case or another. In other words, your digital identity when using business applications should be different than when using personal applications in the cloud. And a cloud identity is different than on-premise – even for root accounts. This requires a little more explanation to understand the nuanced differences.

To start, in Amazon Web Services (AWS), there are two different privileged accounts. One is defined as root user (account owner), and the other is defined as an IAM (identity access management) user. The difference between them is why defining an identity in the cloud can get really confusing for most administrators and end users.

Consider you start a business called "Time Traveler" (if you have read any of the other *Attack Vector* books, you will understand why), and you decided to use the power of the cloud to realize your vision. You create an AWS account with your email address, password, and other relevant details. Your initial setup creates the credentials (email address and password) for the root user, the root user for everything related to the account. Arguably, this is the most powerful account for the instance. Like any other resource, the root user has complete ownership of the instance, and it can do everything with your account. The omnipotent power conferred by root makes this account a prime target for threat actors.

Next, to get your business started, you hire a group of developers to work on your project within your AWS account. The developers need administrative control for your project. However, as a security best practice, you should not give developers your root account credentials – to do so is just a very unwise and risky idea.

In AWS, the role-based access model allows you to create an IAM user (it is another form of an identity). As the owner of the instance, you, therefore, create this IAM user for each developer, assign them permissions based on least privilege (hopefully), and allow them to begin working.

As an IAM user, they should only be able to perform tasks you have defined as a part of their entitlements. This forms the foundation for a least privilege security model.

Even if an IAM user is granted every permission, the fundamental differences between these identities can be classified by their foundational entitlements. The overlap is why they generally become confusing to team members. To start, let's break down an AWS root user vs. an IAM user:

a. **Root User**

- The root user is the first cloud service identity created by default when you create your cloud account. This account should be disabled, or even deleted, for security if the provider allows it.

- You can log in as a root user using the email address and password that you used to create the account, but as a security best practice, you really should not. This holds especially true in a production environment.

- All cloud service providers have a root account. Depending on the provider, you may be allowed to have more than one such account. The more root accounts you have, the larger the risk surface.

- A root user (identity) has full access to all the resources in the account and associated instances. This explains the risk they represent if compromised.

- The only way to restrict permission to a root user is by having a Service Control Policy applied to your account. But even this control has its limitations.

- You should not use your root user for your everyday tasks (even administrative ones). As a best practice, you should create an IAM user with administrative-like privileges and lock down the root account, as previously discussed.

b. **IAM User** (typically used to describe an AWS identity, but applies to other identities in different cloud service providers)

  - An IAM user can be created by a root user or another IAM user who has entitlements to create additional IAM users.

- You can authenticate or start a remote session using your IAM user credentials and your account ID or alias (if required) if entitlement is granted. It is best to enable MFA and disable all single-factor authentication for IAM user accounts.

- An IAM user should be created using least privilege. Consider this identity "fully closed" since most cloud service providers do not grant any privileges upon account creation.

- Organizations should absolutely implement a policy based on current security controls to restrict the access of any IAM user against inappropriate behavior.

- An IAM user can be a human, application, process, or another machine-based identity to implement a use case. This is a big difference from traditional definitions for identity.

- Depending on the use case, you can assign entitlements to individual IAM users or role-based access groups.

With this in mind, an IAM user granted administrative privileges can pretty much do everything that a root user can do, except for a few tasks that are restricted to the root account. Among the differences, the following list highlights some of the more critically important privileges only available to root:

- Closing your cloud service provider account

- Changing many of your cloud service provider account settings, like the root email address

- Changing your support plan and billing information

- Enabling or disabling specific security controls, like MFA, to manage key runtime parameters, like deletion

Regardless of the account type, the cloud represents unique challenges for all identities. Consider these best practices when managing cloud identities:

- Do not use your root user access key for anything except extreme use cases. If the cloud provider allows for it, consider disabling it or even deleting it.

- Enable MFA for all your root users, as well as for all IAM users. Single-factor authentication should never be used for the cloud.

- Don't share your root user/IAM user's credentials with anyone for anything, at any time.

- Create separate IAM users for anyone who needs access to an account. Accounts should never be shared – even for machine identities

- Grant least privilege access to your IAM users – always!

- Have a robust password policy in place for all users, and consider a privileged access management solution to safeguard them and to perform management.

Many of the attack vectors later discussed will explain why all this is so important. By the way, for a complete and formal definition of identities, and their associated threats and risks, please reference the book *Identity Attack Vectors*[1] by Haber and Rolls (2020).

---

[1] www.springer.com/us/book/9781484251645

Finally, as a wicked twist to identities, consider BYOI (bring your own identity). All the methods we have spoken about are considered Federated Identities that have a registered entry in a company-authorized, third-party directory service. Unfederated Identities use a third-party directory service for authentication and permissions that are user maintained and trusted via an external provider. Entitlements, permissions, rights, etc., are all linked via an API (Application Programming Interface) to allow an identity to be authenticated without any other details about the user, profile, or account being stored locally.

The most popular current methods for registering and authenticating into a third-party cloud service are via Google, Microsoft, Apple, Facebook, LinkedIn, etc. The identity is hosted and managed elsewhere, which is why it is called unfederated. Real-world use cases include authentication into services like PayPal and Amazon for financial transactions based on attributes stored in the unfederated account. All of these are instances of BYOI being used to pass identity information from a directory service to a system that has no knowledge of, or storage requirements for, the identity that is being authenticated. In this author's opinion, this will be the future of identities in the cloud. Your employees will bring their digital identity to your workplace. This practice will bridge the gap between work and personal data, which could include banking information, vaccination status, right to work, and voter registration – information that is transportable between jobs and maintained solely by the human identity, as well as machine-to-machine linkages via state, local, and federal governments. Cloud-based technologies, like blockchain, that are hosted in a CSP are the future of how this will be deployed.

Accounts

An account is an electronic representation of an identity and can have a one-to-many relationship with the identity. One identity can, therefore, have multiple accounts. These accounts reference a set of permissions, rights, entitlements, and privileges needed for an application or asset to connect or operate within the confines of a system. While the definition of an account is obvious for an identity, it can take on a variety of forms when used electronically for services, impersonations, application-to-application functions, and when defined within proprietary cloud assets.

To unravel the complexity around accounts, consider that accounts can have intricate relationships with identities, and they can either be defined locally, grouped, nested in groups, or managed via identity infrastructure, such as directory services or in the role-based access model for a cloud service. Accounts can have role-based access applied to them either directly, at the group level, or based on a directory entry. These roles can implement a wide range of capabilities – from disabling access to providing privileged capabilities, such as root, to providing privileges over an entitlement, its usage, and its assignment. The level of privileges and role-based access is dependent on the security model of the cloud service that is implementing them, and it can vary significantly from one vendor to another.

Linking accounts to identities is how we gain access to the functions within the cloud. Technically, an account is simply a vehicle for authorizing usage and controlling operational parameters. Excessive assignment of privileges to any given account goes against the principle of least privilege (PoLP)[2]. This will significantly increase cyber risk and the potential for a cloud attack vector. Therefore, consider this basic approach: an account is the digital representation of a human or nonhuman identity.

Principals

In cloud computing, "principals" are a concept that maps an identity (normally by account name) to an entitlement, permission, and rights. Each entry for this combination is a single principal. When managing

---

[2]https://en.wikipedia.org/wiki/Principle_of_least_privilege

entitlements in the cloud, the Principal Name is associated with the Account, Group, or Role, regardless of directory service source, and the Principal Type is a reference to the actual identity, like User, Role, Group, API, etc.

In managing cloud security, the total number of high-risk principal entries helps gauge the security level of an instance. A lower number of risky principals generally help support a model of least privilege, as long as the principals themselves are not overprivileged. Figure 4-1 helps illustrate this in practice. This concept supports the notion of intelligent identity and access management.

Recommendation	Risk Level	Principal Name	Principal Type
Remove Permissions	High	sjennings_beyondtrust.com#EXT#@btengcpb.onmicrosoft.com	User
Enable MFA	High	BT_PB_Test_User_SBQA	User
Remove Permissions	High	BT_SWATHI_TESTUSER	User
Enable MFA	High	BT_SWATHI_TESTUSER	User
Remove Permissions	High	joutlaw_beyondtrust.com#EXT#@btengcpb.onmicrosoft.com	User
Enable MFA	High	BT_PB_API_User	User
Remove Permissions	High	BT_PB_Test_User_SBQA	User
Remove Permissions	High	BT_SJ_QAUser	User
Enable MFA	High	infra-admin	User
Remove Permissions	High	it-admin	User

Figure 4-1. *Discovered principals within a cloud environment*

Secrets

Whether on-premise or in the cloud, the credentials processed by nonhuman or machine identities are often called "secrets." In rare instances, these secrets rarely apply to humans as well.

By definition, secrets refer to a private piece of information that acts as a secure key, providing authentication or validation for authorization. Secrets provide access to protected resources, allow for programmatic authentication, expose information between applications, and enable automation in cloud environments. Secrets more typically apply to nonhuman/machine credentials instead of human credentials.

Some of the most common secret types include

- **Privileged Account Credentials**: Traditional username and password credentials.

- **Passwords**: The secret itself without a username qualifier.

- **Certificates**: Used to identify the owner of a resource or communications; these are typically digitally signed to prove validity.

- **SSH Keys**: A type of secret used by the SSH protocol to raise the confidence in authentication above credentials by establishing a secure key pair.

- **API Keys**: An application programming interface key is a unique identifier used to authenticate a user, developer, or calling program to an API.

- **Encryption Keys**: A key in cryptography is a piece of information, usually a string of numbers or letters stored in a file, which, when processed through a cryptographic algorithm, can encode or decode cryptographic data.

Secrets Management

Secrets management refers to the tools and methods for managing digital authentication and authorization secrets, including passwords, keys, APIs, and tokens for use in applications, services, privileged accounts, and other sensitive components within the IT ecosystem. While secrets management is applicable across an entire enterprise, the terms "secrets" and "secrets management" are referred to more commonly in IT with regard to DevOps or SecDevOps environments, tools, website certificates, and other automation processes.

While passwords and keys are some of the most broadly used secrets, credentials for human consumption typically include management via password management or via privileged access management solutions for authenticating applications and users. This is because machine-based secrets should never be exposed interactively during any workflow, while human-based secrets have use cases that can, and should, expose the secret in clear text or allow copying and pasting for insertion within applications. While this is a subtle nuance, once a machine secret is exposed to a human, it is no longer secure, no longer controlled, and, consequently, should be changed.

Secrets can include the following use cases:

- Randomly generated passwords that are complex for humans to write, remember, or even verbally communicate

- API and other application keys/credentials (including within containers) that meet complexity requirements

- SSH keys for application-to-application or user-to-application authentication

- Database and other system-to-system passwords for encrypting or accessing data

- Private certificates for secure communication, transmitting, and receiving of data (TLS, SSL, etc.)

- Private encryption keys for systems like PGP to secure email

- RSA and other one-time password (OTP) devices that frequently change

As the IT ecosystem grows in complexity and the number and diversity of secrets expands, it becomes increasingly difficult to securely store, transmit, and audit secrets. This is why secrets management is important in the cloud.

Common risks around secrets include

- **Lack of Visibility** over all the privileged accounts, applications, tools, containers, or microservices deployed across the environment and the associated passwords, keys, and other secrets. SSH keys alone may number in the millions at some organizations, which should provide an inkling of the scale of the secrets management challenge. Visibility becomes a particular shortcoming of decentralized approaches where admins, developers, and other team members all manage their secrets separately, if they're managed at all. Without oversight that stretches across all IT layers, there are sure to be security gaps, as well as auditing challenges. The compromise of any one secret could be enough to breach an organization.

- **Embedded Secrets**: Privileged passwords and other secrets are needed to facilitate authentication for app-to-app (A2A) and application-to-database (A2D) communications and access. Often, applications and IoT devices are shipped or deployed with hardcoded, default secrets or credentials, which are easy to crack by threat actors who are using dedicated tools or can obtain access via another attack vector. DevOps tools frequently have secrets hardcoded in scripts or files, which jeopardizes security for the entire automation process, should they become compromised. This also compounds the difficulties in managing credentials as it is often unclear where credentials are being used so the risk of taking them under management and changing the password can become debilitating.

- **Privilege Sprawl**: Cloud and virtualization administrator consoles (as with AWS, Azure, GCP, etc.) provide broad superuser privileges that enable IAM users to rapidly spin up and spin down virtual machines and applications at massive scale. Each of these VM instances comes with its own set of privileges and secrets that need to be managed; otherwise, the settings and runtime for the entire cloud environment could be compromised.

- **DevOps Tools**: While secrets need to be managed across the entire IT ecosystem, DevOps environments are where the challenges of managing secrets seem to be particularly amplified based on current solutions and the maturity of the cloud. DevOps teams typically leverage dozens of orchestration, configuration management, and other tools and technologies (Chef, Puppet, Ansible, Salt, Docker containers, etc.), relying on automation and other scripts requiring secrets work. They are all intricately interlinked. Again, these secrets should all be managed according to security best practices, including credential rotation, time-/activity-limited access, and auditing through a centralized solution instead of management via multiple tools.

- **Remote Access**: How do you ensure that the authorization provided via remote access or to a third party is appropriately used? How do you ensure that the third-party organization adequately manages secrets for remote access? These use cases will be explored in more detail later, but secrets management is the key to making sure that remote access stays secure, regardless of employee, contractor, vendor, or auditor.

Leaving secrets management in the hands of humans for manual management is a high-risk security practice. Poor secrets hygiene, such as lack of secrets rotation, default secrets, embedded secrets, and secret sharing mean secrets are not likely to remain secure, opening up the opportunity for breaches. The more manual the secrets management processes, the higher the likelihood of security gaps and malpractices occurring.

As a simple statement, manual secrets management suffers from deficiencies. Security siloes and manual processes frequently conflict with "good" security practices, so the more comprehensive and automated a solution, the better. While there are many tools that manage some secrets, most tools are designed specifically for one platform, for example, Docker, or at most a small subset of platforms. Privileged access management can broadly manage application passwords, eliminate hardcoded and default passwords, and manage secrets for automation. Organizations must consider the end-to-end workflow for optimal implementation of PAM solutions.

For any secrets management implementation, consider these seven best practices (regardless of implementation technology):

1. **Discover/identify all types of passwords**, keys, and other secrets across your entire IT environment and bring them under centralized management. Continuously discover and onboard new secrets as they are created and, importantly, remove ones that have been deprecated.

2. **Eliminate hardcoded/embedded secrets** in DevOps tool configurations, build scripts, code files, test builds, production builds, applications, and more. Bring hardcoded credentials under management by replacing them with API calls, to your secrets or password management system. Eliminating hardcoded and default passwords effectively removes dangerous backdoors to your environment.

3. **Enforce password and secrets security best practices**, including password length, complexity, uniqueness expiration, rotation, and more across all types of passwords. Secrets, if possible, should never be shared. If a secret is shared, it should be immediately changed. Secrets to more sensitive tools and systems should have more rigorous security parameters, such as one-time passwords, and rotation after each use.

4. **Apply privileged session monitoring to log, audit, and monitor all privileged sessions** (for accounts, users, scripts, automation tools, etc.) to improve oversight and accountability. This can also entail capturing keystrokes and screens (allowing for live view (4-eyes principle), searching, and playback). Some enterprise privileged session management solutions also enable IT teams to pinpoint suspicious session activity in progress and pause, lock, or terminate the session until the activity can be adequately evaluated.

5. **Extend secrets management to third parties**, and ensure partners and vendors conform to best practices in using and managing secrets. This is especially true for any interaction that might occur with your organization's assets.

6. **Apply threat analytics** to continuously analyze secrets usage to detect anomalies and potential threats. The more integrated and centralized your secrets management, the better you will be able to report on accounts, keys applications, containers, and systems that are exposed to risk.

7. **DevSecOps**: With the speed and scale of DevOps, it's crucial to build security into both the culture and the DevOps life cycle (from inception, design, build, test, release, support, maintenance). Embracing a DevSecOps culture means that everyone shares responsibility for DevOps security, helping ensure accountability and alignment across teams. In practice, this should entail ensuring secrets management best practices are in place and that code does not contain embedded or reused secrets at any time.

By layering on other security best practices, including the principle of least privilege (PoLP) and separation of privilege, you can help ensure that users and applications have access and privileges restricted precisely to what they need and what is authorized. Restriction and separation of privileges help reduce privileged access sprawl and condense the attack surface, such as by limiting lateral movement in the event of a compromise. The right secrets management policies, buttressed by effective processes and tools, can make managing, transmitting, and securing secrets and other privileged information much easier. By applying these seven best practices in secrets management, you can support cloud security and tighten security across the enterprise.

Virtual Private Cloud (VPC)

For organizations that rely on a diverse quantity and type of servers within their server infrastructure, implementing a VPC (Virtual Private Cloud) to segment public and private infrastructure is an absolute security requirement. Building an environment with VPCs is similar to the concept of VLANs (Virtual Local Area Networks), but it is extended in the cloud using software to build your network segments and access. VPCs are the conceptual equivalent that targets the traffic flowing from the cloud to your network.

Having a VPC configured is essential to protecting your infrastructure from external threats; it is a paradigm that requires continuous maintenance and review, especially for dynamic cloud environments. Cloud administrators must monitor and maintain their VPC to keep it secure and ensure the risk surface is acceptable.

While a VPC can mitigate the attack vectors from a threat actor, it needs to be implemented, secured, monitored, managed, and audited just like any other security implementation at the network layer. Therefore, it's essential to get up to speed with a cloud provider's security and architectural solutions to understand their capabilities for VPC monitoring and management, which will be different for all CSPs. From a business perspective, it ultimately translates in the cloud to simple requirements, like a virtual firewall allowing users to lock down their networks and defend against unauthorized activity.

Entitlements

In the context of a cloud-based access control decision, an entitlement is the approval for an identity to perform an action on, or in relation to, an asset. It is often thought of as a collection of rights, privileges, permissions, authorizations, access rights, or rules at an abstract, higher level to perform a task. However, there is a subtle difference between each when discussing attack vectors in the cloud that needs clarification to formulate attack mitigation strategies. Entitlement management comprises the processes that grant, enumerate, monitor, revoke, and administer fine-grained access entitlements.

To start, there are two typical cloud authorization models, and these should not be confused with authentication. Please reference Figure 4-2. In this model, which is termed the *"Cloud Enforcement Scenario,"* there is a request to authorize an action (in this case, in the cloud) on a resource, by an identity (user, process, or application). The workflow involves a positive response from an authorization, with the potential responses to be Allow, Deny, or Not Applicable. This is the workflow that has been confirmed by the Oasis XACML and IETF OAuth2 committees.

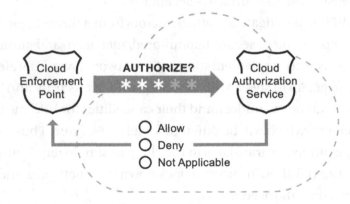

Figure 4-2. *Cloud enforcement scenario*

This workflow is called the *"Cloud Entitlements Scenario"*; it embraces the concept of entitlements. There are services in a cloud-native environment, unique to each vendor's architecture, that determine all the entitlements an identity (user, process, or application) has at any given instance of time. In this workflow, a Cloud Entitlement Point (CEP) asks a Cloud Authorization Service for an identity's entitlements within the current context. The Cloud Authorization Service (based on configured policies) will return a set of entitlements that belong to that identity.

In this workflow, the entitlements become a logical group that can be enumerated during runtime to determine the authorization status and what needs to be acted upon in future requests. Remember, this is about authorization of an entitlement after authentication. Entitlements are not involved in the authentication process.

Privileges

In the context of cloud attack vectors, privileges can be defined as any permissions, rights, or entitlements assigned to an account that will resolve a task to authorize with an "allow." While privileges are generally thought of as being only assigned to administrator or root accounts, in the cloud, privileges are much more granular. They can be any privileged assignment that would be a critical risk to the environment when misused, abused, or hacked. Therefore, the concept of privileges in the cloud is much broader than privileges on-premise due to the potential impact and exposure they can have when assigned or, more importantly, abused.

As a point of reference, a formal definition of privileges and the associated threats and risks can be found in *Privileged Attack Vectors*.[3] A simple illustration of the privileged model can be viewed in Figure 4-3.

---

[3] www.springer.com/us/book/9781484259139

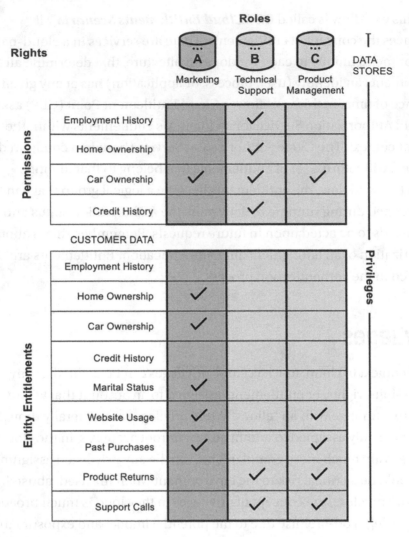

Figure 4-3. *The privilege model applied to entitlements, rights, and permissions*

Rights

A right is defined as a task that identities and their associated accounts (or groups of accounts) can perform for a specific purpose. In the cloud, systems administrators assign rights to identities comprised of accounts (users) or groups of accounts. For example, the ability to manipulate an identity (existing, creation, or deletion) requires role-based access rights to identities and accounts to manipulate the schemas containing these objects.

In general, rights typically translate the security definition for a role in an organization. That is, does the person have the right to perform this task or function? As another example, the role of auditor typically has rights that allow extensive read-only permissions to logs and reports for inspection to conduct an audit. This role (linked to the account) has no permission to alter data or perform additional actions.

Roles

A role is an abstract concept that groups like identities and accounts together based on a technology or business function. In business terms, these collections describe employees and their job functions. As an example, individuals can be categorized by their job role, such as "developer" or "legal team member."

Roles can be abstracted in business terms when discussing the cloud, like quality assurance engineer or automation processes used for the maintenance or deployment of a software. In this example, cloud automation for the role could involve publishing new content and therefore must have the rights and permissions to perform the task. The best way to think of a role is as a group of identities represented by accounts in a collection with a specific function. The role then can have a security model that only allows the activities required for the performance of the desired tasks.

Certificates

The easiest way to understand certificates is by first starting with how they are used in the cloud. Certificates that cloud service providers use contain a public key. By definition, a public key is a part of a cryptographic system that uses pairs of keys. Each pair consists of a public key and a private key. The generation of such key pairs depends on cryptographic algorithms based on mathematical problems, termed one-way functions.

Certificates have a thumbprint based on a public key that provides a means to unequivocally identify the system. This thumbprint is used to validate an identity and determine which certificate a cloud service should use for authentication. It is the primary method for validating the identity of a cloud service (like a website), and it allows for authorized communications. In the cloud, this technology is fundamental to ensuring a website, application, or service responding to requests is genuinely the proper source and not one that has been spoofed.

As you can surmise, if a certificate is compromised or faux certificates are created on behalf of an organization, then threat actors have an attack vector to lure unsuspecting users and Internet traffic to their malicious site impersonating legitimate cloud-based services like the website for a specific company.

Resources

The term "resource" is one of the most misused words when it comes to cloud computing. The definition of resource differs when referring to on-premise technology vs. the cloud. When we refer to a resource as on-premise, we refer to almost any system that can help accomplish a mission. It could be a database, web server, file storage, etc. Almost anything.

On-premise, a resource is different than an asset because the resource may not be tangible, like a physical server, but rather intangible, like the components that are installed and functioning on that server as a system.

When we reference the cloud, the definition of a resource is strictly a subset of the on-premise definition for intangible resources. Resources in the cloud refer to computing services, like memory, CPU, and file storage that can be dynamically managed or fixed to discrete parameters. Since the cloud has no physical attributes for the end user to consume, the asset, system, and similar concepts are not included in the definition. Concepts, like a web server in the cloud, are more commonly (but not always) referred to as an asset, but the dynamic processes that make the web service scale and function are the resources.

While this difference is a slight nuance in insanity to get right, resources are often swapped with other terms like assets when discussing security in the cloud. However, a nuanced understanding of what "resource" means can make all the difference in the world when describing an attack that consumes resources versus an attack that exfiltrates data from an asset. As an attack vector, resource consumption may be an indicator of compromise, and high resource consumption generally equates to the costs of operating in the cloud due to the consumption-based pricing of resources themselves.

Certificate Authorities

A certificate authority (CA) is a trusted entity operating as a business that issues Secure Sockets Layer (SSL) digital certificates as a part of public and private key pairs (previously discussed). These digital certificates are simply files that are used to cryptographically link a resource with a public key. Internet services, including web browsers, use them to authenticate data sent on the Internet (or trusts built internal to an organization), ensuring the integrity and source of content delivered online.

CAs are a reliable and critical trust component of the Internet's Public Key Infrastructure (PKI). They help secure communications between users, services, applications, and cloud providers throughout the

Internet and, thus, the world. When a CA issues a digital certificate for an organization and their website and/or services, users and applications know they are connected with the correct service and not a fake or spoofed website that a threat actor is hosting with malicious intent.

CAs play the following important roles concerning Internet services:

- Issuing digital certificates to reputable organizations

- Verifying the trust for resources communicating over the Internet for a wide variety of use cases

- Verifying domain names and organizations to validate legitimate identities and, thus, avoid spoofing and domain squatting

- Maintaining a certificate revocation list that gets populated based on expiration or reputational abuse of a certificate (it was used, stolen, or issued with malicious intent)

Finally, as a business, every CA requires a processing fee to complete the business verification process and issue a digital certificate.

Permissions

A permission determines what identities (and associated accounts or groups) can do with the rights assigned within a policy. This is typically scoped using roles (but can be as granular as the account level, depending on the system) and includes basic definitions like

- **Read**: The identity or account can view items.

- **Write**: The identity or account can create or edit items.

- **Delete**: The identity or account can delete items.

- **Deny:** The identity or account is explicitly restricted from items.

In the context of the cloud, permissions can apply to other identities, instances, files, logs, runtimes, etc.

If you consider the combination of entitlements, roles, privileges, permissions, and rights, you have a model that allows for the assignment of principals to an identity to perform a task. Figure 4-4 illustrates the complex interaction of users, roles, rights, privileges, and resources.

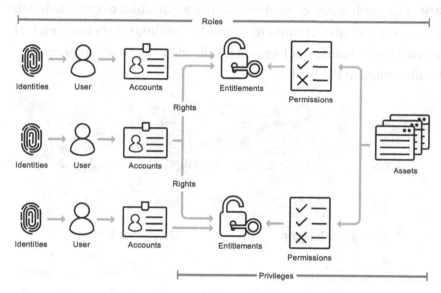

Figure 4-4. *Permissions model illustrated to explain complete interaction*

While the interaction is generally seamless to end users, the difference between privileges, permissions, and rights can be exploited by a threat actor when not clearly defined. Therefore, it is up to cloud administrators to properly provision all accounts and associated identities correctly to ensure there are no security gaps or inappropriate privileges assigned.

Containers

A container is based on software virtualization; it creates an instance in which the host operating system's kernel allows for multiple user space instances to operate. Simply, a container is a concept that creates a unit of software that bundles up source code (and all its dependencies and libraries) for application control and for the application to execute reliably from one computing environment to another, without extra overhead. The complete bundle before deployment is referred to as a container image and is illustrated in Figure 4-5.

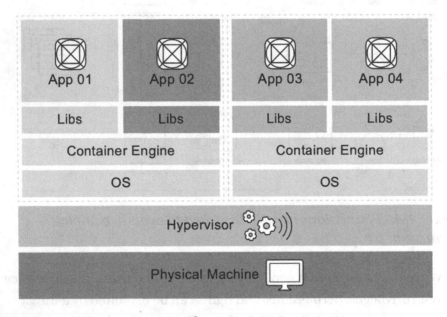

Figure 4-5. *Representation of a container image*

Containers are a foundational component for achieving efficiency and scalability in modern cloud computing. They can be created and destroyed via automation to meet these objectives.

Consider, as an example, a special case of a container based on Docker. A Docker container is a lightweight, stand-alone, compiled version of a container with executable packages of software that include everything needed to execute the actual application. This is a proprietary implementation based on Docker technology itself instead of container technology from vendors like Microsoft.

As a side benefit, containers offer a good security layer to applications in the cloud due to their isolation and encapsulation of the necessary runtime to execute. If one container is compromised, it can be destroyed and subsequently replaced by another container created based on the source container image.

Segmentation

The concept of segmentation can be applied to memory, networks, or any other resource or asset that can be isolated from one another using electronic or physical security controls. The goal is to build a definable boundary in the asset or resource. This creates separation that protects the asset/resource from becoming a liability if some malicious activity occurs in a similar portion of the system.

For example, memory segmentation in an operating system is a memory management technique for partitioning a computer's memory (primary or storage) into sections. This is commonly used to virtualize instances, but it can also apply within an individual instance. If a computing device uses segmentation, a reference to a memory location includes a value that identifies a segment and an offset (memory location) within that segment that will allow the applications and the operating systems to identify the placement of stored information. Applications that utilize the same memory segment each time are typically targeted for exploitation due to the predictability of their runtime location. Randomization of memory allocations, when applied to segmentation, adds entropy to relocations, making their location less predictable. This mitigation technique is called Address Space Layout

Randomization (ASLR), and it is a common method of enforcing security when using segmentation for memory. This helps protect the cloud from memory-based lateral movement attacks between virtualized assets.

Network segmentation is a similar concept, but it is applied to all the addressable assets within a network address. A basic example would be to logically group web servers, database servers, and nonadministrative user workstations into separate network segments. The VPC would then provide appropriate connectivity into those segments from on-premise technology or between these segments. By creating network segments and granting access to only the resources that are necessary within each segment (as opposed to a flat network where everything is visible and addressable), you adopt a fundamental principle of least privilege network access.

Finally, when considering cloud environments, segmentation applies not only to memory and networks but also to storage, access control, databases, and any other object or resource that can be logically grouped to isolate runtime and activity from other resources. This is necessary when considering attack vectors that can leverage lateral movement from one resource to another in multitenant, and even some single-tenant, environments.

Microsegmentation

Microsegmentation is a method of creating zones within segmented environments to isolate workloads from one another and secure them individually, even if they are of the same asset type. Microsegmentation can be implemented on-premise or in the cloud, and it is based on policies that limit network traffic between workloads based on approaches like zero trust.

The primary goal of microsegmentation is to restrict inappropriate interaction between assets and only allow expected communications to occur. Microsegmentation can be implemented using traditional network security controls or using software-defined networks (SDN) to separate and implement policies between control and data planes. Using SDN for microsegmentation is preferred in the cloud due to its flexibility and its rapid ability to adjust dynamic environments.

Microsegmentation benefits include

- **Attack Surface Reduction**: Microsegmented asset communications are no longer flat; the resources contained within, regardless of device type, can be isolated and monitored for inappropriate network traffic.

- **Restricted Lateral Movement**: In case of a security breach, microsegmentation limits the targets that can be compromised by limiting exposed services.

- **Regulatory Compliance**: Microsegmentation allows for the implementation of policies to strictly adhere to data governance and data mapping.

- **Policy Management**: Regardless of hardware or SDN implementation, policies for networks, applications, and zone access can be centrally managed and monitored to ensure proper data flow.

- **Security Best Practices**: The separation of duties for security, development, and operations can be implemented and enforced for production deployment of code and production cloud operations management.

Instances

The term "instance" is one of the most overused and misunderstood terms in cloud computing. An instance should be understood as a single copy of a running program. Having multiple instances of a program implies that it has been loaded and is executing in an asset's memory multiple times. When you use the term in the context of the cloud, it can be any asset, whether dormant or executing. A single file can be an instance, or multiple executions of a file used with microsegmentation can also be considered instances.

The trouble with the definition of "instance" is that it applies to any asset in the cloud that "could" be duplicated and which "could" have multiple identical copies present. When there is only one version, no copies, and no chance of duplicating it, it is commonly referred to as an instance, but that is incorrect. Therefore, only when the instance conforms to a replicable data type definition can it be called an instance, and when it is unique, the term should not be applied. Then it should be referenced by its asset type a configuration file, virtual appliance, template, or image. While there is a subtle distinction here, it is important to understand the nuances as we begin to explore attack vectors against instances as opposed to a specific stand-alone resource type.

Single Tenant

Single tenancy is a solution deployment architecture in which a single instance of an application and supporting infrastructure is deployed, typically using some form of segmentation for an individual customer. Single tenancy is commonly used to deploy solutions on-premise and as a model for implementing SaaS when the deployment model is satisfactory based on costs and security.

In a single-tenant deployment, a customer (referred to as a tenant) will have a singular instance of an application dedicated to them. The service provider will manage the tenant and dedicated infrastructure while still allowing nearly complete control of the implementation, including updates by the customer.

The most common characteristics of a single-tenant SaaS application include:

- A high level of user engagement, user control, and customization to meet business requirements.

- High level of reliability, security, and backup due to the isolation of the implementation and avoidance of potential issues created by other customers sharing the same tenant via segmentation.

- Change control of updates and patches are managed by the end user vs. the provider. This allows clients to maintain a version until they are ready to consume updates.

- The tenant's performance and uptime are solely dependent on the customer's instance and rarely impacted by other customers.

- Sensitive data is independent of other potential tenants from the same provider because they are housed in dedicated instances. This provides security in case of a data breach or in case of faults in segmentation that could lead to lateral movement.

- Single tenancy may also provide an easier migration path to hosting in another cloud computing provider, if a need arises or there is migration from on-premise to the cloud.

Organizations would likely choose a single-tenant deployment and a vendor that supports this model over other possible options if all other things like pricing, security, and service-level agreements are considered equal.

When considering or designing a single-tenant architecture, every tenant will have its own instances that are comprised of software, databases, web servers, etc. With this design, each tenant's data and runtime are segmented from one another. Each instance may be customized based on a generally available template for every tenant to personalize it for their needs. However, customers do not have access to any underlying code or maintenance of the runtime environment. This separates a single-tenant SaaS deployment from an end user deploying an application on their own in the cloud.

Despite some stigma attached to this approach, cloud adoption of single-tenant architectures is very common and even preferred by some, especially in the federal space. If an organization uses a private cloud service or a third-party cloud offering to host an application, it is most likely a single-tenant system. This is because the organization would license its operations solely for them and would have complete control over access to the tenant – and all the security and management options contained within. Figure 4-6 illustrates a single-tenant deployment model.

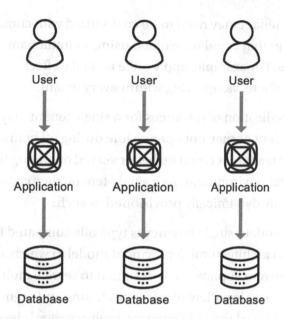

Figure 4-6. *Single-tenant deployment model*

With all the potential advantages to single tenancy, it is still not the preferred approach by cloud software vendors and cloud service providers. Drawbacks of single tenancy include

- The setup, computing resources, customization, security, and maintenance of hosting one SaaS tenant per customer typically cost more for a cloud computing provider than hosting a multitenant version of the solution. This cost impacts the software vendor's profitability and financials and the consumption of cloud computing resources.

- Since the cloud computing provider normally manages the customer's tenant, it then takes more time to update, upgrade, or manage every tenant. This has a distinct overhead cost.

- Every tenant may need to be customized with common settings that could be avoided using a multitenant model. For example, apply once and take effect everywhere, vs. applying within every tenant.

- The dedication of resources for a single tenant may be inefficient or may not operate idle during off hours. These resources could be better served operating in another environment. As a single tenant, they cannot be easily dynamically provisioned as such.

In tenancy models, single tenancy is typically compared to multitenancy, an architectural deployment model in which a single instance of a software application is designed to service multiple customers using a wide variety of resource sharing and segmentation techniques. Compared to single tenancy, multitenancy is less expensive to operate, has efficient shared resource usage, has lower maintenance costs, and, arguably, has larger computing capacity. This will be discussed in more detail in the next section.

From a cloud attack vector perspective, individual instance flaws in a configuration, or missing security patches, can be exploited per tenant. Each tenant would need to be attacked due to the inherent segmentation in a single-tenant model. Thus, within a single-tenant model, it is less likely that every customer could be breached at once or that one tenant could compromise the rest of the hosting environment. This statement has a few exceptions, including vulnerabilities with exploits that affect every tenant or poor security hygiene, like shared credentials, that could impact every instance.

Multitenant

As important as single-tenant deployments are to the cloud, most SaaS services operate on multitenant architectures. That fact is based on cost to operate, performance, human resource requirements to maintain versions, obsolete definitions for cloud applications, and ensuring strict similarity between all subscribers. To that end, we need to understand the reasons behind multitenancy and the justifications beyond risks and costs.

Multitenancy refers to the model of operations for software where multiple clients (businesses, users, organizations, etc.) operate using the same application in a shared, albeit segmented, environment. The tenants (instances) are logically segmented at multiple layers, but they are electronically integrated and coded as a part of the software. The degree of segmentation must be absolute to ensure there is no data bleed, but the degree of actual data segmentation will vary based on the service offering. The tenants are typically represented as organizations with access to the multitenant application via license subscriptions.

To understand multitenancy, think of how social media applications operate from the perspective of the daily user. Multiple people can store and access photos and posts from other people, but their preferences, groups, and friend lists are completely separate, despite being stored in the hosting service. Users of the social media system do interact with each other, but they don't have access to anything that is posted privately or to a limited set of users. This model also holds true for systems like online banking, where family members may be granted access to the same account, but the rest of the service is completely isolated from customer to customer. Unless explicitly permitted, no unauthorized user can see your balance or conduct a transaction.

In multitenant architectures, customers of the application service provider use the same infrastructure, assets, and application, all while keeping data and business runtime separate and secure. Based on the service, some data may be shared between tenants, or it may even be sanitized for some form of statistical reputation. Figure 4-7 illustrates this as a shared application with multiple users.

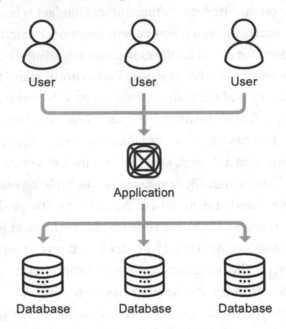

Figure 4-7. *Multitenancy with multiple users, shared applications, and single-tenant databases (not segmented)*

Many cloud benefits are only possible because of multitenancy. First, consider why multitenancy is beneficial for software providers, cloud service providers, and end users:

- **Resource Management**: A single tenant reserved for one client isn't efficient because that one tenant is not likely to consume all the instance's resources. By sharing instances and infrastructure among multiple tenants, consumption of available resources and computing power is optimized.

- **Operating Costs**: With multiple customers sharing resources, a cloud computing provider and application vendor can offer their services to many customers at a much lower cost than if each customer required their own dedicated tenant.

- **Analytics**: Cloud applications and services that can share sanitized data across tenants benefit every customer. For example, a vendor incurring a cyberattack can share indicators of compromise with others to mitigate future attacks.

And, as there are always pros, the cons lead us to the attack vectors that we should be concerned about:

- **Security and Compliance**: Some organizations, like federal agencies, may be unable to store data within a shared infrastructure, no matter how secure, due to regulatory requirements. In addition, security problems or corrupted data from one client could spread to other tenants that share the same resources as a part of the multitenant architecture. While this should not typically occur, mistakes do occur in coding, unpatched vulnerabilities, or other security settings that could allow a threat actor to breach the environment and laterally move between tenants. These risks are managed by cloud and application vendors since they normally invest more in security and testing to ensure these threats do not materialize. However, one mistake can lead to an exposure of every client.

- **Shared Resources**: The performance of a multitenant environment can falter if one tenant uses excessive resources compared to other clients using the same environment. While this is also considered an extreme case and the solution should be architected against this scenario, untested use cases, or other cyberattacks like DDoS (distributed denial of service), can impact the entire service. Again, this should not occur if the cloud and application providers have correctly set up their infrastructure.

- **Updates**: When a cloud provider pushes a solution update, all the tenants simultaneously receive the changes. If the update has a bug or introduces a vulnerability, then all the subscribers typically experience the fault all at once. End users cannot mitigate this risk via their own change control since updates are at the discretion of the application vendor and cloud service provider.

To understand this better, consider a baseball glove that is shared between multiple players, among multiple teams, and across different leagues. Each user plays a different position on the field, and every person has a different sized hand. After the glove has been broken in, it will fit some players better than others, and the webbing will have become uneven because of the wear it has incurred being fit to all the different hand sizes. The player's performance is now being governed by the history of the glove, and, clearly, the adage "one glove fits all" is no longer true.

This baseball analogy captures an unfortunate truth in the way many cloud and application providers implement multitenancy. Most providers implement multitenancy as a shared software instance with multitenancy capabilities. They store configuration information about each tenant and use this data to customize the environment to an individual client's needs. Clients are segmented from each other – even though they all share the same software instance. They each use and experience the solution differently, and the amount of customization available is similar to our baseball glove. It will only fit some clients well. Some clients may use the solution heavily, potentially driving features based on their financial commitment to the solution (how much they spend each year). This solution direction may not lend itself well to other clients, based on the vertical or use cases they need. The difference is like a catcher's glove vs. a first baseman's glove. They are both baseball players, but it will suit neither well if the glove is a mismatch for the position.

Edge Computing

Edge computing is a computing model that distributes computation and data storage closer to the sources of data being processed – typically, the endpoints themselves. The concept improves response time by minimizing factors that could slow down processing, like network latency, insufficient cloud resources, and saturated or slow network bandwidth.

Edge computing is modeled after a topology where the location of the data and edge process the information for the system, rather than sending raw information to the cloud. Unfortunately, the concept is often confused with IoT (Internet of Things) devices, but they are only part of the architecture; they are actually part of the edge. Edge computing is an architecture, not a specific technology or device like IoT.

Consider a home-based camera system with motion detection. In lieu of sending the raw video to the cloud for every camera, the camera processes the video locally, including motion and person detection, before transmitting the results. The bulk of the processing is done at the edge, in the IoT camera, while the cloud provides storage, alerting, and authentication services. It would be ineffective to perform these services in a traditional client server model.

Table 4-1 compares computation traits using a cloud service provider vs. edge computing. Please note, the attack vectors for both are similar, but the impact is different.

Table 4-1. *Comparison of cloud service providers and edge computing technologies*

Traits	Cloud Service Provider	Edge Computing	Attack Vector
Applications	Primarily SaaS-based applications hosted and maintained by a vendor in support of an organization's business initiatives.	Devices with local operating systems and software that perform computation tasks and leverage the cloud for additional data. This includes devices like smart home technology, digital personal assistants, and even smart vehicles.	Vulnerability, misconfiguration, credentials, or secrets
Availability	Regional-based data centers with high availability, disaster recovery, and fault tolerance architected into the solution.	Devices, if designed, can operate without the cloud, but are dependent on the cloud for additional processing and management.	Denial of service
Location	Data centers and computing power can be anywhere.	Primary processing is with the edge device itself, and additional computation requirements can be anywhere else in the world.	Regional to global outage or reduced services

(continued)

Table 4-1. (*continued*)

Traits	Cloud Service Provider	Edge Computing	Attack Vector
Latency	Dependent on latency to and from the data center to the source.	Since the edge device is electronically close or contained with the end user's asset, latency is experienced when additional computation power is needed from the cloud. Typically, latency is not a concern unless cloud dependencies exist.	Regional to global outage or reduced services
Bandwidth	Restricted by the slowest network link connecting to the cloud and network saturation.	Restricted by the local area network on which the edge device and the user reside.	Regional to global outage or reduced services
Scalability	Dependent on the design of the service and capabilities within the data center.	Scalable at both the edge and at the data center, similar to a cloud service provider	Denial of service or distributed denial of service
Security	Attacks are primarily at the data center (electronic, not physical) or with transmission of data itself.	Attacks are localized to the edge device and user, as are any additional communications required from the cloud.	Vulnerability, misconfiguration, credentials, or secrets

Breach

"Breach." The nasty "B" word that every business fears and every cybersecurity professional should use only when appropriate. The word "breach" is more than just a word to describe a threat actors' penetration into an organization or the exfiltration of information. It is a word that businesses, legal departments, and compliance officers fear due to a precise workflow of disclosures and notifications that must occur if the word is used externally to describe a security event or incident. If nothing else, security training for all employees should include the ramifications of using the word "breach" to describe any cybersecurity-related activity until the organization is appropriately prepared to follow through on any, and all, appropriate related activity. The reasons why are quite profound if not understood by everyone.

To begin, let us define a breach. A breach in terms of cybersecurity is a violation in which sensitive, protected, or confidential data is copied, transmitted, viewed, stolen, or used by an individual unauthorized to do so. In addition, it can be the inappropriate usage of assets or resources that can undermine the integrity of a system, application, or infrastructure used to provide services to a business. The outcome will result in unintentional information disclosure, data leak, runtime issues, or sensitive data exfiltration. When a cybersecurity incident takes on these characteristics, public disclosure is often branded a breach vs. a cybersecurity incident due to legal or compliance regulations. Consider what must happen if you label a cybersecurity incident a breach:

- Local, state, or government laws may require notification and disclosure to appropriate governing bodies within a very specific service-level agreement.

- A DFIR (Digital Forensics and Incident Response) may be legally required by a third-party organization depending on the type of data compromised or potential financial loss.

- Your legal, marketing, and executive teams need to be prepared with appropriate public statements based on the vertical, market, and intended audience for the breach information.

- Based on your cyber insurance policy, you may need to notify them and their procedures followed for a formal investigation and release of funds for remediation, compensation, and business continuity.

- Client, vendor, and end-user disclosure should be conducted based on applicable laws and if needed proper mitigation plans announced like credit monitoring before any information is disclosed.

- While not legally required, proper transparency and honesty should always be used in discussing a breach with the public and occur in a timely manner. Attempting to hide or obfuscate facts generally creates a negative feedback in the community.

Sadly, breaches range from targeted attacks by malicious threat actors (black hats), organized cybercriminals (often in countries outside of legal justifications), political activists, and even nation state–sponsored attacks for geopolitical reasons. In addition, if an employee or trusted individual like a contractor assists with the breach, it is generally labeled an insider attack. Contrary, an incident (not labeled a breach) occurs when something suspicious has occurred or an infiltration has happened, but there is no data disclosure, or performance anomalies are benign. These are generally identified promptly and shut down as a part of normal information security operations.

In the end, when classifying a security incident as a breach, there are quantifiable costs that can be associated with the event. This comes in the form of remediation costs, investigation fees, legal or compliance penalties, and any indirect costs to brand reputation, victim compensation, or supplemental services like credit monitoring. Therefore, when you need to label a cybersecurity incident as a breach, be aware of all the ramifications for your breach and most importantly your legal obligations potentially worldwide. As a security best practice, it is always recommended to be transparent and honest about any breaches and disclose information in a timely manner.

Recovery Point Objective and Recovery Time Objective

Recovery Point Objective (RPO) and Recovery Time Objective (RTO) are two of the most important metrics for disaster recovery and data integrity anywhere, including in the cloud. These metrics are not calculated by the end user; they are delivered as a statement[4] from your CSP or XaaS vendors for each solution or system they are offering. The statement should include data from theoretical and empirical testing and any prior experienced failure conditions. This will essentially be the material supporting the claimed RTO/RPO time frames.

In the real world, it would be great to have a service with an RTO of ten minutes and an RPO of zero seconds, but entirely another thing if an actual recovery takes days and loses months of data. This is a real-world consideration that forces a business to formulate scenarios and options for the resumption of business processes in accordance with established RPO and RTO statements. Therefore, RTO and RPO must be correct before establishing any availability of cloud-based services. Availability cannot be calculated without them.

---

[4]https://www.unitrends.com/blog/rpo-rto

To a new security professional, these two terms can appear quite similar or trivial in their functions although they are not. Let's dig in deeper into the definitions for each to understand how they are actually different and why they should not be confused with other terms like MTBF (Mean Time Between Failure) and MTTR (Mean Time to Repair).

For those unfamiliar with RPO, it can seem an odd thing to describe as an objective. The RPO defines the maximum amount of data, in terms of a time period, that the business can afford to lose, e.g., four hours of data. If you ask a business unit how much data they can afford to lose, almost all will say "none" even though that is not necessarily true. What you are looking to discover is the point at which data loss impacts the company's ability to do business and tolerance for a real fault.

As an example, if the RPO is 24 hours, then we need a data backup solution that ensures the maximum interval between backups is 24 hours. At first glance, this may seem easy to achieve with a daily backup schedule. Remember that the RPO specifies the threshold at which the transition between acceptable and unacceptable occurs. It makes sense, therefore, to operate multiple backups within the period to allow for any failure within the backup service. A 12-hourly backup schedule ensures there's at least 1 prior backup available during the RPO period, should the most recent be unavailable for whatever reason.

RTO is the length of time within which a business process must be restored to a service level, acceptable to the business, after a failure, disaster, etc., to avoid consequences unacceptable to the business. Simply put, the RTO answers the question: "How much time can the business operate without this service before there is significant impact to operations?" It's important to remember that restoration of a process is probably not limited to the process being available to operate; there's undoubtedly impact from the outage to consider that will also need to be addressed to achieve true recovery. This is essentially the time needed to catch up from the disruption itself and restore to a proper normal state of operations.

Both RPO and RTO should be an outcome of Business Impact Analysis (BIA) and not driven by the capabilities of the services underpinning them. For example, RPO is not defined by any existing data backup operation. Just because the service or solution already runs on a daily backup schedule does not mean that the RPO is 24 hours. The business defines the tolerances, the processes, and technology services that support the business within those tolerances. Figure 4-8 illustrates how RPO and RTO apply to an incident.

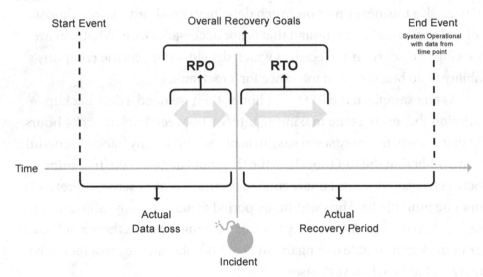

Figure 4-8. *RPO and RTO in relationship to an incident*

While performance BIA is beyond the scope of this book, when looking at operations to determine RPO and RTO, the following offers a list of common data points that should be considered:

- Maximum tolerable data loss for the specific organization or organizational unit in terms of time. How many minutes, hours, or days of data can you afford to lose completely or recover from other sources that might be labor intensive or consume excessive time? Organizations processing sensitive information, such as financial transactions or health records, may have external drivers, such as regulation and law, on what can and cannot be lost and over what time period. There may also be requirements around analysis and reporting that must be performed following any loss – another cost that should be considered when conducting BIA.

- Third-party service dependencies in the cloud that may impact the ability to recover from a disruption. This can be anything from an ISP outage to collateral damage from a third-party cyberattack.

- Data storage options, such as physical files vs. cloud storage, can affect the speed of recovery, especially when full backups are needed from the cloud and bandwidth will be the limiting factor in data restoration. The time to restore backups can be overlooked when looking at BIA as the focus is on the failure and getting operational again. Data can have dependencies over time, meaning backups need to be restored completely prior to new data being added – this highlights the link between RPO and RTO.

- The cost to implement technology to minimize RPO and RTO compared to the cost of reprocessing the lost information. This is of course subject to the fact that the information for reprocessing is not truly lost due to another fault.

- Regulatory compliance initiatives that mandate controls for disaster recovery, data loss, and data availability that may change your calculation.

- The cost of implementing real-time, near real-time, or cold disaster recovery solutions.

With any good plan, there are risks for failure. Once you have established RPO and RTO, consider their counterparts, Recovery Time Actual (RTA) and Recovery Point Actual (RPA). These can only be established during business continuity plan testing and simulated incident response events.

RTA and RPA are empirical values that will help prove that your service-level agreements for RPO and RTO can actually be met. Conducting this testing across all systems and services that support your business's core functions is essential to both prove that they provide and support the business and to expose any flaws in your operations that might need improvement. As we've said elsewhere in this book, wherever your data exists, it's your responsibility. Make sure you don't miss a component in your planning and testing because it's owned or operated by someone else. If it forms part of your service, it needs to be part of your planning and testing.

One last point, when considering RTO and RPO, these are business objectives and are never determined by looking at the technology. It's entirely possible that meeting the RTO and/or RPO demanded by the business with current technology is not possible. Therefore, the business must accept the risk or commit to developing processes that offer alternative operating approaches that mitigate some or all of that risk.

Others

There are so many other words, real or made up, and acronyms associated with the cloud and specific cloud provider services that even the most seasoned professionals have to stop and ask "what is that?" or "what does that mean?" from time to time. This is analogous to finding the definition for self-sealing stem bolts or the origins of a tree octopus. To help streamline our conversation on cloud attack vectors and cloud-specific technologies, consider these additional definitions.

S3 Bucket

An Amazon S3 bucket is a public cloud storage resource available in Amazon Web Services (AWS). The nomenclature S3 is an acronym play on Simple Storage Service (S3 because all three words start with the letter S), and the resource is simply an object storage offering. Amazon S3 buckets, which are like file folders, store objects that consist of data and the descriptive metadata. In the cloud, S3 buckets can have public access and will need to be restricted to only appropriate identities. Lack of proper access controls is the most common mistake that leads to a breach and data exfiltration.

EC2

Amazon Elastic Compute Cloud (Amazon EC2) is a web service that provides secure, dynamically scalable, flexible computing capacity in the cloud. It is designed to make services to develop web applications easier for developers. The implementation of EC2 utilizes a web service interface that allows nearly complete flexibility programmatically, which enables users to configure the service based on technical or business requirements. Configuration mistakes and poor secrets management of unpatched vulnerabilities can lead to the exploitation of EC2.

E5

E5 and its sister Microsoft Offerings, E1, E3, F1, F3, and F5, are cloud-based offerings that provide a wide variety of services and solutions for Microsoft 365, a SaaS suite of productivity applications (Outlook, Word, Excel, PowerPoint, etc.) that have been combined with advanced services for voice, analytics, security, storage, and compliance services, all of which are hosted in the cloud.[5]

Threat actors target all aspects of Microsoft 365 via poor credential management and unsecure API implementations. Microsoft is very good at keeping vulnerabilities patched within their services, but if the API or administrator account is compromised, then all your email and OneDrive files could be exposed to a threat actor. This was one of the results of the techniques used to exploit SolarWinds in 2020.

Kubernetes

Kubernetes (also referred to as K8s) is a portable, extensible, open source platform for managing containerized workloads and services. K8s excels over similar offerings by providing robust automation and enforcement of standardized configurations. The name Kubernetes is derived from the Greek word meaning helmsman or pilot. K8s is a play on the word (also known as a numeronym) based on the number of letters between the "K" and the "s" – yes, it is eight. The solution was originally developed by Google and was made open source in 2014, after 15 years of managing cloud-based workloads. In recent years, it has been a target for attacks based on unsecure implementations used for automated workflows.

---

[5] https://go.microsoft.com/fwlink/p/?LinkID=2139145&clcid=0x409&culture=en-us&country=US

Docker

Docker is a solution that delivers PaaS products that use operating system-based virtualization to deliver software in discrete packages, called containers. As previously defined, containers are isolated from one another and bundle their own software, libraries, and configuration files to provide segmentation for software during delivery and runtime. Containers communicate through well-defined channels, allowing for strict architectures and security monitoring based on segmentation. Docker is a major component of what makes the cloud "the cloud" today.

SCIM

System for Cross-domain Identity Management (SCIM) is a standard for automating the exchange of user identity information between identity domains and information technology solutions that use an identity for role-based access. This can include identity information used for authentication, authorization, or both. The SCIM standard has grown in popularity and importance as organizations continue to use more cloud-based tools. SCIM is designed to solve the problem of provisioning large quantities of applications (internal and external), servers, databases, and storage without the need for multiple directory services and without maintaining separate role-based identity access models in different solutions. SCIM provides a standard connection method for interfacing and sharing identity information everywhere. While some of the definitions discussed have unique attack vectors, SCIM is a standard for simplifying identity access management and reducing the identity attack surface in the cloud.

Service Fabric

Microsoft Azure Service Fabric is a distributed systems platform that makes it easy to package, deploy, and manage scalable and dependable microservices and containers. It is essentially Microsoft Azure's answer to Docker and Kubernetes, albeit with a plethora of differences for managing Microsoft Windows workloads. Service Fabric also addresses the significant challenges in developing and managing cloud-native applications based on the need for stateful services that may be needed in the cloud and in support of hybrid environments.

Directory Bridging

Active Directory (AD) Bridging is a mechanism that allows users to authenticate non-Windows systems using Active Directory login credentials. This is typically an add-on solution to Linux distributions that join the host asset to a Windows Domain and allow for it to be managed like a native Windows operating system. AD Bridging eliminates the need for a separate directory service for Linux, or the management of local accounts in the cloud, by using established best practices of Active Directory or Azure AD.

DevOps Security (SecDevOps)

DevOps security refers to the discipline and practice of safeguarding the entire DevOps environment and life cycles through strategies, policies, processes, and technology. DevOps security should enable a productive DevOps ecosystem, while helping to identify and remediate code vulnerabilities and operational weaknesses long before they become an issue. In simple terms, it is the security of the automation and workflow from code development all the way through quality assurance and automated deployment. It is commonly used with Agile development practices for publishing solutions to the cloud.

Least Privilege

Least privilege, often referred to as the principle of least privilege (PoLP), refers to the concept and practice of restricting access rights for users, accounts, and computing processes to only those absolutely required to perform routine, authorized activities. Privilege itself refers to the authorization to obtain certain security rights to perform tasks that otherwise would be restricted. A least privilege security model entails enforcing the minimal level of user rights, or lowest clearance level, that allows the user to perform their role. However, least privilege also applies to processes, applications, systems, and devices (such as IoT) in that each should have only those permissions required to perform an authorized activity. As a result, if a user or device is compromised, the threat actor would not have the authority to perform inappropriate actions.

Separation of Privilege

Separation of privilege is an information technology best practice that organizations apply to broadly separate users and processes based on different levels of trust, needs, and privilege requirements. Similar to the concept of network and memory segmentation, separation of privileges essentially creates "moats" around specific parts of an information technology cloud environment. It helps contain intruders close to the point of compromise, restricting lateral movement, while also ensuring that employees, applications, and system processes do not have access to more data than needed. Segmenting privileges and the associated tasks also benefit from a cleaner audit trail and simplified compliance reporting.

Cloud Washing

Cloud washing refers to a misleading marketing practice that is used to rebrand old products by connecting them to the cloud, hosting them in the cloud, or marketing them as cloud enabled or ready. In many cases, there is little difference between cloud washing and hosting an application in the cloud as a single-tenant solution. In reality, cloud washing of applications can result in excessive security risks because the source application was probably not designed to be exposed to the Internet. Thus, the security controls necessary to make the application cloud ready have been "bolted" or "retrofitted" instead of being natively designed into the solution. Cloud washing approaches are generally incompatible with strategies like zero trust. This will be discussed in detail later in this book and often associated with the "lift and shift" of an application from on-premise to the cloud.

Content Delivery Network (CDN)

A content delivery network (CDN) is a network of distributed services that deliver content to a designated target audience based on the user's geographic proximity to the designated cloud's actual data center. CDNs allow efficient content delivery based on being electronically close to the consumers of the content. Most CDN content is associated with streaming services and high-bandwidth applications, like real-time video games.

Elasticity

In cloud computing, elasticity is a term used to reference the ability of a system to adapt to changing workload demand by provisioning and deprovisioning assets and resources. Since most cloud service providers bill based on consumption, optimizing the usage allows for the provisioning of assets and resources to match demand. Customers do not overpay a cloud service provider for services provisioned, but not consumed.

CloudTrail

CloudTrail is an AWS-specific service that enables governance, compliance, monitoring, and auditing of your AWS account and interacting services via logs. Any activity invoked by an identity, role, or other AWS service is recorded as an event in the Cloud Trail logs. These events include, but are not limited to, activity in the AWS Management Console, AWS Command Line Interface entries, and AWS software development kits and APIs that are invoked against your instances or account.

CloudTrail is one of the most powerful AWS tools for threat hunting and for determining evidence of compromise. By default, CloudTrail is enabled on your AWS account when it is first created, and it must be turned off manually, if logging is not required. It is a security best practice to leave CloudTrail always enabled. With the proper role-based access, identities can easily review events in the CloudTrail console by searching the event history based on the specified data retention period in settings. This may need to be adjusted based on your compliance and security requirements and cloud storage costs.

Open Source

Open source is a development model in which a product's source code is made openly available to the public by the developers or organization that created it. Open source products promote collaborative community development and rapid prototyping and identify vulnerabilities that could affect all entities that leverage the solution. Kubernetes is an example of an open source orchestration platform.

101

As an attack vector, open source vulnerabilities can affect multiple companies simultaneously, if they leverage the source code (libraries) within their products. The exploitation of Log4J[6] and previous vulnerabilities like HeartBleed[7] demonstrate how broad of scope an open source vulnerability can be.

Service-Level Agreement (SLA)

A service-level agreement (SLA) is a measurement used to determine whether an arrangement between a customer and a cloud service provider for levels of service, availability, and performance is operating as specified. An SLA is typically documented in a contractual agreement. Violations of an SLA can range from refunds and service credits all the way through "no action" except "we are sorry we had an outage."

Outside of purely technical issues, outages and disruptions caused by a cyberattack can also affect a stated SLA. Organizations may require an SLA for notification, if their data or business has been compromised as a part of a cloud attack. Typically, this is stated in hours or days after a positive determination.

Virtual Machine

A virtual machine (VM) is a software-based computer (asset) that runs an operating system and application environment hosted on a hypervisor (virtual machine hosting system) in lieu of physical hardware. The administration and configuration of the virtual machine has virtually (pun intended) the same experience as setting up dedicated hardware. For lack of a better explanation, a VM is a machine (asset) within a machine (hypervisor).

---

[6] https://www.cisa.gov/uscert/ncas/current-activity/2021/12/10/ apache-releases-log4j-version-2150-address-critical-rce
[7] https://heartbleed.com/

By running virtual machines simultaneously, a physical hardware computer running a hypervisor can execute multiple virtual machines simultaneously, in parallel. In this model, applications running on separate virtual machines do not interfere with each other. If one application crashes, it should not affect other resources in other virtual machines.

Virtual machines can host other virtual machines, similar to the concepts shown in the movie *Inception*. Such a practice can help obfuscate attack vectors by nesting malicious activity in virtual environments using other virtualized technology. Figure 4-9 illustrates this three levels deep and how threat actors can obfuscate malicious behavior in virtual machines or even nested virtual machines.

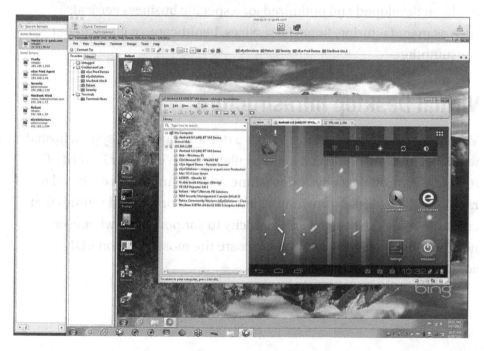

Figure 4-9. *Nested virtual machines containing VMware ESXi, Windows, and Android operating systems*

Finally, attack vectors affecting virtual machines can start in the virtual machines themselves or the hosting hypervisor. This even includes ransomware[8] that targets the hypervisor and encrypts every virtual machine instance as a hostage. Lateral movement between virtual machines is possible when segmentation flaws exist in memory and are exploited with techniques like Rowhammer[9] or when the configuration of virtual machines is not sufficiently hardened to prevent inappropriate communications between them.

Vertical Cloud

A vertical cloud is a solution offered by a cloud service provider and has been developed and optimized for a specific business vertical, such as manufacturing, financial services, healthcare, or government consumption.

Virtual Desktop Infrastructure

Virtual desktop infrastructure (VDI) is a desktop operating system hosted within a virtual machine and made available to an end user instead of remotely controlling a physical machine. VDI technology is designed to rapidly create a desktop environment with saved or cleaned settings that can scale using the principles of elasticity to support users whenever needed. Microsoft, VMware, and Citrix are the most common VDI solutions in the market today.

---

[8] www.truesec.com/hub/blog/secure-your-vmware-esxi-hosts-against-ransomware

[9] https://www.techtarget.com/searchsecurity/definition/Rowhammer

SAML

Security Assertion Markup Language (SAML) is an open standard for exchanging authentication and authorization data between resources, typically between an identity provider and a service provider. SAML is an XML-based markup language for security assertions that enables authentication technologies, like SSO (Single Sign On), to mitigate the risks of multiple credentials, one per website, from being stored or remembered. Its primary function is to allow gated access to additional web applications once a user authenticates via a secure method like multi-factor authentication (MFA).

OpenID

OpenID allows you to use an existing account to sign into multiple websites without needing to create new passwords for each web application. OpenID conceptually builds on the use case of SAML, but it adds attributes to the authentication request that can be used for additional processes. As a user, you can specify what information from your identity it should associate with your OpenID so that it can be shared with the websites you visit. This can include details like your name, phone number, or email address. With OpenID, you control how much of that information is shared with the websites you visit without ever sharing, or having the potential to enter, a password for authentication.

Identity Proofing

Identity proofing is a concept and the associated process by which a cloud service provider collects, validates, and verifies information about a person and their real-world identity. Identity proofing uses knowledge-based attributes and public and private national identity systems to confirm that a person's identity actually matches who is behind the keyboard (or mobile device). This allows users to self-identify and provide verification, enabling a secure authentication process that offers a high level of confidence for the provider – without degrading the end user's experience.

OAuth

OAuth is an open standard for access delegation. It is commonly used as a way for identities on the Internet to grant websites or applications access to information on other websites. The purpose is to enable identity information sharing that never requires the sharing or disclosing identities, secrets, or passwords.

FIDO

FIDO (Fast ID Online) is a set of technology-agnostic security specifications for strong identity authentication. It was developed by the FIDO Alliance, a nonprofit organization that provides standardized authentication at the client and protocol layers. The FIDO specification includes multi-factor authentication (MFA) and public key cryptography support. Unlike traditional password databases, FIDO stores personally identifiable information (PII), such as biometric authentication data, locally on the consumer's device to protect it, typically using advanced storage technology like TPM (Trusted Platform Module). FIDO's local storage of secrets (passwords, certificates, biometrics, etc.) is intended to address concerns about personal data stored in the cloud.

CHAPTER 5

Asset Management

Asset management is one of the most fundamental cybersecurity best practices. Regardless of whether the technology is on-premise, in the cloud, or operating in a hybrid environment, understanding and documenting all your assets is critical. After all, you cannot adequately develop a security strategy against threats if you are unaware that an asset exists and needs protection. And in the cloud, even though it may not be your computer or resource, tracking and classifying the asset is crucial. This will help ensure that it does not become a risk from identity management attacks, data governance issues, and the persistence of exploitable vulnerabilities.

While this discussion on asset management could focus on performing an inventory of everything your organization has in the cloud, one form of Cloud Security Asset Management (CSAM) is critical to protecting against cloud attack vectors. Therefore, this asset management discussion will focus on the identities and, specifically, privileged accounts that are crucial to your asset management and cloud security strategy.

Privileged accounts are a key part of the cyberattack chain. These accounts and their credentials are estimated to be involved in at least 80% of breaches, according to Forrester.[1] Protecting privileged user accounts and, increasingly, machine accounts (nonhuman accounts) is a key

---

[1] www.securitymagazine.com/articles/91830-surge-in-attacker-access-to-privileged-accounts-and-services-puts-businesses-at-risk

M. J. Haber et al., *Cloud Attack Vectors*, https://doi.org/10.1007/978-1-4842-8236-6_5

priority for every security-conscious organization. They are also central to addressing many regulatory requirements and enabling zero trust (will get to this discussion a little later as part of a zero trust common office environment strategy). Privileged account access can enable a threat actor to acquire sensitive information, make system changes, manage resources, and even override security controls and erase traces of their actions, depending on the type of privileges obtained.

As enterprises become more complex and decentralized, embrace the cloud, and as more users work from home, the number and diversity of privileged accounts is exponentially expanding. Every cloud asset needs at least one privileged account at some point in its life cycle. Many of these privileged accounts are proliferating unseen, unmonitored, and unmanaged, presenting dangerous backdoors to the environment for threat actors. Asset management is a critical starting point for getting on top of this risk.

While some privileged users are employees, other privileged accounts are associated with contractors, vendors, auditors, or even automated third-party services and nonhumans who are accessing on-premise, in the cloud, or hybrid environments. As a part of any cybersecurity strategy, the most important first step is to perform an asset inventory and, in this case, to ensure that inventory discovers all accounts and their associated privileges. After all, if you do not know what exists in your environment, you cannot design an appropriate strategy to manage and mitigate their risks. This strategy is most effective when the entire cloud environment and the privileges that exist therein are identified and well understood based on function.

Many organizations rely on asset discovery to perform the most basic asset inventory. This technique ideally identifies every asset, active or dormant, in the cloud and provides details on the associated services, accounts, applications (software), configurations, operating systems, etc. This information then helps the organization classify assets and accounts based on sensitivity, data, ownership, geolocation, and potential attack vectors.

While digital discovery is never perfect, and often suffers from some blind spots based on technology limitations, it does help generate the much-needed baseline for organizations. Ongoing discovery then becomes a routine part of the cybersecurity practice of identifying new assets, shadow IT, nonconforming systems, and even assets that should be deprecated, if not managed via automation. With all this information, privileged account asset management in the cloud can begin to take shape.

In this author's opinion, the best way to embrace asset management of privileged accounts in the cloud is by using a privileged access management (PAM) solution. To start, PAM enables the management and protection of accounts (both human and nonhuman/machine) and their associated privileges throughout an on-premise, hybrid, and cloud environment. Common use cases can include secure storage, rotation, and retrieval of privileged credentials, removing administrative rights, secure session access, and managing secrets used for automation.

All of the above PAM use cases share one common requirement: you must discover or have some foreknowledge of the credential or secret to be managed. To make this process easier to digest (and not like the last supper on the Nostromo), consider these steps:

1. Perform a discovery and enumerate accounts associated with each asset.

2. Identify your sensitive assets and crown jewels. If possible, identify any asset that stores or processes PII (personally identifiable information).

3. Perform a classification of the account to determine if it is local or directory based.

4. Classify whether the account is interactive or machine based. If the account is interactive, ensure it is not using single-factor authentication.

5. Determine all the privileges associated with each account.

6. Identify all assets, applications, services, scripts, etc. that utilize shared accounts. By definition, a shared account is any account used by multiple identities for authentication.

7. Rate each account in terms of importance based on asset inventory. This will include personally identifiable information, trade secrets, financial information, payroll, etc. The list will vary per company, but the compromise and disclosure of any asset that could cause extreme embarrassment, market or financial stress, or is a "game over" event is typically classified as "critical."

8. Associate which accounts have access to these resources and place them under privileged access management. The process should continue through your inventory until you have covered every asset and account that you deem important or that is required to mitigate perceived risk. New accounts should always be added, and deprecated assets should have all privileges removed.

9. If possible, remove all excessive privileges and administrative rights.

Note   While many asset management solutions allow you to discover an account, if you do not classify how it is used or the source of the account, then anything you do next is a moot point. A list of accounts, with no relevance nor context, will not provide you with any assessment around impact, should an account be compromised.

While the process we outlined in steps 1–9 has been admittedly simplified for this book, there are a few accounts in particular that pose the most risk to your cloud attack vector mitigation strategy, if they are not discovered and adequately managed.

So, what are the most important privileged accounts to find across your cloud environment for asset management, and why?

- **Domain Administrator Accounts**: The most important privileged accounts in your cloud or on-premise environment are ones that have access to virtually any and every asset. These are typically domain administrator accounts. These accounts represent the highest value to a threat actor. Organizations should strive to minimize the number of domain administrator accounts – and who has access to them – and should place all of these accounts under privileged access management.

- **Nonhuman Automation Accounts**: Next, seek out any account associated with an application, operating system, database, service, network device, etc., that is shared among multiple assets to enable functionality. While these generally do not have blanket administrative rights, compromising one asset with the shared account can easily be used for lateral movement. This authenticated "hop" to other assets typically occurs by a threat actor until some form of privileged escalation can occur and the compromise of administrative privileges is achieved. In general, the existence of shared accounts represents a poor security practice. Yet, shared accounts persist because they offer the most workable and convenient way to enable some use cases. Therefore, these accounts should always be identified and placed under privileged access management as well.

- **Management Solutions**: Technology used to manage, monitor, configure, automate, and install/modify a cloud environment – from directory services to security solutions – should never have shared accounts. While this may not always be technically possible, they should always be minimized. Security best practices dictate that access from a user to these solutions should absolutely always have a one-to-one relationship. Therefore, all the accounts used by application, network, security, and operating system administrators should be placed under management. This can ensure the one-to-one relationship is maintained and all access is monitored for appropriate behavior. This encompasses any access that occurs on-premise or in the cloud and any work performed remotely by employees, contractors, vendors, auditors, etc.

- **Service Accounts**: The most under-the-radar accounts in every cloud environment are associated with running services and processes. Service accounts represent the plumbing for applications in a cloud environment and are often assigned credentials that cannot log in locally, yet they can be abused or misused to compromise the operating system or an application. Service accounts are generally a form of shared account that, depending on the application, can be shared on multiple assets in order to operate as a single system. When service accounts are placed under management by a PAM solution, changes (such as for credentials) must be synchronized; otherwise, connected resources will not seamlessly stop and restart their services. This is why attributes are such an important component of discovery. It is imperative to identify all the locations for service accounts and to automatically link shared ones so the accounts can be managed as one group. Otherwise, some accounts could be missed, they could fail to correctly rotate credentials, and new assets that utilize the same service account will not be placed under proper management. Each of these events can contribute to security holes and cascading outages.

- **Cloud Accounts**: When using the cloud to manage your workloads, vendor-specific IAM accounts are created to manage instances, runtime, and resources based on an identity, entitlements, and permissions model. As a discovery function, these accounts should be enumerated across multicloud environments and represented in a common format for risk assessment (principals). By uncovering and onboarding these cloud accounts, you can manage cloud account entitlements and determine when accounts are over-provisioned, stale, or even misused during operations.

- **Specialty Accounts**: Some of the most overlooked
  types of accounts for discovery and management
  are specialty accounts that are created on endpoints,
  locally, to support reimaging, by the help desk, and
  for other information technology functions. Often,
  these accounts are created as a local administrator
  and represent a legitimate backdoor into the host
  by authorized sources. As you can surmise, these
  accounts frequently lack unique passwords, or they
  may have passwords that have been shared between
  similar devices based on age, geolocation, or owner.
  As a security best practice, each one of these accounts
  should have a unique password. Access should be
  monitored and managed for each device, especially
  if they communicate with cloud assets, because they
  can be the initial entry point in an attack, should they
  become compromised. This represents a unique
  challenge because on-premise and cloud-based
  password management solutions are typically unable
  to establish a network route to a remote host to manage
  these credentials. This is especially true with work-
  from-anywhere users. In addition, basic endpoint
  hardening would prevent any inbound connection
  that could administer these accounts. Therefore,
  management of these accounts is typically done with
  a PAM agent. The discovery functions are performed
  using the same, or similar, technology to populate
  an asset management database with the attributes
  necessary to onboard accounts and ensure that
  privileged accounts on endpoints do not become the
  entry point into your environment.

- **Accounts with Embedded Credentials**: There are
  a myriad reasons why a developer, administrator, or
  even an application may have credentials embedded
  in scripts, configuration files, or compiled code.
  This is typically tied to DevOps automation for Agile
  development, but best practices may be beyond the
  control from a development, quality assurance, and
  automation perspective. The files could be scripts
  created by any department looking to automate a
  task (e.g., business logic) or a third-party program
  that self-compiles code once a credential is set. Many
  older ERP (enterprise resource planning) solutions
  suffer from this type of flaw, which highlights why
  cloud washing is a bad idea. The practice of embedded
  secrets is well recognized as a high security risk, so it's
  important to discover and onboard these credentials
  for management, if even possible. However, once
  discovered, secrets and passwords stored in files may
  need additional automation tools to replace them or to
  have code recompiled within your PAM solution.

Aside from these important privileged account types, there are a wide variety of other accounts that should be discovered. Security best practices suggest that your environment identify, classify, and rate the risk for each one to determine the sensitivity and prioritization for onboarding and management via continuous monitoring. An automated discovery process can also pinpoint risks related to the password/account attributes that were found in the discovery process, such as passwords that are defaults, reused, or which have not been changed for a long time and have become stale.

Following a proven privileged account asset management plan can help you improve your cloud security posture. By leveraging an asset management database and discovering all your accounts, you can effectively manage this critical threat to your cloud environment. And, as a best practice, the discovery, onboarding, and offboarding of privileged accounts should be an ongoing process that is baked into daily operations.

CHAPTER 6

Attack Vectors

The first step in establishing a secure cloud environment is understanding the threats it's likely to encounter. The attack vectors that your environment will be subjected to will form the to-do list of the areas you need to secure first and foremost. This can seem like a daunting task, even for those who are well versed in the subject matter or particularly for those who are well versed in the immensity of the space. You need to avoid analysis paralysis, getting caught in a loop of trying to address everything at once. We'll come back to that later in the book, but for now, the best advice we can give you is to look at the cybersecurity frameworks that exist; many intelligent people have thought about the attack surface and identified the attack vectors, so you don't have to. Treat these as toolkits, guidelines, and, in some cases, gospel in understanding cloud attack vectors.

No one should be looking to find a single framework that will address every concern. Identify the elements from each toolkit that come together to meet your organization's needs. In the coming pages, we'll walk you through several resources suited for building your understanding of attack vectors (not mitigation strategy yet), which might apply to your organization. As you read through these resources, begin sorting them into groups, like sorting the wheat from the chaff, or Gryffindor from Slytherin (the latter suggestion was on behalf of my youngest daughter). This will help you decide what applies to your organization, and that will help you create success criteria that quantify progress in securing your cloud environment.

© Morey J. Haber, Brian Chappell, Christopher Hills 2022
M. J. Haber et al., *Cloud Attack Vectors*, https://doi.org/10.1007/978-1-4842-8236-6_6

Finally, remember – the more things change, the more they stay the same. This is because the attack vectors in the cloud are nearly the same as with on-premise, but they are different when measured as a risk to your organization. If you have not made this connection yet, you soon will. Consider Figure 6-1, types of attack vectors.

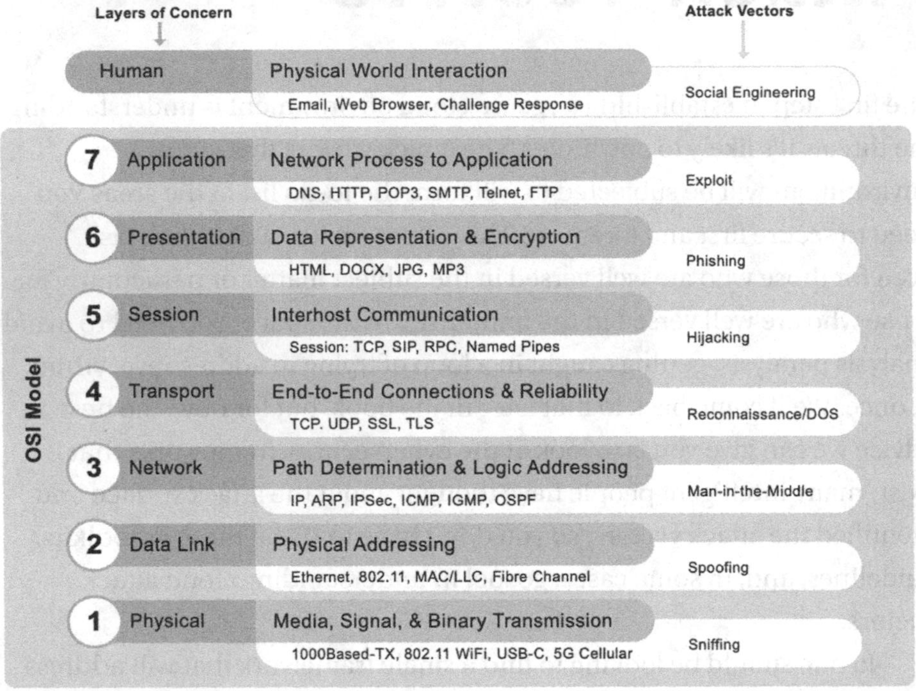

Layers of Concern			Attack Vectors
Human	Physical World Interaction		Social Engineering
	Email, Web Browser, Challenge Response		
7 Application	Network Process to Application		Exploit
	DNS, HTTP, POP3, SMTP, Telnet, FTP		
6 Presentation	Data Representation & Encryption		Phishing
	HTML, DOCX, JPG, MP3		
5 Session	Interhost Communication		Hijacking
	Session: TCP, SIP, RPC, Named Pipes		
4 Transport	End-to-End Connections & Reliability		Reconnaissance/DOS
	TCP. UDP, SSL, TLS		
3 Network	Path Determination & Logic Addressing		Man-in-the-Middle
	IP, ARP, IPSec, ICMP, IGMP, OSPF		
2 Data Link	Physical Addressing		Spoofing
	Ethernet, 802.11, MAC/LLC, Fibre Channel		
1 Physical	Media, Signal, & Binary Transmission		Sniffing
	1000Based-TX, 802.11 WiFi, USB-C, 5G Cellular		

(OSI Model – layers 1 through 7)

Figure 6-1. *Types of attack vectors*

If you are a student of networking and computing technology, you know the OSI model[1] divides a network implementation into seven layers. Some joke there are really eight layers when you add the human element on top as an attack vector, but that is not officially a part of the model. When you consider the cloud, it truly is an attack vector layer. Therefore, as illustrated in Figure 6-1, the layers are

---

[1] www.techtarget.com/searchnetworking/definition/OSI

1. **Physical**: The lowest layer of the OSI model focuses on the electrical or optical characteristics required for transmitting raw, unstructured data bits across a network. This includes all the physical specifications, such as voltages, pin layout, cabling, shielding, hardware, and even radio frequencies for transmission. Devices at the physical layer include network hubs, cabling, repeaters, network adapters, or modems. This layer is susceptible to Sniffing[2]-based attacks. For the cloud, this is primarily wireless network based.

2. **Data Link**: At the data link layer, directly connected assets are used to perform node-to-node data transfer. Data is packaged into frames for transmission. The data link layer also corrects errors that may have occurred due to problems at the physical layer. The data link layer specification contains two components. The first component, media access control (MAC), provides flow control and multiplexing for device transmissions over a network. The second component, the logical link control (LLC), provides flow and error control over the physical medium and also identifies line protocols. As an attack vector, spoofing[3] is the highest risk at this layer.

---

[2] https://intellipaat.com/blog/tutorial/ethical-hacking-cyber-security-tutorial/sniffing-attacks/

[3] https://www.veracode.com/security/spoofing-attack

3. **Network**: The network layer is responsible for receiving frames from the data link layer. Once confirmed to be transmission error-free, the network layer then forwards them to their intended destinations based on the addresses contained inside the frame. The network layer finds the destination by using logical addresses, such as IP (Internet protocol), to route source and destination traffic. Network routers are typically associated with this layer to perform this function. For the cloud, almost all communications go through the Internet and are potentially susceptible to man-in-the-middle[4] attacks, even for private clouds.

4. **Transport**: The transport layer manages data packets' delivery and error checking for contents. It regulates the size, sequencing, and, ultimately, data transfer between assets. Transmission Control Protocol (TCP) is the most common transport layer protocol and is susceptible to denial-of-service[5] attacks.

5. **Session**: The session layer controls the conversations between assets. A session or connection between machines is set up, managed, and terminated at this layer. Session-layer services also include authentication, reconnections, and statefulness. At this layer, hijacking[6] attacks are the most prevalent.

---

[4] https://www.imperva.com/learn/application-security/man-in-the-middle-attack-mitm/

[5] https://www.paloaltonetworks.com/cyberpedia/what-is-a-denial-of-service-attack-dos

[6] https://owasp.org/www-community/attacks/Session_hijacking_attack

6. **Presentation**: The presentation layer formats and translates data for the application layer based on the protocol, design, and contents that the application accepts. This layer is crucial for cloud services because it also handles the encryption and decryption required by the application layer. The presentation layer is also the largest risk surface for end users; it is responsible for phishing[7] attacks.

7. **Application**: At this layer, both the end user and the application layer interact directly with the application. This layer enables end-user applications, such as a web browser or mobile application. At this layer, vulnerabilities and exploits[8] dominate cloud attack vectors and are responsible for the vast majority of the breaches that make the news.

In the cloud, these layers loosely map to attack vectors, just as with on-premise. Arguably, it is easier to conduct many of these attacks on the Internet and in the cloud vs. on-premise. For example, a man-in-the-middle attack intercepts network traffic in the middle of a session to sniff and spoof network traffic for a future attack. That would require the installation of an asset to perform this attack within a corporate network that can intercept, decode, and route, or forward, traffic. This is not necessarily an easy task to perform for a remote threat actor. Such an attack requires some good hacking skills, even for an insider. However, this is easier to accomplish through the Internet when network connections are dependent on insecure Wi-Fi to provide services. Therefore, consider

---

[7] https://cybersecurityguide.org/resources/phishing/
[8] www.techtarget.com/searchsecurity/definition/exploit

each attack to have a different potential risk severity and ease of execution compared to on-premise. This is where the more things change (ease of execution), the more they stay the same (attack vector). Consider Table 6-1 as an opinion on this topic.

Table 6-1. *OSI and attack vectors, comparing ease of execution in the cloud vs. on-premise*

OSI Layer	Attack	On-premise	Internet/Cloud
1. Physical	Sniffing	Difficult	Variable
2. Data link	Spoofing	Difficult	Moderate
3. Network	Man in the middle	Difficult	Moderate
4. Transport	Reconnaissance/DOS	Moderate	Moderate, depending on the target
5. Session	Hijacking	Moderate	Moderate
6. Presentation	Phishing	Easy	Easy
7. Application	Exploit	Moderate	Easy
8. Human (unofficial, but relevant)	Social engineering	Easy	Easy

The primary reason on-premise is more difficult to compromise in lower layers is because the network is physically secured and there are mitigations in place to prevent physical network tampering (lock doors and wire closets) by those threat actors who've obtained inappropriate access. Hybrid and private cloud environments should be considered nearly the same since the physical security of the cloud service provider is inherently protecting you, just like your own building. Public clouds are different due to their exposure to the Internet – the only exception is at layer 7.

External vulnerabilities with workable exploits are generally fixed first on the Internet to prevent an intrusion. They are then patched internally later (if at all) based on criticality and timing. Thus, threat actors generally find more exploitable vulnerabilities externally than internally since the perimeter provides some layer of protection. Unfortunately, this is also becoming more relevant as people continue to work from anywhere, and the resulting security maintenance of remote devices becomes more challenging from layer 5 and up.

As we also have discussed at length, cloud attack vectors can be identity based. This poses a challenge to securing everything in the cloud that uses a secret for authentication. Even with the best multi-factor authentication and security tools in place, poor policies and lack of privileged access management can threaten cloud resources. And if your identity management is poor, then your risk surface expands to not only exploits and secrets but potentially also to rogue identities that threat actors use. Therefore, we need to blend sound identity management, access management, and policy management for all authentication in the cloud. Thus, it's really layers 6, 7, and, unofficially, 8 that we worry about the most for cloud attack vectors.

Consider the flowchart in Figure 6-2 for identity-based authentication and how it applies to higher layers.

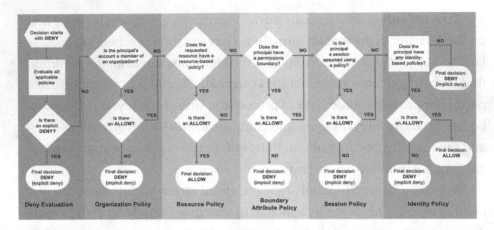

Figure 6-2. *Identity-based authentication in the cloud*

Each set of identity-based decisions used to provide authentication and access can be divided into six categories:

1. **Deny Evaluation**: This models least privilege and zero trust. Start with a deny and then prove. The process for access should only be started if an explicit deny is not present.

2. **Organizational Policy**: Does an organizational policy exist to allow access for the identity?

3. **Resource Policy**: Does the resource (asset or application) allow for access? This ensures that only authorized devices or assets under proper management are allowed to authenticate.

4. **Boundary/Attribute Policy**: Is access permitted based on attributes governing the identity, such as geolocation, time, date, etc.? In many cases, this is one of the most important steps to proving appropriate access to cloud resources.

5. **Session Policy**: Does the requested session have a policy that would allow or deny access based on all previous decisions and attributes? This is typically implemented in real time using behavioral analytics, machine learning, and/or artificial intelligence.

6. **Identity Policy**: Does the identity itself have a policy that can confirm access based on all previous decisions? This final step links identity proofing to all the other access decisions.

If this logic is applied to your environment, and if policies can be implemented at a technology level, many of the identity attack vectors that impact the cloud can be mitigated.

Finally, now that we have reviewed attack vectors from an academic perspective and an identity-based policy perspective, the next section will cover how they empirically apply to real-world threats and how they are classified.

MITRE ATT&CK™ Framework

The MITRE ATT&CK Framework[9] is a knowledge base of the methods of attacks and exploits used by threat actors. It was founded in 2013 to bring together the common tactics, techniques, and approaches that hackers, in particular the teams or groups identified as advanced persistent threats (APT), used primarily in hacking Microsoft Windows at that time. Like so many useful tools, ATT&CK grew out of a research project (Fort Meade eXperiment – FMX) that was initially looking at using endpoint data to improve post-compromise detection.

---

[9] `https://attack.mitre.org/`

Based on the information gathered, MITRE decided to build a framework bridging the gap between the high-level cyber life cycle and kill-chain concepts and the defenses that can be implemented. This effectively brings the theoretical knowledge of an attack vector forward in a more tangible form. Unifying this knowledge within a single framework also helped enforce common terminology for all attacks. This is an area that information technology regularly falls afoul of (please no references to Hawk in Buck Rogers).

At its best, ATT&CK provides a tool to model attacks, which is useful for the teams looking at attack vectors, but also for the teams staffing the defenses to gauge their progress. Fortunately, MITRE decided that everyone could benefit from this framework and they released the first version to the public in May 2015.

Since then, the framework has been expanded to incorporate more operating systems, such as macOS and Linux, as well as platforms, such as mobile devices and (most relevant for us) the cloud. Figure 6-3 is a summary of the current MITRE ATT&CK™ Framework.

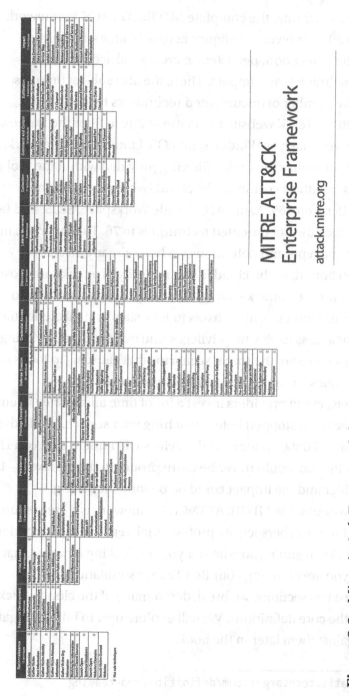

Figure 6-3. Mitre Att&ck Framework for attack vectors

At the time of writing, the complete MITRE ATT&CK Framework includes over 200 top-level techniques across 14 areas, including reconnaissance, execution, persistence, credential access, lateral movement, exfiltration, and impact. There are also sub-techniques, catapulting the number of documented techniques to around 600.

The MITRE ATT&CK website offers the ability to filter the framework for specific targets, such as Windows, macOS, Linux, cloud, network, and containers. If you utilize the online filtering provided within the tool and apply settings for attack vectors in the cloud (which includes the sub-targets Microsoft 365, Azure AD, Google Workspace, SaaS, and IaaS), the results reduce the documented techniques to 76. To that point, many reference the concepts and definitions we have already discussed.

Being web bound, as the cloud is, the majority of attacks are closely related to a web-based attack strategy. Looking for opportunities to compromise credentials, routing users to fake sites to steal credentials, and using that access to elevate privileges and exfiltrate data or bring the system down – these are the threat scenarios that cause us to focus so much on identities, accounts, credentials, and secrets.

Fortunately, cloud providers invest a lot of time and money to ensure that most attacks are stopped before reaching your service. While that's great, that mass of data, systems, and services will remain a bit of a Holy Grail (Monty Python would never be more proud) to the attackers – breach a cloud provider and the impact could be beyond imagining.

Without a doubt, the MITRE ATT&CK Framework is a great source of information for any cybersecurity professional, regardless of experience. The framework can guide you whether you are looking for areas that need attention or you are planning your Red Team[10] simulations.

In the next few sections, we break down many of the cloud attack vectors into the core definitions. We will explore how to build mitigation strategies against them later in the book.

---

[10] https://whatis.techtarget.com/definition/red-teaming

Entitlements

If there's a poster child for an attack vector, excess entitlements must be it. Across the world, organizations still regularly assign entitlements to users in a very broad fashion, that is, admin or root access, when a more specific grant would enable the user to complete whatever task spurred the initial request. It's important to bear in mind that very few users wake up in the morning thinking, "I'd really like to be an administrator." They tried to do something that they often believe is entirely reasonable, and the system told them that they had insufficient permission to do so – their entitlement was inadequate.

After potentially being irritated, they will raise a request for sufficient access to complete the task they started. The smart ones will add that the inability to complete the task will prevent them from doing their job. In our experience, the #1 reason for the removal of controls or the assignment of excess entitlements is so people do not complain. As this seems to be a minor issue among the myriad of concerns the security team has, the quick and dirty answer to the end user's request will be granting superuser access, which should be removed at some point in the future. In all likelihood, that point will be when the next audit highlights how many people have superuser entitlements in the system. If this is you, please do not feel bad; it's far more common than anyone imagines. But equally, don't accept it as a reasonable risk – these risks need to be addressed immediately.

When looking for a way to authenticate into an asset, overly entitled user accounts are a pot of gold for a threat actor. Everyday user accounts tend to have easier passwords to guess or derive from all the wonderful information people post on social media about themselves. Their systems are less secure than the core network, and they are vulnerable to social engineering attacks. Users are also consistently active on systems. Spotting the malicious activity among a lot of legitimate activity is difficult.

Between the unnecessary entitlements and the smoke screen of activity, effective entitlement control must rank highly on any cybersecurity strategy, and as mentioned, it must follow the principle of least privilege.

Vulnerabilities

An area that many organizations struggle with is the management of vulnerabilities. In this context, we are characterizing a vulnerability as one of the following:

a)   A technical issue with a piece of software that may enable a threat actor to gain additional access to a system

b)   A mistake in the coding of a solution that can be exploited via additional nefarious code

c)   A misconfiguration that provides an entry point that otherwise would not have been available

d)   A person who, through whatever mechanism, enables unauthorized third-party access to your systems

First, let's take a closer look at the first two of these, which represent technical vulnerabilities.

A litany of cyber threat and data breach reports, including the *Comparitech*[11] and Check Point Cyber Security Report for 2021,[12] have reported that in excess of 75% of successful attacks are the result

---

[11] www.comparitech.com/blog/information-security/cybersecurity-vulnerability-statistics/

[12] www.checkpoint.com/downloads/resources/cyber-security-report-2021.pdf

of vulnerabilities that are over two years old! This refers to technical vulnerabilities, where software errors allow threat actors to gain access to systems and/or elevate their account privileges on systems. The figure hasn't changed significantly in recent years, indicating that we need to continue to remediate this threat. This applies to all assets, regardless of their location or whether they are cloud native or cloud washed.

Technical vulnerabilities are logged and reported through the Common Vulnerabilities and Exposures[13] (CVE) (another service provided by Mitre), which provides a unique identifier for each vulnerability (CVE ID) that is registered with the service. The service delivers a list of known vulnerabilities, with details and references to help remediate/mitigate each.

While many of the services offered in the cloud will place the onus on identifying and mitigating vulnerabilities with the cloud service provider, we mustn't lose sight of the potential for a vulnerability to have a substantial impact on our systems and data. Cloud service providers are also only ever going to be responsible for the aspects of vulnerability that are within their control. Even within the most abstracted services, that is, SaaS, misconfigurations and excess permissions represent aspects beyond the service provider's control and, therefore, beyond the scope of their remit to protect. You and your teams must be clear on this demarcation and are thinking clearly and carefully about everything that is under your control and about what vulnerabilities need to be managed. Depending on the cloud service type, some will be yours to remediate, some will be for the cloud service providers to address, and others will be delegated to third parties that contribute to your success in the cloud.

---

[13] https://cve.mitre.org/

Hardening

If, like me, you look at this section title and think, "that's a mitigation, right?", then at least you are not alone. With that said, system hardening is, without a doubt, a complex and challenging activity that is hard to get right (another pun). When it's not right, it can become an attack vector. There are several key areas where hardening can become a problem rather than a solution.

If you are following one of the published system hardening (secure configuration) standards, for example, CIS (covered later in the regulatory section), then you will undoubtedly find that there's some application server or service that needs to have ports left open for normal operations. So, we've implemented a hardening standard and then degraded it to accommodate our environment. This could be for running services or open network ports. This is not bad in itself, but what ports are left open and who can access them is definitely an area of concern (for this section, we will focus on port hardening). Therefore, it is simply required to find those ports, identify acceptable communications, and lock them down with some of the techniques we have discussed, like access control lists. While that sounds easy, in many cases, and especially in the cloud, this is downright difficult.

To start, TCP/IP ports are often poorly understood. Historically, they could be an absolute nightmare because listening ports and sending ports are not always the same. Today, however, stateful firewalls can allow certain communications based on a valid initial connection, that is, you connect to an SSH server on port 22 from port 65000 on your client, and the firewall automatically allows the inbound traffic from the SSH server to port 65000 on your client.

For something as simple as email, you want outbound port 25 and inbound 25 because email servers send data to other email servers. To support email clients, you'll also want the POP3 and IMAP ports inbound – ideally the secure versions.

These port-based hardening functions should be applied across every application and operating system in the cloud. In addition, all unnecessary or unused ports should be disabled. This is another example of why basic asset management is so important. The asset management process can help build an architectural map for what hardening is required and what will need to be unhardened for a system to operate correctly.

Maintaining the hardening profile can be a challenge. It is not a one-time function – it must be reviewed regularly. Changes to a system's function, whether in total or due to expanding use cases, will result in expanded port requirements if network services are added. Another area of potential risk is in user modifications – but no one is going to add their workstation IP address to the acceptable list for port 1433 connections to enable them to admin the Microsoft SQL Server from their desktop. That never happens (or at least, we hope this never happens).

The last area where hardening can become an attack vector is somewhat indirect: complacency. Don't assume that because the system is hardened, it is safe. It will be as safe as you can make it, assuming the hardening is correct, but that's not a fixed state and not purely affected by internal factors. Newly discovered vulnerabilities may still be entirely exploitable, despite your hardening. This is why hardening is about so much more than disabling services and ports. Implementing settings and configurations, like password complexity, makes an asset difficult to compromise through known weaknesses and poor methods for authentication.

In the cloud, everything is accessible via open ports. So, if the port is closed, but the application is running, then an attack vector is potentially mitigated. Proper hardening, however, requires both the application and the port to be disabled. Many applications may need a specific service and its processes operating locally to complete a specific task but can tolerate that no inbound connections are accepted via a closed port. This is a tolerable risk in many environments, but a misconfigured port can result in an unexpected attack vector.

Web Services

Web services offer a potentially rich crop of attack vectors (this is how the Cylons infiltrated the 12 colonies and disabled their military resources). Normally accessed via APIs, these services often offer broad initial access (as they are multitenant), secured through good authentication mechanisms. However, they do not regularly lock accounts upon multiple credential failures. This may seem counterproductive, but an open interface where I can lock you out of your account(s) is an effective denial-of-service attack.

As will be mentioned elsewhere, secrets (in whatever form) remain a key aspect of API authentication because we are working with machine, system, or functional accounts rather than individuals. In contrast, individuals can carry mobile devices or dedicate key fobs to provide secondary factors of authentication (2FA); web services do not. This makes it important to secure all systems using web services and secure web services themselves from secrets-based attacks. This applies to any assets that are effectively using machine-to-machine single-factor authentication – even if the secret is dynamic and frequently changing. Understanding the limitations of system-to-system authentication will help reduce the attack surface that this mechanism inevitably introduces.

Local web services (constrained to your cloud architecture or within your private clouds on-premises) offer the opportunity to restrict traffic to the web service to only those IP addresses that are associated with the systems that need to access them (access control lists maintaining allow and block IP addresses or ranges). This offers a significant mitigation control and a cost-effective measure for securing point-to-point web service API communications. Where this can be applied to public cloud-hosted services, do so. Avoid dynamically assigned addresses, even if these are being processed through dynamic DNS as well. Static addresses for the source IP are vital for ensuring the controls are effective. It's easier to spoof an unassigned IP address or change a DNS entry than it is to compromise a fixed IP address.

OWASP Top 10

The Open Web Application Security Project (OWASP)[14] is a community
effort led by a nonprofit organization, called the OWASP Foundation,
to help organizations get started with the secure development of web
applications. The project started in 2001, with the foundation being
registered in 2004 in the United States (there is a nonprofit entity registered
in Belgium as well: OWASP Europe VZW).

The OWASP team published their first Top Ten list in 2003,
documenting the critical risks facing organizations and their web
applications. OWASP updates the list almost every year, informed by the
survey data the organization collects.

Many groups have adopted the OWASP Top Ten as the basis for their
web application security strategy, aiming to assess against and address the
listed items as their foremost priorities. The OWASP Top Ten has also been
used as a pseudo-standard for many other groups and testing systems and
implementation tools.

The OWASP Top Ten for 2021, published in September 2021, is as
follows.

A01:2021 – Broken Access Control

This item is focused on the approach to access control within an
application. It provides best practices, such as least privilege in the
permissions model, zero trust for all page accesses (not assuming that the
URL provides protection, but rather verifying access is appropriate), and
not allowing manipulation of requests to gain access to data. This item
links to 34 Common Weakness Enumerations (CWEs)[15] that document
specific scenarios relating to broken access controls.

---

[14] https://owasp.org/
[15] https://cwe.mitre.org/

A02:2021 – Cryptographic Failures

Encryption tends to focus on two key scenarios: at rest and in transit. In both of these scenarios, there exists the opportunity for poor implementations to result in the exposure of sensitive data. The CWEs linked by this (29 in total) focus on ensuring the encryption is appropriate and sufficient for protecting the data that is being processed. With data protection legislation continuing to expand and pose more significant penalties, this entry will become increasingly more important in the coming years.

A03:2021 – Injection

This item previously occupied the top spot in the OWASP Top Ten, in 2017. This doesn't diminish its importance, but it does highlight that more applications are addressing the concern. Injection relates to the ability for a malicious user to add to or substitute the commands for data access within a URL to bypass the application-level controls for data access. The "Bobby Tables" cartoon strip by XKCD[16] (Figure 6-4) is a classic example of this kind of attack.

Figure 6-4. *XKCD cartoon for sanitizing database inputs[17]*

---

[16] https://xkcd.com/327/

[17] https://xkcd.com/327/

A04:2021 – Insecure Design

This item is different than most of the others since it is focused on the design rather than the implementation. A perfectly implemented bad design is still a bad design. This highlights the need to bake security into the application architecture, and it is commonly referred to as secure by design. It's a seemingly simple and innocuous change in wording from "how do we develop the application and secure it" to "how do we securely develop the application." There are 40 CWEs linked to Insecure Design, which indicates how badly we're generally doing this one today.

A05:2021 – Security Misconfiguration

Misconfiguration is, from an implementation and operation perspective, one of the most common issues reported in the press. This cloud attack vector can easily be avoided if you know your environment is misconfigured. The first of these findings, ironically, is entirely implementation driven. Even the most secure applications in the world hold the potential to be misconfigured by users, opening them up for abuse by threat actors. Common elements here include default passwords and superuser permissions being given unnecessarily and not removed. There are 20 CWEs linked to this recommendation, which can be taken to indicate that the scope isn't broad. But keep in mind, the impacts can be dramatic.

A06:2021 – Vulnerable and Outdated Components

This item relates to the software components used to develop and deliver applications and services that are often overlooked as a potential route for exploitation. This item is even more critical in cloud environments because those components are more exposed to attack than in on-premise scenarios. Ensuring that components are actively updated to the latest supported components is critical.

As an organization, you should be querying your vendors on the techniques they have in place to safeguard your use of their solutions. This category is unusual among the OWASP Top Ten because it has no CWEs mapped to it. The vulnerable and outdated components are an ever-evolving list, making it difficult to track all potential candidates and even harder to assess complete coverage. Good vulnerability management software should give you a view across all the installed elements in the environment; it should also allow you to track them as a part of your assessment strategy. An active patch management and update program will ensure that software in the environment is up to date and as secure as possible.

A07:2021 – Identification and Authentication Failures

In this context, failures of identification and authentication primarily relate to failure to prevent identification and authentication attacks. This item's attacks include credential stuffing, brute-force password attacks, weak/well-known/default passwords, poor password recovery processes, and session hijacking. Authenticating the identity of a user is the primary mechanism used in granting access to systems in the cloud, regardless of how that authentication is achieved (i.e., username/password, biometrics, smart cards).

Today, it's clear that single-factor mechanisms for authentication (for individual accounts) should be deprecated. That said, most authentication falls back to a password, so while biometrics becomes more popular, organizations must not forget about good password practices and good password hygiene. In total, 22 CWEs cover the multitude of ways in which identification and authorization should be secured, particularly when developing software. This is equally applicable in all aspects of authentication within your environment, from end users to support staff.

A08:2021 – Software and Data Integrity Failures

Software integrity has become a significant problem in recent years, with major breaches originating in the update processes of critical software. These have been coined as supply-chain attacks. Threat actors are targeting the software vendors not to directly exploit the vendors, but to gain access to their customers. From a software vendor perspective, it's important to ensure that the components being managed in OWASP A06 are from trusted sources, are appropriately signed, and have not been tampered with. From a software user's perspective, they want to make sure that software updates follow the same management and source verification process.

Within critical applications, data integrity is vitally important because the data is often stored outside of the application itself, within database servers that are often managed by the end users in cloud services. Data can be manipulated to affect the operation of software and disrupt or misdirect the organization's activity. The potential impact of data manipulation could be greater than the impact of a software vulnerability because it can be harder to uncover. As you can see, data integrity is key for critical applications. That said, ensure data integrity requirements are appropriate for the data in question.

A09:2021 – Security Logging and Monitoring Failures

Visibility is essential in cybersecurity, both in prevention and defense. It's clear that wherever you aren't looking or can't see is where you are most likely to have a breach turn up. Failures due to logging and monitoring of security events not being comprehensive enough, or clear enough, have driven this item to move up the Top Ten by one place for the 2021 list. Logging key activities, such as authentication into and out of a system, as well as changes to configuration, including access permissions, are essential to distinguish between legitimate activity and malicious operations.

In addition to logging, we also need event monitoring, which, ideally, is correlated to approved activity. For example, missing change management tickets ensure that the malicious activities present a strong enough signal to trigger an active response.

While the OWASP Top Ten is focused on software development, this item depends on external log storage and assessment in the mitigation of the threats associated with it. Just four CWEs belie the importance and reach of this item. Logging for logging's sake doesn't improve security; it actually makes it less effective because there's more noise in the system. Like so many security aspects, appropriate controls maintain a vital balance, and behavioral monitoring, machine learning, and artificial intelligence can all help achieve intelligent identity and access security.

A10:2021 – Server-Side Request Forgery

Server-Side Request Forgery (SSRF) is facilitated by the increase in functionality that is being offered to users and enabled by some offerings. This is more likely to be relevant in a cloud scenario because it's common for cloud-based services to rely on other cloud-based services to produce a final offering. Applications and supporting services often require users to provide the URLs for those other services, while interacting with the primary application via some form of configuration. This is typically GUI or a file-based configuration.

Someone gaining access to the URL configuration elements could misuse the shared URLs to attack other systems or even discover aspects of the systems sitting behind the application itself. The threat actor can do this by trying URLs with address and port combinations to find open ports and services. While software vendors need to implement mechanisms to prevent misuse as much as possible, it's another area where appropriate permissions (least privilege) can provide a significant benefit in defending against this kind of attack. This is illustrated in Figure 6-5.

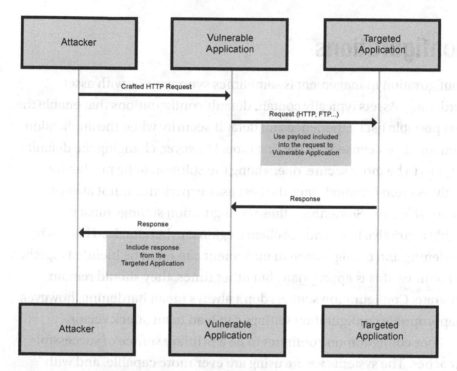

Figure 6-5. *Server-Side Request Forgery*

The OWASP Top Ten has evolved over time, with elements entering, leaving, rising, and decreasing throughout the list. Occasionally, entries have been combined with other areas as technology and architectures have evolved and as some threats have matured.

While the OWASP Top Ten is targeted toward the development of web applications and making those applications secure, as the security community has realized, that same criteria can be used when evaluating the security hygiene of any web application, even off-the-shelf solutions that are either hosted internally or available via the cloud.

Configurations

Configuration management is sometimes synonymous with asset hardening. Assets typically contain default configurations that enable the best possible user experience and default security when the application is enabled, or licensed, for the first time. However, changing the default settings to be more secure, or enabling the solution to be production ready, is often required since the best user experience is not always the most secure. Sometimes, these configuration settings must be highly restrictive to provide resilience against cyberattacks. This is why hardening and configuration management can often be blended together. Sometimes, this is appropriate, but other times, they should remain separate. Configuration settings don't always mean hardening; however, inappropriate configuration settings can lead to an attack vector.

Poor configuration continues to be a primary source of successful breaches. The systems we are using are ever more capable, and with growth comes a growing list of configuration items to consider. It's hard enough to keep track of the configuration settings in a single, complex application or service. This can equate to keeping track of tens, hundreds, or even thousands of possible configuration settings. The task can become impossible.

A report compiled by McAfee[18] indicated that, on average, organizations use 1,935 cloud-based services. This clearly indicates the scope of the problem that configurations represent. How do you ensure every one of them is configured correctly, and none are an unwarranted liability (and thank you Commander Decker for defining unwarranted risk in *Star Trek: The Motion Picture*)? Admittedly, some cloud services may have very simple configurations, although we should remember that the permissions assigned to users and administrators of those services are part of that configuration, including default accounts and passwords.

PKI (Public Key Infrastructure)

A Public Key Infrastructure is a set of roles, policies, hardware, software, and procedures needed to create, manage, distribute, use, store, and revoke digital certificates. This commonly consists of four elements:

- The certificate authority (CA), the ultimate source of certificates. CAs own the root certificates that are used to sign other certificates that the CA issues to prevent tampering and to provide credibility for the issued certificates.

- The registration authority (RA) verifies the identity of anyone requesting a certificate. The RA is essential in validating both the request for a certificate and the assurance that the root certificate provides. Confirming the requester is who they say they are, and that they own the identity that the certificate will be validating,

---

[18] www.mcafee.com/enterprise/en-us/security-awareness/cloud/what-is-saas.html

is the cornerstone of the value of digital certificates. It's possible for the CA and the RA to be the same organization or entirely different organizations.

- The certificate database holds the certificates issued and the information (metadata) relating to the certificate.

- The certificate policy enables other assets to assess how secure certificates are stored and managed and any anomalies with the usage of certificates in an environment. Without confidence in the CA and RA, the PKI is worthless.

The digital certificates produced from a PKI are designed to enable secure electronic information transfer. This is achieved either through encrypting the data (using public and private key pairs as previously discussed) in a way that only enables the correct parties to decrypt it or as a verification of identity – in essence, a digital passport.

As an end user, we encounter PKI, or the output of PKI, daily – in many cases, an hourly basis. Every time you visit a website and you see the padlock icon in the address bar of your favorite browser, or the address bar turns green to indicate security, you are doing so because of a certificate-based secure connection, typically under PKI control.

While a certificate proves the identity of the data source, it's no guarantee that the data itself is safe – just that the source is who they claim to be and the data is encrypted during transmission.

Attack vectors either directed at or associated with PKI tend to focus on gaining unauthorized access to certificates that have been issued to others or on having new certificates issued that provide validation that isn't warranted.

Credentials

Toward the end of every year, we are asked to make some cybersecurity predictions. One prediction has been featured every single year – that we will continue to see poor implementation of security basics. Credentials are at the very heart of cybersecurity for authentication and continue to prove what is possible, not only to gain inappropriate access to systems and infrastructure but also to move laterally across an environment, resulting in significant business risk of a catastrophic breach.

While news stories of this proportion have been primarily on premises, as organizations move to the cloud, those same practices find their way into the new environments, and the attacks themselves almost always originate from the Internet. Credentials of almost any type are how authentication happens. Most commonly, when we think of credentials, we are thinking of username and password. The dictionary definition of "credential" is "a document proving a person's identity." Certificates, keys, passcards, etc., are all credentials in the strictest sense of the term, and this is why identity proofing is so important. Just because you know a password does not prove your identity.

As an attack vector, privileged credentials remain the ultimate objective for a threat actor. However, even unprivileged accounts provide the access needed for threat actors to gather additional information, leading to an escalation of privileges. As previously discussed, the majority of successful attacks start with stolen, purchased, or compromised credentials. There are literally billions of credentials available on the Internet. While we may tell ourselves that **our** team members won't use their company credentials or reuse their company password on public websites, the truth is that they will, and they actually do!

Today, the sheer number of passwords needed to operate is immense. The average user has over 100 accounts in their daily life, and each account needs a password. Trying to remember a handful of passwords, or reusing just one password, isn't uncommon. This is why we have credential theft issues – these are stolen once and reused by the threat actor everywhere.

To mitigate the password problem, many solution providers recommend MFA. This can entail using physical credential solutions, like smartcards, passcards, near-field communication (NFC) fobs, proximity devices, and mobile authentication applications. These all promise to improve the situation because each device is unique. However, devices are frequently "lost" and subject to their own attack vectors, like SIM Jacking.[19]

For shared accounts, commonly the most utilized accounts in any system, the credentials are normally based on single-factor authentication using a username and password. Using other layered security mechanisms with those accounts reduces the risk of them being compromised. This is yet another reason to consider privileged access management for these accounts and management of privileged credentials that are inherent in almost every system.

To that end, we cannot discuss credentials without covering the most dangerous ones – default accounts. While accounts such as "root" in Unix, Linux, and macOS, as well as local and domain administrator accounts in Microsoft Windows™, are easily remembered, the explosion of the Internet of Things (IoT) has resulted in a plethora of new, seemingly harmless devices making their way onto our networks. Each of these devices has at least one default account, probably with administrative privileges. Unfortunately, it's not uncommon to find these devices in our production networks with the factory default credentials (47% according to Internet

---

[19] https://www.coindesk.com/markets/2020/02/26/coindesk-explains-sim-jacking/

of Business[20]) still active. Neglecting to change the default passwords continues to provide a rich vein of opportunity for threat actors, both on-premise and in the cloud.

As a key target for any attacker, it's vitally important that we understand the risks of credentials when planning our mitigation strategies. The two riskiest credential categories are unsecure default credentials and poor security hygiene for shared credentials/accounts. While stolen or weak credentials present risks, basic MFA can help mitigate them. It is when the account is secured by only a single factor that we have the greatest risk for an incident.

Keys

While keys are identified as credentials in the previous section, they have their own special place in the list of attack vectors. Keys are commonly used for nonhuman entities: machines, systems, and applications to intercommunicate. What's also common about nonhuman entities is the high level of privilege needed to successfully execute their functions.

Administrators for your company application may have a lot of control over what other users can do in the system, but the application itself probably has complete control over the database that stores all the information and access via web service APIs. Another application may interact with the system using APIs. Keys are a common authentication mechanism to grant access, particularly in cloud environments.

The use cases that require keys lend to complex scenarios. The best practice of key rotation, particularly in large environments, is often ignored for long periods of time. This often leads to key rotation not being done and consequently a threat actor to successfully obtain keys that provide unfettered access. We must not think for a moment that a threat actor

---

[20] https://internetofbusiness.com/password-iot/

won't discover the lack of key rotation and adapt their approach to avoid detection. Based on the threat actor's goals, they may choose to create their own keys and avoid detection by mimicking existing behaviors. Key rotation may stop their initial compromise, but once a threat actor is inside, management of keys is not an effective breach mitigation strategy. From an attacker's perspective, the key that provides access to the application is the proverbial "pot of gold at the end of the rainbow," and they will go to great lengths to obtain them. Changing the key after it has been obtained will only delay their attack – it won't prevent it from happening again.

S3 Buckets

S3 buckets feature far more regularly in the news as the source of a data breach than many security professionals would like to admit. Misconfiguration of the buckets' access profile is their biggest cause of data loss, and this highlights the importance of knowing where your data resides and how it's secured, regardless of the platform.

A 2021 report by cloud security firm, Ermetic,[21] found that a "toxic combination of overprivileged identities and poorly configured environments" existed across all AWS accounts. Ermetic testing found 90% of the S3 buckets to be vulnerable to attack. How those attacks can be achieved is multifarious, and we cover many of the other attack vectors throughout this book.

Vulnerabilities are so rampant across S3 buckets that the very use of S3 buckets becomes an attack vector that every attacker will seek out. Attackers appreciate that the S3 buckets can store almost any data type,

---

[21] https://ermetic.com/blog/cloud/93-of-security-professionals-say-their-identity-breaches-could-have-been-prevented/

and the permissions model can allow even wide-open public access. With such a massive attack surface, how do you begin to understand what attack vectors are present?

When auditing S3 bucket security, break down the risk into some quantifiable categories:

- **Data**: What is the risk and sensitivity of the data being stored in the S3 bucket?

- **Access**: Audit the identities that have access (read/ write) and ensure they are appropriate. Remember, this is true for human identities, machine identities, and application programming interfaces (APIs for anything operating from machine to machine).

- **Logging**: All access to S3 buckets should be logged using CloudTrail in AWS. This will allow the identification of any appropriate access or usage of the data contained within. Logging by default is set to 90 days. Based on your own individual business or compliance requirements, you may need to increase this setting or archive the data in a secondary solution.

- **Monitoring**: It is one thing to log all activity as mentioned earlier, but active monitoring to look for indicators of compromise is crucial. Too often, data is collected that would indicate an attack, but no one, human or machine, is monitoring the events for evidence of compromise. Therefore, logging and monitoring go hand in hand. Absent monitoring, you might as well not log at all – and that is just a terrible idea.

Identities

We've already explored credentials as a mechanism for confirming identity and the significant attack vector that credentials present. While credentials are the most common mechanism for impersonating an identity, the theft of identity itself offers an attack vector that is not limited by credentials alone. In this context, we are talking about theft of the digital identity of an authorized user within a system. A classic scenario here would be the hijacking of a session token used to maintain authentication across multiple web pages within a site.

It's often forgotten that each HTTPS request is entirely independent and that state is not maintained within the protocol; it's the website code that authenticates you and then provides a mechanism to maintain that state between requests. This is normally achieved through the use of a token that's generated at the time of authentication and then passed back and forth with each subsequent request. The token is either passed as a cookie or within the request URL. When the website receives the token, it checks to see if it's still valid (tokens commonly have an inactivity expiration to prevent old tokens from being hijacked or reused). If the token is still valid, the website will reset the expiration time to the current time, plus the inactivity period, and update the token. As a user, this little ballet happens behind the scenes; you just keep interacting with the site. Should the user be idle for longer than the idle timeout period, the server will consider the token invalid at the next request, and the user will be logged out.

In the early days of this mechanism, there was a significant risk of the token being captured on the wire using sniffing since the HTTP (HyperText Transfer Protocol) is not encrypted. Gaining access to the token is effectively like gaining access to the user's identity because the website will treat any request that provides a valid token as a request from the identity the token is associated with. So much of the underlying technology of the Internet is designed to maintain connectivity across a potentially unreliable infrastructure. Tying the token to an IP address has the potential to drive users to need to log in again just because their client obtained a new IP address via dynamic host control protocol (DHCP) or roaming Wi-Fi connections. This is something that can happen due to idle connections or momentary disconnects, a symptom of the limited IPv4 address space, and the pervasiveness of network address translation (NAT), which is notorious for permitting more devices than can be allocated with unique addresses.

These limitations have been an issue for websites for many years. Until the advent of the cloud, IP and identity correlation issues were limited in impact to just the website that was being accessed. With the cloud being managed through multiple consoles, we now have the risk that compromising an identity with significant access to manipulate the environment could result in a catastrophic loss of service, systems, and data. Whatever authentication mechanism is being used, with as many authentication factors as is reasonable to impose, the outcome is that the token that's used to maintain identity between requests could be compromised. Once stolen, the token will be accepted for all interactions with the target system.

Today, it's unusual to see an HTTP connection. All connections should be HTTPS, with the S standing for "Secure." This means that compromising the token in transit is significantly more difficult, yet it doesn't eliminate the risk. The user's workstation, often necessarily less restricted than the systems being accessed, offers an opportunity to hijack the tokens, should those systems become compromised. No significant privilege is needed because the user must have access to the token for it to be sent to the server. Any attack that compromises the user's desktop offers the opportunity for the attacker to launch another browser window from which they can interact with the cloud console without needing to do anything else. While it may seem that the user would notice the additional window appearing, there are mechanisms that mean the window would not be visible. The user closing their browser would not prevent the attacker from continuing their activities. Also, consider other identities within your environment, including the users logged into workstations or servers, as well as the identities that are not HTTP or HTTPS based that are being used by servers, systems, and applications to communicate across the network. Regardless, authentication results in a token of some kind that eliminates the need to store credentials (to authenticate on each request) or ask the user to authenticate themselves with each interaction.

The cloud's web-based nature brings the risks into sharp focus because of the inherently stateless nature of the ongoing communications. A boon for efficiency, but a challenge to secure reliably, tokens are an attack vector that can be a gold mine for threat actors.

Entitlements

Entitlements, as covered earlier, refer to privileges, authorizations, access rights, and permissions. To rephrase some words of wisdom from the indomitable Yoda (yes, a *Star Wars* reference, and no, not baby Yoda), credentials lead to identities, identities lead to entitlements, entitlements lead to access, and access can lead to "suffering." Or rather, they can lead to suffering from a breach.

For the legitimate user, entitlements are an essential part of their lives and are critical to being able to do what they are employed to do. For the cybersecurity professional, entitlements are often the bane of their lives. Standard user accounts are generally enabled to do very little within the environment, and rightly so. Launching a word processor or spreadsheet, being able to create, read, update, and delete files that they are working on – this, for many, is the extent of their need for daily, work-related access.

To understand entitlements as an attack vector, consider this scenario. One day, a user is tasked to do something that's outside their normal scope of access. A request is raised and an entitlement is added to their account to facilitate that task. Months or years later, that entitlement, long since forgotten, may still exist on their account. The entitlement may remain until their termination or even retirement. This entitlement offers a tempting target to the threat actor who just compromised the employee's workstation. It allows the attacker to perform a task that a standard user could not do on their own, potentially advancing their malicious activity.

Knowing who is entitled to do what, where, when, and how is vitally important in any system, but it is vastly more important when we look toward environments that we don't own, like the cloud. IGA (identity governance and administration) is the IT practice area around providing certifications for identities and their corresponding entitlements, rights, privileges, and permissions.

Consider that even legitimately entitled users, such as the administrators of the systems, are likely to have entitlements that may be too broad for their role. This is not uncommon, particularly when security teams are stretched or when no one is dedicated to identity management. There is no available time to work out exactly what set of permissions the individual (or group) will need across their role, so "give them everything and keep an eye on it" is a fairly common outcome.

Even where entitlements are managed well, entitled users still offer an enticing opportunity for the skilled threat actor. Moving back up the chain of authorization, more attack vectors exist, all leading to entitlements that will facilitate a successful attack.

Short-term entitlements also offer opportunities for a successful attack. It's not uncommon for a compromised account to be monitored by automated processes that are lying in wait for the account to gain a needed entitlement. Once given, the automated process will leap into action and possibly have completed its task before the user has even used the entitlement, further compromising the identity.

It's also possible for vulnerabilities within a system to elevate the entitlement level beyond that granted by the system. This is a type of privileged escalation and is another route for the threat actor to obtain the necessary rights to exploit the system and conduct lateral movement.

API

APIs (application programming interfaces) provide simple mechanisms for applications to interact with other applications, scripts, programs, and automation services. Each API offers services to other applications while abstracting the inner workings of the service. This allows for stability of the API, even while the implementation behind it may change entirely. This also means that APIs can be long lived, meaning that integration work between applications does not have to be changed every time a new version of the API host is released.

While the concept of an API is a standard one, how the APIs are implemented and used can vary greatly between vendors, even for similar web service functions. There have been, and continue to be, many standard mechanisms for APIs to be implemented, but none have become ubiquitous in nature. The API endpoints, the individual functions the API offers, all have been implemented in many different ways; however, with all that variation, some consistency has emerged.

In the cloud, APIs are the control points behind the machine. Much of the advantage of the cloud and the service-based approach is entirely driven by the availability of APIs, with services calling other services to deliver everything from the user interface to the dynamic provisioning of the infrastructure on which the cloud itself resides.

It's useful to think of the APIs as the user interfaces for the nonhuman users (machines) to interact with the cloud. The most common standard used in API implementations in the cloud is REpresentational State Transfer, or REST. This architectural style allows for creating reliable, web (stateless) APIs that leverage the HTTP or HTTPS protocol for communications. APIs that conform, even loosely, to the REST style are said to be RESTful APIs. All cloud-based RESTful APIs should only be addressable via HTTPS for the same reasons we use it for human UIs – for securing the connection and the data in transit with encryption. Just like a human UI, APIs require accounts to authenticate and use tokens to maintain enough state that they can avoid having to reauthenticate with every request.

While they are very much software to software oriented, RESTful APIs benefit from the simple nature of the HTTP protocol, and the endpoints tend toward a very human-readable experience. While many people are familiar with the GET and POST verbs associated with HTTP interactions (GET being used to request data from the endpoint and POST being used to send data), there are other verbs that come into their own within a RESTful API. The most common among these are PUT and DELETE for updating data and deleting data, respectively. With these verbs in place, it's normal for API endpoints to provide all four common data operations (Create = POST, Read = GET, Update = PUT, Delete = DELETE) on a single endpoint. This is also referred to as CRUD. Using these four verbs, any API can be greatly simplified into these core functions. The upshot of this is simple: you get an easy-to-understand architecture for APIs, upon which the entire cloud is foundationally supported.

CRUD also makes APIs a prime cloud attack vector. If you could compromise some of the key APIs used to run the infrastructure for each cloud vendor, then you could potentially compromise every customer on any cloud service provider. Those targets are too attractive to be ignored. Fortunately, protections around APIs tend to be very robust. That doesn't stop organizations using the APIs from allowing their keys and secrets (the two elements commonly used in API authentication) from being exposed. This could be through the hardcoding of these elements, which may be visible in available source code or within live sites by accident (it's happened). Either way, an attacker gaining access to the API credentials that have been used by the systems that run your cloud instances could be catastrophic for your organization.

With over 1,900 cloud services being used, on average, by organizations, the API attack surface is probably the largest risk for any organization that is in, or moving to, the cloud. APIs provide the agility, flexibility, and simplicity that are cornerstones of the cloud itself. As the saying goes, with great power comes great responsibility, and keeping your APIs secure is your responsibility.

Denial of Service

Denial-of-service (DoS) and distributed denial of service (DDoS) are probably the most well-known attack vectors, prior to the rise of ransomware (which is also, by definition, a denial-of-service attack). It's true that a DoS attack still presents a clear and present danger (yes – a shout-out to Tom Clancy) to networks; there are multiple services that can provide protection at various levels. Of course, there are also actions that you can take locally and with your cloud systems, all of which will be covered later.

The objective of a DoS attack is generally to prevent your system(s) from being able to respond to legitimate requests. The attack accomplishes this by disrupting the services that the system(s) uses to respond in the first place.

A DDoS attack will commonly flood publicly accessible connection(s) with more traffic than they can handle. To do this, the "distributed" component is key in two ways. First, it's unlikely that a single device can produce enough traffic to bring the larger networks to their knees. To achieve this, threat actors need to compromise a plethora of assets to pump traffic to the target. Unsecured video or closed-circuit cameras and many other IoT devices make excellent sources for DDoS traffic. The attack does not necessarily care which ports are used or if they are open or closed; the attack is just a flood of direct traffic. The idea is to fill the pipe (the network connection) with more data than it can carry. Every point along the route to your web server, for example, has a capacity. The closer we get to your web server, the more each of those devices contributes to the likelihood of taking your website offline – or appearing to be offline, which, for potential customers, are indistinguishable states.

If the flood of data directed by the DDoS attack reaches your web server, then, even with every port except 443 (the default HTTPS port) closed, the server is still receiving every packet (a discrete block of data sent across the network) and discarding them. That takes much less processing power than actually hitting the right port – you can guarantee that port 443 will be a target – but it's still stopping your web server from dealing with yet another packet.

With sufficient volume, even hitting a closed port will mean the pipe is saturated, and it cannot carry any more data. If you block the port at the firewall, in front of your web server, the firewall can become overwhelmed, too. This is true for the routers, switches, firewalls, and network infrastructure on route, even if it is virtualized in the cloud. These enterprise networking devices are rarely deployed in isolation to address single point of failure (SPOF), but even so, a DDoS attack can overwhelm the infrastructure if adequate security controls are not in place to mitigate this attack.

The second way the distributed nature of the DDoS attack comes into effect is in trying to block the attack. A single device, with a single IP address attacking your environment, can be quickly and easily blocked. Thousands of devices from IP addresses worldwide (IP addresses are regionally allocated), some of which might actually be the compromised devices of legitimate customers, pose a significant challenge. Doubly, threat actors can use IP Spoofing to disguise the real source of the flooding traffic. It's possible that every single packet sent by a compromised machine could appear to be from a different source using this technique.

In the cloud, we may feel that automatic sizing is dealt with both by our cloud service vendors and our elastic scaling, but the ability of the cloud to allow us to respond to demand can be used against us as well. In a yo-yo attack, the attackers apply enough pressure to cause the environment to expand to compensate and then drop the attack. Automated scaling will subsequently cause the environment to shrink back, at which point the attack resumes. This sounds pointless, but scaling either way takes time, resources, and changes the configuration. If you haven't limited your scaling sufficiently, the attacker can simply apply pressure continually, keeping your infrastructure way above the normal operational limit, generating cost beyond what has been budgeted, and impacting your bottom line.

If your cloud system provides service to others, DoS attacks can also target legitimate API endpoints with bad data (see "Server-Side Request Forgery" earlier). They don't even need to breach the system. Flooding a service with bad data that will cause a legitimate error will still prevent the system from operating correctly. The service needs to verify every attempt to determine the validity of the data – that takes time and resources, both of which are finite.

While a DDoS attack wages large volumes of traffic, threat actors can also cripple a cloud service with attacks that are designed to be slow. For example, consider a deliberately slow attack in packet response time based on a communications request. Open the connection and then wait until the connection almost times out before sending the next byte, and then repeat the step over and over. This ties up a connection for a long time and prevents the system from processing another request. If enough connections occur during a slow-rolling attack, your system could experience another form of DDoS attack based on idle resource exhaustion.

DoS attacks have garnered so much attention by leveraging the fundamental principles of the Internet against us. The Internet is designed to try and get packets of data from A to B, even when large parts of the network have been damaged or destroyed. It's designed to be resilient, making it very hard to stop the flood of data in the best place possible, near the source. Threat actors, therefore, leverage the benefits of the cloud against us: elastic scaling, availability, ease of use, simplicity, resiliency, and economy of scale.

As we have said before, more times than anyone wants to hear, the more things change, the more they stay the same. Knowledge to be aware of so you can consider it in your plans because DoS and DDoS are not new because of the cloud. Threat actors have just learned how to take advantage of them to achieve their goals. In fairness, DDoS attack vectors could be a book all by itself. We can't address all the DoS/DDoS possibilities, here, but there are plenty of good resources on the Internet to read more – assuming you can get to those websites.

Authentication

When thinking about attack vectors, authentication probably doesn't come to mind straight away, despite it being the front door, back door, and side door to your systems. We will think about the credentials used and how we protect those, but not so much the mechanism itself. If you have already thought about this, then I commend you. It took a deep look at modern attack vectors and resulted in a moment of enlightenment (like accession in *Stargate*).

User authentication, regardless of user type, is a process. That process takes time, and while processing, the authentication service is tied up. There may be multiple threads running (concurrent authentication services all processing individual authentication requests) to give the impression that it is multithreaded, but you would not want to batch process authentication requests; they require more immediacy.

If you've just finished reading the DoS section, you're probably already seeing a DoS attack on the authentication mechanism. You don't even need to be trying to compromise credentials; just fire random nonsense at the authentication mechanism and consume all the resources available. It will probably happen pretty quickly if the requests are unfiltered and full of garbage. After all, authentication isn't necessarily a simple mechanism; there is commonly at least one encryption process being used, as well as some kind of database or data storage search, in even the most basic methods. Now consider more extensive authentication, one that uses multiple attributes, processing time, and algorithms to result in identity proofing that can be computationally expensive. If all possible authentication threads are consumed, you cannot authenticate to take remedial action. This is even more of a problem in the cloud, where you will not have physical access to crash cart[22] for the asset.

Many systems operate an account lockout process, primarily to hamper brute-force attacks, which try every possible password combination in an attempt to find the correct, current password. In these mechanisms, you generally get between three and five failed attempts before the account is marked as locked, and the system will not accept any attempt to authenticate the account – even with the correct password. Sometimes, there will be a timeout period for the lock that will automatically expire, and the account will become available for login attempts once more. Sometimes, it's a manual process leveraging a higher-privileged account to unlock. Some systems will also implement a progressive approach to lockout; each subsequent incorrect attempt results in an increasing delay before another attempt is possible and before the eventual lockout comes into effect. All of these approaches are great at hampering the brute-force attack, but they also offer opportunities to make the lives of legitimate users difficult, should they just happen to forget their password.

As a threat actor, you can leverage the account lockout to amplify the effectiveness of a DoS attack, while also lowering the frequency of the attack to possibly drop below the levels that might be useful for automatic traffic management. If usernames are easy to discover or derive from email addresses or employee social media postings, then the threat actor can lock your organization's accounts in a few attempts, possibly for significant periods. Worse still, if you use the default database administrator account

---

[22] https://datacenterresources.com/articles/what-is-a-crash-cart/

to allow your application to access its database, I can target that account and prevent your application from accessing data or operating correctly. If a threat actor has leveraged your authentication defenses to disable your systems and has hit enough key accounts this way, it's unlikely that you can respond effectively. For this reason, it is common for a default administrator account to not lock out. The downside is that it does make these accounts susceptible to brute-force and persistent attacks.

It is also important to consider how authentication is set up and secured. There are numerous potential authentication mechanisms for web servers, from the basic authentication to passing a username and password, through to multi-factor authentication leveraging a mobile device for biometrics. It's possible that the developers enabled the site for all possible authentication approaches or that the site implementer has left a default setup in place, either of which potentially leaves an exploitable authentication method available.

Given the loosely coupled nature of the cloud, all steps along the authentication path need to be appropriately secured. A step in the process that is considered hidden does not need an authenticated connection exposed on the Internet, or it will be discovered and exploited. Ironically, there is nowhere to hide in the cloud. If you can get to it, someone else can find it and get to it.

Authentication is a service we cannot deny access to for specific individuals (only attributes like geolocation) since we have not yet validated their identity. IP addresses are relatively easy to fake, so those cannot be relied upon. Even validating IP addresses takes time and could form part of a DoS attack.

Multi-factor authentication (MFA) can eliminate the need to lock out accounts by adding one or more authentication steps that rely on data that changes with every attempt and that cannot be brute forced. Again, the validation of these takes time, and time is a constrained resource that can be abused as an attack vector.

Certificates

Digital certificates offer some very creative attack vectors for cloud-based systems. Certificates themselves are a secure mechanism, but they are not independent entities; they rely on a chain of authority that leads back to a certificate authority (CA) that can be validated against. A threat actor will look to access the organization's CA account. From there, manifold attack vectors exist.

To begin, two primary attack vectors exist for the CA account: social engineering and stolen credentials. With social engineering, the threat is twofold, both at the CA and at the organization. Social engineers will attempt to convince CAs to release new certificates against existing company domains, allowing them to stand up fake sites (using some of the other attack vectors mentioned in this book to redirect traffic) or perform man-in-the-middle (MitM) attacks. The MitM attack is potentially more damaging because it has a high chance of going undetected until the damage has already been done.

MitM attacks present a secure connection in the browser, while decrypting traffic arriving at their system and then re-encrypting it to the legitimate target and vice versa. The user feels they are connected directly to the legitimate target system and successfully completes whatever activity they were planning; nothing appears out of the ordinary. Even changing response times will be treated as acceptable, in most scenarios, because the Internet can be highly variable. The attack can capture credentials and information about the organization's operation with the target system. This kind of attack is typically associated with watering hole[23] attacks.

---

[23] www.proofpoint.com/us/threat-reference/watering-hole

Imagine a MitM attack leveraged against a business with their banking partner. The attacker can monitor connections and harvest the necessary credentials to perform any banking activity, as well as banking habits. This can enable the attack to keep their activities within the scope of normal transactions, frequency, and value, thwarting many protections that the organization and the bank may have implemented to detect fraud. Social engineers will not stop there. Getting key credentials released to gain access to CA accounts, accessing key systems to steal or to scam authorized staff to share client certificates (used for authentication), and signing certificates (used to sign applications and/or emails) are all important attack vectors to consider.

As an example, in 2011,[24] a hacker managed to gain legitimate server certificates for multiple high-profile websites, including Google, Microsoft (Skype and Live), Yahoo, and Mozilla. This was achieved through a compromised partner account used with a CA (for reselling their CA services) and led to a well-documented breach.

Next, consider the nonhuman requirements for certificates. Client certificates are often used for API access and generally need superuser access to install and manage. These are, thus, relatively hard to steal. A threat actor needs administrative or root access to a system with the certificate installed. Once the attackers have a copy of the certificate, they can install the certificate onto their system and are one step closer to gaining access to something of value.

Like credentials, certificates can represent keys to the most valuable assets within an organization; they need to be treated as sensitive data and properly secured, both at rest and in transit. Being a complex concept that's dependent on external resources, it's not unusual to find certificates that have been poorly implemented, left on unsecure file systems, and with excessive permissions that can lead to other attack vectors.

---

[24] https://slate.com/technology/2016/12/how-the-2011-hack-of-diginotar-changed-the-internets-infrastructure.html

BGP/DNS

While BGP (Border Gateway Protocol) and DNS (Domain Name Service) are different technologies, they both offer potential mechanisms to misdirect network traffic toward faux cloud locations or to force a system outage. The latter happened due to a simple mistake and created an outage for Facebook[25] that lasted the better part of a day.

BGP is a routing protocol used by ISPs, specifically autonomous systems (AS), to exchange routing information. An autonomous system is another name for a routing domain, a group of machines and/or networks under the same administrative control or authority. You'll probably have seen. AS numbers in IP address assignment information seen through WHOIS, indicating the administrative control or authority that owns the assigned address or range. While an AS is never assigned to more than one organization, however, it's not uncommon to find multiple AS assigned to a single organization particularly where the organization is large. For example, how to get from A to B, but more specifically, where is B and how do I get there? While BGP is commonly referred to in two forms, iBGP (internal BGP) and eBGP (you guessed it, external BGP), that's a qualification on where it's used rather than separate protocols; it's all BGP. However, BGP does use the source (internal or external) in route selection. The nuance is similar to saying my house has stairs inside, but steps outside. iBGP is used within an ISP to maintain routing tables, and eBGP is used between ISPs.

When a link is first established between two routers, they exchange their entire routing tables via BGP and, subsequently, only exchange changes to routes. This is part of the resilient design of the Internet. If a route fails for whatever reason, traffic can be rerouted automatically through these exchanges of routing information. An analogy would be your satellite navigation system receiving live updates on traffic and road closures and automatically adjusting the route to your destination; you may drive the

---

[25] https://cisomag.eccouncil.org/facebook-outage/

same route for months or years without alteration, but one day, someone breaks down and blocks a road and you are rerouted "automagically."

It's the same for BGP, although you, as an Internet user, are unlikely to be aware of the change. Your traffic to and from your favorite websites arrives as it always has, and unless you are monitoring the route the traffic is taking, you'll be none the wiser. This technology is fundamental to how the Internet works, but it has the opportunity to be abused as an attack vector. There is no authentication between routers for BGP, and there is no hierarchy of authority regarding the routes; therefore, there is no way of identifying the "correct" route. As BGP is only exchanged between routers, the connections between them are manually established, and so somewhat trusted, but that doesn't entirely prevent abuse.

If an attacker can gain control of a legitimate BGP router that links two autonomous systems, they can inject fake BGP data, claiming ownership of IP addresses and redirecting traffic to and/or through their own systems. This makes it much harder to detect that you are not communicating with the legitimate target you intended. Everything can be configured to look exactly like the official site, including certificates, because you are getting to the "correct" IP address. It also offers opportunities for malicious actors to cause your traffic to pass through their systems while you continue to communicate with the legitimate sites and targets you expect. The ability to then examine the traffic being sent could offer the opportunity to discover secret information or to misdirect you with fake responses. TLS[26] (transport layer security) does offer some security here, but if the target server isn't the legitimate one, your system will establish a secure link to the threat actor's system, leaving your traffic entirely exposed once it arrives. An attack on MyEtherWallet[27] showed how transparent this attack can be – and cost an unsuspecting user thousands of dollars.

---

[26] www.internetsociety.org/deploy360/tls/basics/
[27] https://www.helpnetsecurity.com/2018/04/25/myetherwallet-dns-hijacking/

BGP rerouting has been used by attackers to redirect traffic and also to break legitimate connections. As BGP relays changes in routing almost continuously across the Internet and less frequently between individual routers, there is an opportunity for DoS attacks to repeatedly advertise routes as available and unavailable to other routers, causing them to relay that information onward. BGP has built-in protections to avoid this kind of activity (legitimate or not) from causing a routing storm (where the routing updates flood out across the Internet). Ironically, those protections can extend the time it takes for routing to return to a steady state after an attack because the routers cannot distinguish between legitimate and fake routing updates.

BGP is not the only mechanism that's available for allowing attackers to misdirect your traffic; DNS provides another way – one that makes it easier to compromise cloud traffic. The Domain Name Service (DNS) was created to help prevent humans from having to remember hundreds of IP addresses and instead represents them as human-readable names, like `www.beyondtrust.com`, for the company BeyondTrust. Systems communicate using IP addresses, and a network infrastructure uses IP addresses for remote connections and MAC (media access control) addresses for local ones. Neither IP addresses, for example, 192.168.0.1, nor MAC addresses, for example, 01:FE:23:24:33:B4, make a lot of sense to humans (they are not easy to remember, document, and even verbally communicate), but they contain enough information for machines to use.

Humans much prefer descriptive domain names, with letters or words that make sense and are easier to remember. When we type a DNS address into a lookup tool, the first thing it does is contact the DNS servers configured for our workstation to look up that name and retrieve the IP address that it believes is the target for routed traffic. This allows the workstation to ultimately communicate with the asset. DNS was originally a very static mechanism, with the lookup tables being manually managed.

You can still find the "hosts" file on your operating system, which was used to look up domain names before DNS was a ubiquitous standard. All of the lookups were stored locally on every machine, which presented a management nightmare for updates and synchronization.

When DNS itself was young, it used (and still does in some implementations) text files to hold the look up tables on each DNS server centralizing that configuration file. Today, most DNS implementations maintain dynamic lookup tables that can be modified by appropriately permissioned systems and for the basis for most of the directory systems used, such as Active Directory and LDAP. Given the critical nature of DNS in the operation of networks today, it's remarkable that it's also one of the most commonly misconfigured networking technologies.

Anecdotally, a colleague of mine who worked in sales throws out the statement, "It's DNS," in response to any problem that comes up – and is painfully right a fair proportion of the time. We don't have an answer to why it's such a challenge, but we suspect it has more to do with the mundanity of the technology leading to less attention being given than any technical complexity. DNS is another scenario of "getting the basics right," being a mantra we should all have pinned to our wall. In the cloud, it demonstrates the same discussion point we have revisited repeatedly. The more things change, the more they stay the same. Getting DNS correct in the cloud is just as important as getting it correct on-premise.

That aside, as you can imagine, a directory that converts domain names to IP addresses is a prime target for an attacker wishing to get you to a system under their control. A poorly secured DNS server can offer the opportunity to modify the lookup table to redirect you to a fake website, although this will be a different IP address, known as DNS Poisoning.[28] We don't normally see IP addresses, so this may be invisible to us.

---

[28] https://www.okta.com/identity-101/dns-poisoning/

The prevalence of digital certificates for public websites will tend to alert us to the unsecure nature of the connection, but, as we've already covered, it's not impossible to generate or steal a certificate to complete the deception.

On the Internet and, consequently, in the cloud, domain names are not a free for all; you have to register your domain name with a registrar (a company that manages domain name assignments for a fee), which will record the IP addresses for the authoritative DNS servers for your domain name. This helps prevent just anyone from wresting control of your domain name, but should someone gain access to your domain registrar account, then those authoritative domain names are open to hijacking.

In addition, within your local infrastructure, it's possible for an attacker to change the DNS servers that are being used by your systems for name resolution and redirect connections for their malicious intent. This is particularly effective when DHCP (Dynamic Host Control Protocol) is in use, providing a single location to update that information for all connected systems. DNS is a hierarchical system where lookup requests are forwarded to authoritative servers for initial resolution and the responses are passed back to the originating DNS server, where they are to be delivered to the system. The responses are cached locally to avoid overloading those authoritative servers. This means your systems accept the response from the DNS server they query without question, and, thus, this process can be abused.

We have highlighted a few examples for potential attacks affecting DNS. To be fair, this topic could be a book in itself. It is, however, a cloud attack vector we must consider and protect.

Ransomware

Over the years, ransomware has grown from an annoyance to an attack vector that can take down any business, organization, or a nation's critical infrastructure in nearly an instant. Today, ransomware not only threatens workstations and servers but also cloud resources and hypervisors, encrypting virtual machines and instances. It's no surprise that just the thought of this crisis can induce cold sweats and panic among investors, executives, and security professionals who are tasked with preventing these attacks from occurring in the first place.

At its core, ransomware is a form of malware that cybercriminals use to infect computers or cloud resources and then to encrypt files and data, making them inaccessible until the owner has paid a ransom or extortion demands are met. Of course, even paying the ransom is no guarantee that the perpetrators will restore access, especially if they have exfiltrated sensitive information.

The worst part about ransomware is that you no longer need to be a technical cybercriminal to conduct an attack. Ransomware as a Service (RaaS)[29] allows virtually any threat actor to conduct attacks from cloud and profit share on extortion attempts. The service is not much different than other cloud services we have discussed, outside of its illegality in most regions of the world.

Unfortunately, the results are the same from RaaS to organized cybercriminals. From downtime, economic devastation, to loss of life, today's ransomware is clearly beyond the scope of just being a nuisance. It has already been attributed to the loss of life[30] when critical medical systems have been compromised, impeding patient care. So, why are organizations still getting the threat wrong? And what changes can you make to protect against ransomware, particularly in the cloud?

---

[29] https://www.crowdstrike.com/cybersecurity-101/ransomware/ransomware-as-a-service-raas/

[30] https://www.nytimes.com/2020/09/18/world/europe/cyber-attack-germany-ransomeware-death.html

All security professionals will be able to tell you that there's no silver bullet to defend against every variety of ransomware. But there are strategic security practices and key technologies that can help mitigate the threats of ransomware outright and dramatically reduce the overall risk of suffering a devastating attack.

So, how can your organization significantly improve its chances of mitigating a potential ransomware attack against cloud resources? Consider these recommendations:

1. **Secure Remote Access into/out of the Cloud**: Remote access, particularly by third-party vendors, is often the weakest link in network security. Many factors contribute to the unique difficulties of securing third-party access. Vendors authorized to access the network and applications might not adhere to the organization's same level of security protocols. Perhaps they use weak or, worse yet, default passwords or share a single set of credentials among numerous people or multiple third-party vendors. As a note, remote access will be covered in depth later in the book as we explore remote access protocols like RDP, their risks, and mitigation strategies. This is because in 2020, 52% of ransomware was associated with publically accessible RDP Servers according to Group-1B.[31]

   Another risky practice is the use of virtual private networks (VPNs) to extend "secure" access to vendors. Threat actors often target vulnerabilities or misconfigurations in VPN technology to

---

[31] https://explore.group-ib.com/ransomware-reports/ransomware_uncovered_2020

compromise the supply chain and then steal sensitive company data. VPNs generally provide broad, often excessive, access to network resources. Not only does this create a potential surface for mischief, but it also gives even the legitimate third-party user access to far more than the one or two applications they might really need.

Organizations can take control of remote access by eliminating "all or nothing" remote access for vendors – this means ditching those VPNs, especially when VPN software and certificates are provided to a third party for use on their own systems. This changes the paradigm of requiring all connections to be brokered through a single access pathway to a newer model. Now, in lieu of performing protocol tunneling or using access control lists (ACL) to limit network segments, role-based access is granted at the identity level to specific resources and applications vs. networks or hosts. This is commonly referred to as vendor privileged access management (VPAM). Vendors or internal users should only be permitted access to specific resources for a specific allotted time and to specific applications or workflows – nothing more. Administrators should also be able to approve or deny access requests to any resource, which goes far beyond the capabilities of any VPN solution today.

2. **Manage Privileged Secrets**: Compromised credentials are a well-known ingredient of almost all IT security incidents, and ransomware is no exception. To execute, ransomware needs privilege.

It is a critical path for ransomware's persistence. That's why it's essential to secure privileged credentials with an enterprise privileged password management solution that will consistently discover, onboard, manage, rotate, and audit these powerful credentials. Automated rotation of credentials and consistent enforcement of strong password policy protects your organization from password reuse attacks and other password exploits.

3. **Apply Least Privilege**: As G. Mark Hardy, CISSP, CISA President, National Security Corporation, noted,[32] "Ransomware is not magic – it can only run with the privileges of the user or the application that launches it. Therein lies its weakness, and our chance to leverage tools to contain it before it starts." Removing local admin privileges and applying least privilege access across all users, applications, and systems won't prevent every ransomware attack – but it will stop the vast majority of them. It will also mitigate the impact of those ransomware payloads that make their way into an environment by closing down lateral pathways and reducing the ability to elevate privilege. Least privilege can even mitigate the impact of stolen credentials. If the credentials are for a user, endpoint, or application with limited or no privileges/privileged access, then the damage will also likely diminish.

---

[32] www.beyondtrust.com/blog/entry/ransomware-a-problem-of-excesses-access-privileges-vulnerabilities

4. **Implement Patch Management**: Of course, one of the most fundamental ways to reduce ransomware and other vulnerability-based exploits is simply by staying up to date with the patching and remediation of known, published vulnerabilities. This condenses the attack surface, reducing the potential footholds in your environment that are available to attackers. In the past, significant ransomware attacks have been blamed on unpatched vulnerabilities that have been exploited. If you are looking for details, consider WannaCry[33] and NotPetya.[34] Very few ransomware attacks leverage zero-day vulnerabilities in the cloud that target the cloud (with web services being the most common to date). If you're effective at patching, that's good news, and the best mitigation against the most common ransomware attacks directly related to the cloud.

The end goal is to prevent ransomware from having direct access to your cloud environment. Unfortunately, this all too often starts with exploitation at the endpoint and ends with lateral movement that will ultimately compromise the entire environment. This highlights the importance of thinking in terms of an attack chain and following attack vectors in both directions to understand the start and end of your security controls.

---

[33] https://www.cisa.gov/uscert/sites/default/files/FactSheets/NCCIC%20ICS_FactSheet_WannaCry_Ransomware_S508C.pdf
[34] www.hypr.com/notpetya/

Crypto Mining

Crypto mining as an attack vector stretches the concept of hacking and attacking to new frontiers. It involves making money with someone else's resources and assets, often without the victim even knowing they have been hijacked.

If we consider all the attack vectors that are in the cloud already, attacking Internet-facing resources, and potentially compromising devices that are used for edge computing, a threat actor can truly "destroy" the technology that has been implemented. However, destruction is not the goal of crypto mining attacks. Mining for cryptocurrency is processing intensive; it uses excessive resources and energy (electrical power), and it generates few rewards compared to the cost of modern hardware. In lieu of threat actors building crypto mining farms (which plenty of legitimate people do), threat actors attack vulnerable resources in the cloud and elsewhere on the Internet to run malware that performs crypto mining for them. The goal is to offset the cost of hardware and electricity by using someone else's computers, without their knowledge, to do the mining for them.

Crypto mining attacks can leave you vulnerable to future attacks and consume precious resources needed to deliver the services your organization has built a business model around. If you think this is crazy, consider the attack on a Ukrainian[35] power plant that drew excessive energy production for crypto mining, including installing custom hardware locally to conduct the attack. So, how do you detect a crypto mining attack and prevent it? Consider the following for detection and potential prevention:

---

[35] https://www.codastory.com/authoritarian-tech/cryptojacking-at-a-ukrainian-nuclear-plant/

- **Processing Performance**: Crypto mining is resource intensive. Monitor for excessive CPU performance, especially for unknown and/or unsigned processes. A low and slow resource (CPU and memory) approach to avoid detection does not work well with crypto mining since it does not yield results.

- **Foreign Processes**: Basic application control in the cloud and for Internet-facing assets is a security best practice. Consider allowing listing, block listing, and only permitting digital-signed applications with a valid certificate to operate. This will prevent the vast majority of crypto mining attacks, except for the very few based on living off the land attack vectors.

- **Command and Control**: For crypto mining as an attack vector to succeed, a foreign server must assign work (proofs, depending on the cryptocurrency) and collect the results. Using native monitoring tools in the cloud or cloud-based firewalls, identify traffic patterns that could indicate a command and control service for your assets.

- **Anti-malware**: The cloud is not immune to malware and other forms of malicious code. Regardless of whether you use side scanning technology, agents, authenticated antivirus scans, etc., always deploy and manage an anti-malware solution to detect, and potentially remove, malicious code. Full stop.

- **Security Basics**: As we have stated multiple times, the best way to mitigate most attack vectors is to implement security basics and do them well. This includes privileged access management, identity

175

access management, vulnerability management, patch management, and change control. The vast majority of crypto mining attacks leverage the compromised credentials of unpatched vulnerabilities. Keeping systems and identities up to date is the best method to ensure your cloud assets do not become a victim.

In the end, crypto mining threats are just another form of malware. Their goal is to steal computing resources to make money.

Phishing

Phishing comes in many forms – not just as messaging-based attacks within email applications. In fact, many unsuspecting users have been duped via text message phishing (SMishing) and through social media. The threat of malicious messages luring users to click a link, open a malicious web page, download malware, or provide credentials on a spoofed site continuously proves that threat actors are creative in their methods to hijack your assets and steal your credentials. And, as we have discussed at length, if they have your credentials, that probably means they have access to one or more of your cloud applications.

While traditional phishing attacks use electronic written words to lure a user into their scam, and some of the messages may be hosted in social media, a new form of messaging attacks is emerging via other cloud and SaaS (Software as a Service) platforms that provide in-application messaging between users. Take, for example, these messages between users on a popular online auction platform:

Hi there, regarding my purchase, I have to go to California, my sister has mental health issues so I'll be there for couple of days. It will be very helpful if you send this item to new address (See attachment). Kind regards.

And,

Hello, I want to ask you about my item, if you can send it to the address below, because due to an accident my house was burned out and I got to change my address. Thanks!

These messages appeared in the online platform messaging system after the auction concluded and did not originate from the legitimate winner. The threat actors created or hijacked accounts and sent messages appearing to be from the winning buyer in an attempt to trick the seller into routing the merchandise to their address vs. the proper recipient. If the seller does not carefully check the message sender ID, they may fall victim to the attack and route the merchandise to the wrong place. The online auction strongly recommends sending winning bids only to the address on file, but it is conceivably very easy for someone to fall for this attack. And, if the merchandise has significant value, the seller could be liable for the merchandise and revenue because they sent it to the wrong place. It was not lost, stolen, nor were there insufficient funds. If the seller is duped, they may ultimately need to refund the buyer. The seller is out both the money and the product – a double whammy.

While this real-world example blends a traditional phishing attack with an online auction, the crime is physical and borderlines on mail fraud. However, the seller intentionally mailed the package to the wrong address after receiving the phishing email. So, how do you pursue justice? It is not that simple, especially if the scam involves more than one party. According to the FTC[36]

Question: Am I obligated to return or pay for merchandise I never ordered?

Answer: No. If you receive merchandise that you didn't order, you have a legal right to keep it as a free gift.

---

[36] https://www.consumer.ftc.gov/articles/what-do-if-youre-billed-things-you-never-got-or-you-get-unordered-products

So, if one threat actor is sending the phishing email in the cloud application and another is receiving the merchandise, you would have to prove to law enforcement the relationship between the individuals and that one executed the email and the other was the recipient for the merchandise. And, even if it was one person acting as the attacker and recipient, you would need to prove they sent the phishing email in the first place with receipt of the merchandise to themselves. That might be very difficult to prove if they are using burner phones, public computers, or if they leveraged a compromised account in a cloud application for which they had access. Ultimately, it is a very simple scam that could have significant financial implications.

Phishing attacks can truly occur anywhere that messaging applications are present. When users are online using a SaaS or cloud application, they might be more susceptible to clicking or performing an inappropriate action because they have a level of false security while operating within that application. The attacks themselves may not be strictly electronic, as we have just seen, but the results are similar to other common crimes, in this case the theft of merchandise.

For end users, there is a lesson to be learned. Threat actors use the written word, the power of language, social engineering, and blending attack vectors (messages and postal mail) to dupe unsuspecting individuals for their own financial benefit. Phishing attacks can occur anywhere you are reading text and observing a message. When they are present in cloud-based applications, we need to screen them just as vigilantly as when receiving a malicious text message. And most importantly, check and double-check your reactions before you commit to performing an action that is out of your normal behavior. In our example, the winning bidder should receive the merchandise, and it should not be rerouted based on a simple, anonymous, online, and in-application message. Phishing attacks can truly happen anywhere.

178

Now, what if those phishing attacks come in the form of solicitations? As a part of any mature security management process, providing security awareness training and penetration testing via phishing helps protect the organization and boost immunity against myriad threats. And while there are various products to help automate and measure detonation of emails, the effectiveness of any phishing testing is all in the content. If the sample phishing attacks are blatantly obvious, the expected click rate should be low. For example, "click here and I will deposit $9420.00 in your account" (from a "Nigerian prince").

If the phishing samples are targeted, have few misspellings, and contain spear phishing or whaling attributes, the click rate and detonation should be significantly higher. There is one flaw in this approach, however. Each phishing test is generally a snapshot in time and a single-email campaign. Rarely are they part of a series of similar emails within a campaign that builds end-user confidence in their authenticity. One such very successful phishing campaign-style attack relies on the "Unsubscribe" feature that is built into many email solicitations, turning them into watering hole attacks and credential theft. If you think this is a crazy example, read on – you will get the scenario pretty quickly.

Reliably, every day, I get a slew of marketing emails from my favorite vendors selling furniture, clothes, and electronics. These arrive at nearly the same time daily, and all of them have an "Unsubscribe" link or button. Once clicked, some sites require authentication before modifying your preferences, while others do not. Any site that requires authentication is a red flag. If the email is a phish in the first place, then asking for credentials is potentially an attack vector. Why should you have to authenticate to manage your email preferences? So, here is how the phish works and why it is a great way to penetrate your employees with a continuous campaign, regardless of the type of phishing attack.

First, let's start with your favorite vendor that sends you spam every day. Copy the contents into your favorite phishing penetration tool (daily), and change the unsubscribe link to a faux authentication page (watering hole). Most phishing tools can create this type of website out of the box and customize it to look legitimate. Now, send the email to your targets multiple times a day, and then change the content every day based on the latest advertisements. If they click the link, they get a real product, so the email looks legitimate. Soon, they will get annoyed at the volume and eventually click "Unsubscribe" based on sheer irritation. Once they try to unsubscribe, and if they fill in the credentials or launch another payload, they have been owned for that site.

Now, we know this is devious. We get it. But it illustrates a very important point in cyber education and phishing attacks. Often, training and testing is a point-in-time exercise and is not continuous. And when continuous penetration testing with phishing is applied, many tests do not provide a sequence of emails or related emails that can break down the end user into falling for an attack. From our observation, these campaign-based tactics are some of the most successful ones. The attributes demonstrate continuity and set expectations that the end user is "expecting" the email. That creates a basic level of trust. And with that, those phishing emails are the ones employees are most likely to click. All users tend to trust emails they expect to see regularly. Thus, they are more likely to interact with these emails, such as by link clicking, responding, or unsubscribing.

Lateral Movement

To a cyber threat actor, lateral movement means all the difference between compromising a single asset and potentially navigating throughout a cloud environment to establish a persistent presence. A threat actor might initially succeed in infiltrating an environment via a number of methods, such as an opportunistic phishing attack or a targeted attack based on stolen credentials or an exploit. However, lateral movement is the means to find data of value, compromise additional assets, and, ultimately, execute malware for reconnaissance and command and control of any compromised asset. Figure 6-6 illustrates this for simplicity and can be found in the second edition of *Privileged Attack Vectors*.[37]

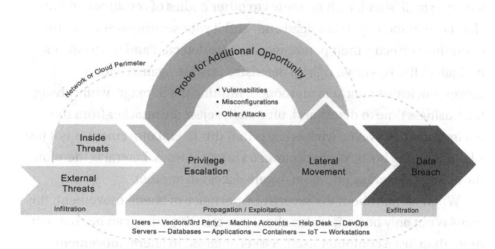

Figure 6-6. *Attack chain from Privileged Attack Vectors, Haber 2020*

As a simple definition, lateral movement refers to the ability to pivot from one asset (identity, account, database, asset, container, etc.) to another. Lateral movement is a key stage of the cyberattack chain, and published studies have found that it occurs in about 70% of cyberattacks.[38]

Try thinking of the approach to stopping lateral movement in these terms. An attacker opportunistically exploits a vulnerability or uses a compromised credential to gain an initial beachhead in your cloud environment. It's very unlikely that this initial entry point will give the

---

[37] https://link.springer.com/book/10.1007/978-1-4842-5914-6
[38] https://www.carbonblack.com/global-incident-response-threat-report/april-2019/

threat actor direct access to what they want. Again, it is merely a weak spot that they found in your security and were able to exploit. However, the danger is that this foothold in the environment can be used as a pivot point to obtain additional privileges and access to get closer and closer to the more desirable assets the threat actor seeks. With the right security strategies, you can ensure that the threat actor's beachhead is essentially a (very) small island, with no routes to other bodies of resources and no chance to island hop. It is a dead end, and if your security solutions are operating correctly, their penetration can be detected and the weakness mitigated. If this is done right, a defensive posture against lateral movement leaves attackers marooned, limiting the damage, while giving the business time to detect and, ultimately, eject the attacker from the environment. However, what is key is that this lateral movement is not just island jumping hosts; it can occur in a variety of ways. Lateral is therefore the ability to leverage one asset to gain access to another.

When we talk about the security importance of lateral movement, the focus is not only hosts, it is also about "assets," since they can be so much more than just a computer itself. Assets engaged in lateral movement can be any of the following and, most importantly, any combination of them. This is illustrated in Table 6-2, comparing of attack vector categories to assets:

Table 6-2. Comparing assets to attack vectors

Assets	Privileged Attack	Asset Attack	Identity Attack	Determination in the Cloud
Operating system	Credential, hash-based attacks or golden ticket	Vulnerabilities, exploits, and misconfigurations	Credential, defaults, guest/anonymous, and shared accounts	Compromise of virtual machines, hypervisor, or containers
Applications	Credential or application-to-application attacks including man in the middle threats	Vulnerabilities, exploits, misconfigurations, insecure architectures, and end of life	Credential, defaults, guest/anonymous, and shared accounts	Compromise of runtime, exfiltration or ransom of data, or denial of service
Containers	Credential or insecure connectivity	Vulnerabilities, exploits, misconfigurations, insecure architectures and Agile DevOps	Automation compromise of credentials or secrets	Compromise of instance, data, automation, or workflows

(continued)

Table 6-2. (*continued*)

Assets	Privileged Attack	Asset Attack	Identity Attack	Determination in the Cloud
Virtual machines	Credential, hash, or hypervisor-based credential attacks	Vulnerabilities, exploits, misconfigurations, insecure architectures and Agile DevOps, and CPU and memory-based vulnerabilities	Credential, defaults, guest/anonymous, and shared accounts in the virtual machine or hypervisor	Compromise of operating system, other virtual machines, hypervisor, or containers
Accounts	Credential theft or abuse or identity theft (including brute-force, spraying, reuse, etc.)	Credential theft, abuse, memory scraping, and insecure credential storage	Credential, defaults, guest/anonymous, and shared accounts	Lateral movement to other assets sharing the account, privileged escalation
Identities	Credential reuse and account-to-identity associations (i.e., via email account names)	Inappropriate account linkage	Lateral movement between accounts and privileged escalation, if possible	Lateral movement to other accounts linked to the same identity, privileged escalation

While the techniques for lateral movement vary substantively between these assets (including for privileged and asset attack vectors), the threat actor's objective is the same. Their goal is to laterally move between assets that are similar or share underlying services. For example, a threat actor may laterally move from an operating system to an application and then compromise additional accounts using any combination of the attack vectors (and there are definitely more) referenced previously. This raises the obvious question: How do you protect against lateral movement when it can occur in so many different ways? First, consider the underlying faults that allow lateral movement to occur. They occur due to attacks leveraging privileges against the asset and the identity that affect operations in the cloud. Network segmentation is one way to restrict lateral movement in broad stroke across the cloud, but to stop threat actors in their tracks, we need to understand and implement security controls specific to privileged, asset, and identity attack vectors.

Asset attacks are typically addressed, or at least mitigated, through vulnerability, patch, and configuration management. These are traditional cybersecurity best practices that every organization should be doing well, but as we all know, very few organizations have them working like well-oiled machines. The conversation we need to have with our teams is that due to poor basic cybersecurity hygiene, lateral movement is the primary attack vector for modern threats, like ransomware, crypto mining, and other malware.

Contemporary concepts like zero trust and just-in-time privileged access management provide a foundation to mitigate the threats from privileged attack vectors, but do not mitigate asset or identity-based attacks. Therefore, for lateral movement based on asset attacks, we need to ensure the basics are being done well week after week, month after month, and year over year. This constancy can help ensure we do not expose weaknesses in our cloud security posture that could lead to a vulnerability and exploit combination or authentication attack based on compromised credentials. This is covered next in the form of privileged attacks.

The second method of lateral movement is based on privileged attack vectors. This typically includes some form of privileged remote access and, in today's world, is the easiest attack vector for a threat actor to compromise an asset and conduct lateral movement.

The most popular techniques to infiltrate a cloud environment include

- Password guessing
- Dictionary attacks
- Brute-force attacks (including techniques like password spraying)
- Pass the hash
- Security questions
- Password reset
- Multi-factor authentication flaws
- Default credentials
- Backdoor credentials
- Anonymous access
- Predictable password creation
- Shared credentials
- Social engineering
- Temporary password
- Reused or recycled passwords

If multiple accounts are compromised for the same identity, then the attack vector can evolve into an identity attack vector. In such an instance, everything a person owns (and their accounts), is responsible for, or has privileged or unprivileged access to becomes a form of lateral movement based on the account-to-identity relationship. This is important in our conversation about lateral movement because the asset is not always electronic. An asset can be abstract, like an identity or software in the form of a container. Regardless, the movement is a pivot and a form of lateral movement between the assets.

Lateral movement potential by privileged attack vectors can be drastically curtailed by effectively executing several security best practices:

- **Applying the principle of least privilege** will not only reduce the risk that a threat actor gains a foothold in the first place (executing privileges to install malware), but it limits the access pathways available to the threat actor. Removing administrative rights can broadly reduce access to those internal corridors across the entire cloud environment. An important piece of enforcing true least privilege requires just-in-time privileged access management, a strategy that aligns real-time requests for usage of privileged accounts directly with entitlements, workflow, and appropriate access policies. By enforcing true least privilege, the lateral access pathways are limited in both number and in the windows of time and duration in which they can be accessed. In other words, least privilege eliminates persistent access.

- **Enforce privilege separation and separation of duties.** When applied to users, this involves segmenting user privileges across separate users and accounts and ensuring certain duties can only be performed with specific accounts. Thus, if one account is compromised, the range of privileges it affords the threat actor is restricted in scope. This also implies that an administrator should not use their IAM user account for administration to access email.

187

- **Implement privileged identity management**, such as privileged credential management (rotation, eliminating default/reused credentials, etc.). This best practice eliminates a broad swathe of attack methods, while reducing the effectiveness of others. For instance, implementing one-time passwords (OTPs) for highly privileged accounts will prevent password reuse attacks. Frequent rotation of credentials also means that the threat window for which an account can be compromised via stolen credentials is time limited.

- **Intelligent identity and access management** for the rapid detection and response to indicators of compromise. This is an important part of stopping attacks before they become worse. All privileged sessions should be monitored for unusual activity (trying to execute inappropriate commands). Additionally, a powerful defensive capability is the ability to centrally assert control over sessions, including pausing, transcribing, and terminating sessions.

Additionally, the concept of zero trust (discussed in detail later as a part of a common office environment accessing the cloud), which requires a multifaceted approach, can be applied to defend against lateral movement attacks. A zero-trust approach emphasizes upholding strict access controls and not trusting anyone, anywhere, at any time – even those already inside the cloud environment, by default. Zero trust strives to ensure that authorization or authentication is not allowed between assets unless a third-party trust and subsequent approval have been granted.

Remember, lateral movement can happen in between any assets, and it is that inappropriate trust between them that should be prevented. Consider the illustration in Figure 6-7 covering how different exploits (vulnerabilities, secrets, keys, and identities) can be used to laterally move between assets.

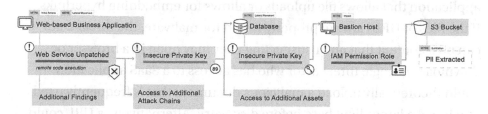

Figure 6-7. *Lateral movement using multiple techniques for exploitation*

There are many forms of lateral movement, all of which allows for the expansion of the threat actor's coverage area into an environment and potentially the compromise of more resources as they conduct their mission. As a reminder, lateral movement does not always require credentials to be compromised. Lateral movement can occur through vulnerability and exploit combinations, misconfigurations, and, most importantly, through files and resources shared by assets on-premise or in the cloud.

Now that the fundamentals of lateral movement have been explored, from assets to privileges and identities, consider how lateral movement works in a cloud-based application. There are two primary attack vectors to consider:

- Movement within the cloud, jumping from asset to asset via the same or different types

- Interaction with the cloud by an end user or on-premise assets with a machine-to-machine connection

Movement from identity to identity is typically difficult within a secure SaaS platform unless the threat actor knows the credentials for another user or it has been poorly configured to allow the impersonation of another user, including escalation of privileges. However, resources that are shared between users can allow for lateral movement. Consider a SaaS application that allows file uploads or allows for embedding hyperlinks. If the files or URLs are not properly vetted for malware, the threat actor can post content that an unsuspecting user may open in a browser or download. A single threat actor who has access to a SaaS application could theoretically upload a malicious document that is frequently used and infect a large client base before discovery. Alternatively, a URL could be embedded in a frequent link that was innocuous when posted, but altered afterward to host some malicious intent. The results are the same: movement between identities in a SaaS application can occur via shared resources in the application, and a malicious or hijacked user can enable a vehicle to compromise other users. And since no anti-malware solution is perfect, the more advanced the threat, the more likely this type of scenario could succeed. Once it does, the same vehicle is used for lateral movement.

Next, consider interaction between a cloud-based application and remote assets. As we have seen with the SolarWinds Orion incident, a compromise in the supply chain allowed the auto-update services for Orion to contain malicious code that was delivered to SolarWinds clients. Essentially, any downloads from a cloud-based service could impact a remote device, whether the intent was malicious or not. Unfortunately, we have seen this several times throughout the years with bad antivirus signatures that caused inappropriate file deletions, poor performance, or even system outages (like blue screen of death). With the knowledge that a service in the cloud or SaaS application that downloads and executes code on a remote device could be a threat, the potential for a supply-chain attack, SaaS hijacking, or even poorly crafted update that was missed in quality control practices could impact an environment. And, if the update contains malicious code, then the peer-to-peer lateral movement begins to expand to all systems in scope. The SaaS application becomes the unwitting delivery mechanism of malware or unwarranted configuration changes to allow a threat actor to engage lateral movement. Today, this is primarily a supply-chain issue, but SaaS hijacking is a real thing and was attributed to the shutdown of a cryptocurrency, LiveCoin.[39] Everything from back-end servers to social media was compromised, and the cryptocurrency exchange grinded to a halt and stopped providing services.

Change control is king to verify all updates to combat both of these threats. As a security best practice, all cloud-based solutions should have MFA enabled for all users. Single-factor authentication is just not acceptable, considering the modern attack vectors we have seen used to compromise credentials.

Finally, using an identity-centric security approach with privileged access management can solve many of these problems. This includes ensuring all identities for humans and nonhumans are as unique as possible, applications are implemented using least privilege principles, and secrets (like passwords and keys) are unique and never reused. This helps ensure that if a SaaS application does manage to infect your assets, other accounts and privileges cannot be used by traditional lateral movement techniques. These recommendations have been repeated throughout this book and emphasize again that the more things change, the more they stay the same. In this case, our recommendations are still the same. This is because lateral movement is no longer strictly host to host nor device to device.

To a threat actor, lateral movement is a crucial attack strategy. It allows them to move from where they opportunistically landed within an organization via the initial exploit to other, more desirable assets.

---

[39] https://beincrypto.com/livecoin-closes-permanently-following-suspicious-hack/

The techniques for lateral movement can be based on asset, privileges, or identities and can include traits that span a human identity all the way through unpatched vulnerabilities on an operating system.

Remote Access (RDP)

RDP (remote desktop protocol) is a technology that allows for a complete desktop experience, including remote sound, clipboard, printers, and file transfers with high-resolution graphics (which can be scaled down based on bandwidth) for a remote user. Jokingly, some security professionals have recently dubbed RDP as "Ransomware Distribution Protocol" due to excessive vulnerabilities that plague its installation and poor authentication hygiene.

In 1998, Microsoft introduced Windows Terminal Server as an add-on to Windows NT Server 4.0 Operating System. This add-on capability enabled remote desktop access over a network using TCP/IP. Every Windows OS release to follow has also included this capability, which became mainstream with the release of Windows XP (circa October 2001). Since the release of XP, RDP has been the de facto standard for remote session access for Windows Desktop and Server Operating Systems.

At 20+ years old, RDP has seen multiple versions, with new capabilities added to mature it as a reliable remote access protocol. Over this time, RDP has also had its share of security issues. However, with the emergence of a "new normal" that entails more remote working, increased reliance on cloud computing, and ever more distributed environments, RDP is now commonly being stretched for use cases far beyond what was intended. Numerous threat[40] and breach research reports over the last 18+ months have indicated that this misuse of RDP is helping fuel the success and onslaught of ransomware and other cloud-based cyberattacks.

---

[40] https://explore.group-ib.com/ransomware-reports/ransomware_uncovered_2020

At its core, remote desktop protocol utilizes a single TCP/IP port to initiate a connection (default 3389) and is a derivative of the T.128 application sharing protocol. Without going into technicalities of how each packet and frame is constructed, the important takeaway is that all traffic is generally point to point, encrypted, and contains all the data to efficiently transmit and process an entire user experience remotely and with various mechanisms for fault tolerance, authentication, and even multiple monitor support. This is all done without the need for HDMI, USB, and other types of cables, but rather everything is sent over the network from one asset to another. In fact, RDP can work just fine over Wi-Fi, and even cellular, as long as TCP/IP is available. This is illustrated in Figure 6-8.

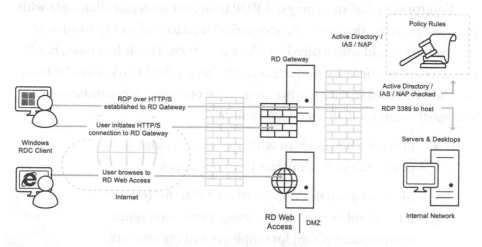

Figure 6-8.   *Remote desktop protocol (RDP) network communications through the Internet*

The diagram in Figure 6-8 helps illustrate typical scenarios for connectivity. A client can use a browser or remote desk client through the Internet to connect to remote desktop gateways on-premise or in the cloud. While these are based on running RDP over HTTPS (blue and black connectivity lines), the risk is much higher when running

RDP (orange line) directly to cloud resources. To mitigate this risk, authentication and abstraction controls in the RD Gateway or RD Web Access Server (defined as Policy Rules) shield any malicious activity via direct access.

However, the highest risk with regard to RDP is when it is directly exposed to the Internet via port 3389 or when RDP is allowed to traverse directly through the firewalls to a target on the internal network. This practice is common and should absolutely be avoided at all costs. To that end, if you are familiar with using a Citrix Server or Microsoft Windows Terminal Services, you are probably using RDP all the time and may not even be aware of it.

Enterprises of all sizes may use RDP to access servers, collaborate with other employees, and remotely access desktops to perform tasks similar to how they would with a physical office presence. This is less risky, but it is still a concern because perimeter controls can shield an external attack, but they also lend to lateral movement once one asset is compromised. The most common RDP use cases include

- Provide a bastion host with applications into an environment that mimics local resources.

- Allow a virtual desktop interface (VDI) for (or into) cloud environments using a common office environment (COE) for employees or contractors.

- Provide a graphic user experience to remote servers for maintenance, setup, and troubleshooting regardless of their location.

- Provide access for help desks, call centers, and service desks into remote users that provide technical support.

- Allow employees, contractors, vendors, or auditors access to a desktop to provide a similar user experience as being in an office.

These are all valid use cases that are extremely relevant and important in a work-from-anywhere world. However, some of these use cases pose far more dangerous risks than others. In ideal and environmentally controlled situations, the remote desktop protocol works great. However, securing RDP to prevent rogue sessions, hijacking, inappropriate access, exploits, privileged escalation, and so on requires a level of information technology and security maturity that goes far beyond default RDP settings.

RDP's default settings only provide a baseline for encryption and basic security. If these settings are solely relied on for security and used as is, they create a situation that presents an unacceptable risk to most organizations. With that said, how do you secure RDP for both internal and external operations when connecting to and from the cloud for Windows assets?

The first security rule of RDP: it is absolutely unacceptable to leave RDP exposed on the Internet for access, no matter how much endpoint and systems hardening is performed. The risks of such exposure are far too high and are exploited regularly. RDP is meant to be used only across a secure network segment. Why? Since RDP hosts support a listening port awaiting inbound connections, even the most secure installations can be profiled as a Windows Operating System and its version. Once this is known, social engineering, missing security patches, zero-day exploits, credentials on the dark web, and insecure password management all could allow inappropriate access via RDP.

So, let us take securing RDP on external hosts off the table. It is just a bad idea (just like time travel). This scope even encompasses mobile devices like laptops used by employees at home or to support a mobile workforce. No devices that can have, or do have, a public TCP/IP address should have RDP enabled. This is why many organizations require VPN or modern remote access solutions to connect to external resources.

This is true even if they are in the DMZ or cloud to mitigate these potential risks. But what's involved with adequately securing RDP for a secure cloud segment? We can start with what we know about the default configuration:

- **Access Lists**: Enabling RDP on Windows hosts, by default, only allows access by the local or domain administrators (depending on its current configuration). While this prevents access by a standard user, it represents an unacceptable risk, since only administrators can authenticate via RDP into the asset. This does not follow the security best practice of least privilege. Therefore, access for administrators should be eliminated. Only the appropriate standard user accounts should be granted RDP access, and this should adhere to a just-in-time model, meaning access is for the briefest duration needed to complete a task. Moreover, session activity should be fully monitored and recorded to ensure it is appropriate. The necessary least privilege, just-in-time access, and session monitoring controls can be most thoroughly enforced via a privileged access management (PAM) solution.

- **Default Accounts**: If the access lists recommendation provided earlier is not strictly followed, a threat actor can easily hack the administrator account for access from another asset. And, if the administrator's default username is "administrator," a breach, at least on some level, is almost foregone. Therefore, we recommend that the administrator account for the local machine or domain be renamed to something different, unique, and not guessable. While this does not protect the SID (Windows Security Identifier), it does at least obfuscate the username. In addition, RDP'ing (yes, it commonly used as a verb too) as an administrator should only be performed in use cases where it is unavoidable, but not for daily remote access needs. That should be performed using a dedicated solution with all the traits we have currently discussed.

- **Authentication**: Network-Level Authentication offers the strongest available method for authenticating RDP communications. If this is not turned on, credentials are sent in clear text to a remote host or domain controller. Non-Windows implementations of RDP, unfortunately, may only allow this older and insecure authentication mechanism.

- **Encryption**: The "high" encryption level offers the strongest available encryption for RDP network communication. If this is not set, the maximum key strength supported by the target is negotiated (instead of the maximum key strength set by Group Policy Options) through a domain controller.

- **Clipboard Redirection**: RDP Servers offer clipboard redirection, so remote sessions can easily copy, cut, and paste content from remote systems to the connecting device and vice versa. This practice is ripe for abuse, such as by data extraction, or pasting of system information, like passwords.

- **Network and LTP Printer Redirection**: RDP Servers offer printer redirection for remote access sessions. This feature allows for the connection of network and LTP (Line Terminal Printer) printers from local devices and domain controllers to the remote assets.

This can allow the printing of critical information and the introduction of malicious printer drivers into an environment. RDP should be configured without redirection for network and LTP printers so data cannot be printed remotely and exfiltrated.

- **Session Management**: Windows Servers allow for multiple RDP sessions per user account. If a user is unintentionally disconnected, the results could be a loss of productivity or information, because a new session does not reconnect to the previous session. The session is considered orphaned. This situation can be mitigated by restricting access, especially by limiting administrators to one session. This setting also acts as a rudimentary session management solution for malicious RDP since only one session can occur at a time, which makes tracking access easier.

To implement these settings, organizations should configure them all in Group Policy Options and apply them via Active Directory. Resources that are not domain joined must be individually set and hardened to match this configuration. Regardless, for both configuration scenarios, if one host is misconfigured, it could represent an enormous risk. Yet, this happens all the time.

While we keep security best practices for the configuration of RDP in mind, there are other risks that must be regularly monitored and managed:

- **Vulnerabilities**: Since the inception of RDP, various versions have had myriad vulnerabilities, including a few, such as BlueKeep[41] and DejaBlue,[42] that

---

[41] www.cisa.gov/uscert/ncas/alerts/AA19-168A

[42] www.coresecurity.com/core-labs/articles/dejablue-vulnerabilities-windows-7-windows-10-cve-2019-1181-and-cve-2019-1182

have allowed remote code execution and privilege escalation. For any environment (cloud or on-premise) using RDP, information technology administrators need to stay apprised of security updates and apply them in a timely manner. Without many of these security patches, few mitigating controls can prevent exploitation.

- **Clients**: The RDP protocol is well documented. Many third-party products support acting as an RDP client. In addition, other operating systems, such as macOS and Linux, also contain native RDP clients based on open source and proprietary code. If a vulnerability is discovered in any of these clients, then the risk can be propagated back to an RDP host server. Therefore, controlling, limiting, and managing the RDP clients allowed in your environment (such as via application control) are critical to ensure the end user's access does not become the attack vector.

- **Licensing**: Microsoft requires licensing of the RDP protocol for its use in an environment. Deploying a third-party solution or open source versions may violate your licensing agreements with Microsoft. As silly as this sounds, ensure any third-party solutions using RDP that you deploy have a proper license with Microsoft in order to instrument their technology.

RDP security risks are unjustifiable for many organizations. Even the slightest incompliance, whether internally or externally when using RDP, is unacceptable. Such organizations require a strategic solution for remote access that is not dependent on native operating system functionality.

This leaves a few choices for modern Microsoft Windows assets and other operating systems that support RDP as a client or server. Consider these alternative remote access protocols when managing the cloud:

1. **VNC (Virtual Network Computing)**: VNC is an alternative remote access protocol that competes with RDP. It is a graphical desktop sharing solution that uses the remote frame buffer protocol to control another computer's screen, keyboard, and mouse by relaying screen updates. The primary advantage of VNC over RDP is that it is platform independent and has multiple server and client implementations from various sources on the same platform. With VNC, you can basically pick your vendor, open source, or style and implement it.

   Unfortunately, VNC suffers many of the same security and hardening shortcomings as RDP, including potentially weak encryption, clear text transmissions, and limitations for hardening authentication. While some proprietary solutions have been built upon VNC to solve these issues, they are paid solutions just like any other proprietary third-party remote access implementation. And like RDP, assets using VNC should never be exposed directly to the Internet, and internal assets should be managed accordingly.

2. **SSH (Secure Shell)**: Modern versions of Microsoft Windows allow almost every function to be executed via the command line. In 2018, Microsoft formally added native Secure Shell (SSH) to the operating system to facilitate this functionality remotely.

While not graphically based, SSH allows a secure method to log in remotely to a Windows host and execute commands and scripts. Hardening of SSH entails similar steps to RDP. SSH needs to be properly configured for account access, encryption, and access control lists. To that end, it should only be used internally and never exposed directly on the Internet. This will be covered in more detail in the next section.

3. **Third-Party Solutions**: Proprietary implementations of remote access technology are typically architected in a vastly different manner than RDP, VNC, and SSH. In lieu of opening a listening TCP/IP port on a host, these technologies tend to use agent-based technology to call out to a manager, appliance, SaaS solution, or gateway technology and await an inbound connection request. Such implementations are ideal for placement within the cloud because the exposure has been mitigated by no open ports, and authentication is performed at the remote access manager vs. at the target itself. In addition, traffic is routed through the service to secure the network path as opposed to point-to-point communication that firewalls may block.

Some vendors that supply proprietary implementations for remote access have solved all the challenges and deficiencies associated with RDP. However, these are enterprise solutions and not free. The underlying protocols used for

these solutions are also proprietary to obfuscate
the technology from reverse engineering by
threat actors.

The most advanced of the third-party secure remote
access solutions may offer features like screen
recording, multiscreen sharing, safe mode booting,
and even remote registry access without the need
for a full session or an open port. However, account
management can remain a challenge because every
solution needs to grant authentication privileges
based on a directory service or through a local role-
based access model to each potential target. This
needs to be set up regardless of whether the users
and assets are grouped in Active Directory, LDAP,
or Azure AD. Administrators need to set up who has
access to what, and when, in lieu of allowing wide-
open access, which poses a more significant risk
to the business. And by default, no one has access,
unlike RDP, so the solution starts with the least
privilege access model.

Remote Access (SSH)

Before tackling SSH (Secure Shell) exposure on the Internet, a quick
reminder of cybersecurity basics. Any and all unneeded ports should be
closed when publicly facing. We have covered this already in detail and
will repeat it until it becomes like the song *Baby Shark* ("do do da do").
And, all remote access ports should be disabled at all times when publicly
facing, too. SSH is no exception.

So, why are we covering SSH in this section? For the simple fact that SSH is used to administer almost all of the cloud, but TCP/IP port (22) should never be publicly facing. The port should only be privately accessible, and when appropriate, security controls have been applied.

Consider the following best practices for securing SSH:

- Implement complex (non-default) usernames and passwords (using a privileged access management solution).

- Disable logging in as "root" (PermitRootLogin no).

- Configure an idle timeout interval (ClientAliveInterval 360, ClientAliveCountMax 0).

- Disable empty passwords (PermitEmptyPasswords No).

- Limit which accounts can actually authenticate via SSH (AllowUsers User1 User2).

- Ensure your system is using the latest versions of SSH (Protocol 2).

- Change the default port from 22 to something much higher to obfuscate access (Port 2025).

- Allow access via only specific IP addresses that act as proxies, bastion hosts, or jump points (iptables -A INPUT -p tcp -s [Your IP] --dport 22 -j ACCEPT).

- Enable multi-factor authentication (depends on your build and third-party integration).

- Use public/private keys for authentication (ssh-keygen -t rsa) in lieu of complex credentials.

- Bind SSH to a non-Internet facing TCP/IP address that is private and only accessible internally and potentially through some form of bastion host. It should never be directly exposed to the Internet.

These recommendations make it more difficult for a threat actor to compromise your assets. If credentials are compromised, vulnerabilities are unpatched, or another host is compromised, SSH provides lateral movement for a threat actor to conduct their nefarious mission. The same is true for all remote access protocols. These recommendations help secure SSH access to only assets with strong authentication to verify a user's identity. However, the most important recommendation is true for all remote access protocols: never expose their open ports on the Internet!

Remote Access (Others)

Management of cloud resources requires remote access of some form, regardless if they are virtual machines, based on orchestration tools, serverless, or modern workloads that have been optimized for cloud services. The biggest risk for any remote access is the exposure of the listening port itself. It provides a distinct target for threat actors to focus their efforts. The most common method of identifying listening ports is simply via a port scan. Therefore, the recommendation to never expose it publicly should always be held sacred.

The most common remote access protocols provided with the operating systems themselves are RDP, SSH, and VNC. All of these have listening ports to support a direct or proxy-based connection. Third-party solutions, however, typically use agent-based technology and do not require a listening port. They do not support direct connections, but rather, the agent communicates with a bastion host, authorized proxy, appliances, SaaS solution, or a jump point using an outbound persistent connection to broker a remote access session. The middleware service is typically managed by a cloud-based service that does accept an inbound remote access request (typically HTTPS over 443) and relays the request to the middleware (bastion host, proxy, or jump point) to form a connection. This is illustrated in Figure 6-9.

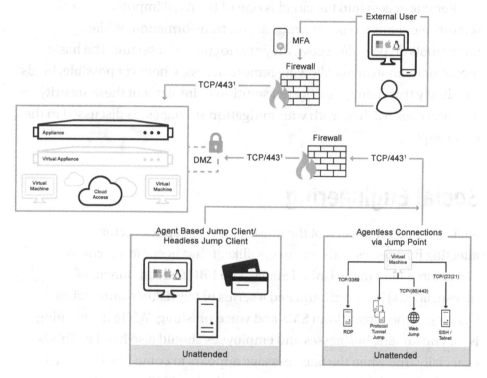

Figure 6-9. *Remote access using a third-party solution and proxy technology*

The best practice architecture is to secure remote access through another layer that can be monitored for proper activity, record sessions, and apply policies to the remote access session itself – all of which does not require a listening port of any type on the cloud-based target, except port 443 (HTTPS). If an agent is not permitted on the target based on technology or environmental conditions, most proxy and jump technologies can perform a traditional remote access connection themselves (RDP, SSH, VNC, Telnet, etc.) and continue to broker the connection. This allows for the monitoring previously discussed, preserves native operating system remote access protocols, and provides the crucial segmentation needed to operate properly in the cloud.

Remote access into the cloud is one of the most important cloud security elements as you embrace digital transformation. While native tools do provide access, they are not the most secure. The basic recommendation of not allowing remote access, whenever possible, holds absolutely true. Using a dedicated solution to implement these security best practices will help with your mitigation strategies, as discussed in the next chapter.

Social Engineering

Social engineering is one of the most significant attack vectors affecting businesses and consumers alike. It has become a focus for law enforcement in the United States. The FBI (Federal Bureau of Investigations) has even launched a series of television commercials warning of the threats from SMS and voice phishing. While the warning is for consumers, businesses and employees should also heed it. This is especially true when the faux message appears to come from a trusted individual within the organization. Consider the SMS screenshot in Figure 6-10 from John Titor.

Figure 6-10. *SMS phishing attack claiming to be from a CEO (John Titor, Time Traveler)*

The screenshot is from an employee that received a faux text message from their CEO. The employee responded, but realized their mistake when the "urgent" task was to purchase gift cards for a client. If the attack vector of "gift cards" was not a part of cybersecurity training or they knew the message was an attack at that point, the employee could have been socially engineered into performing a malicious, and potentially costly, task. Imagine if the request was to reset a password or provide access into an asset. For example, the faux CEO message to an IT administrator could be to unlock their account and forward a new password. Consider what happened to Twitter in 2020[43] when a large portion of their premiere client base was compromised via the help desk and a social engineering attack.

Social engineering to and from the cloud is no different. We have a blind trust in the text messages, emails, and even confirmation notices we receive when we believe the source of the content is trusted and especially when the communication is expected. If the message is crafted well enough, and even potentially spoofing someone we already trust, then the threat actor already gained the first step in deceiving us. If we act on the fake correspondence that targets our cloud assets, we could be exposing a large portion of the business to exceptional risk.

Considering the modern threats in the cyber world – from ransomware to deepfake voice technology – the outcome can become much more severe than just gift cards. At the risk of becoming paranoid about every email we receive, and every text message and phone call we answer, we need to understand how social engineering works and how to identify it in the first place, without losing our sanity. This learned behavior is no different than basic intuition, but it does require some skill sharpening to identify attack vectors – and to pinpoint our own behaviors that make us susceptible. Regardless, you always need to verify the message before acting and understand the risks. To start, threat actors attempt to capitalize on a few key human traits to meet their goals:

- **Trust**: The belief that the correspondence, of any type, is from a trustworthy source. The target believes they recognize the source.

---

[43] https://nypost.com/2020/07/16/twitter-blames-coordinated-social-engineering-attack-for-hack/

- **Credulous**: The belief that the contents, as crazy or simple as they may be, are in fact real.

- **Sincere**: The intent of the content is in your best interest to respond or open.

- **Suspicious**: The contents of the correspondence do not raise any concern by having misspellings and poor grammar or by sounding like a robot corresponding on the phone.

- **Curious**: The attack technique has not been identified (as part of previous training), or the person remembers the attack vector but does not react accordingly.

- **Laziness**: The correspondence initially looks good enough, and the lethargy of the individual to investigate the URLs and contents for malicious activity does not seem worth the effort.

If we consider each of these characteristics, we can appropriately train team members not to fall for social engineering. The difficulty is overcoming human traits and ensuring the material is flexible to cover direct attacks, as well as broad attempts that appear to come from cloud resources.

Consider the email attack that originated from the FBI in late 2021.[44] A threat actor compromised mail services in the cloud and used the FBI to send malicious content to countless individuals. The source was trusted, the messages appeared relatively real, but the threat actors' goal, in the end, gave them away. Figure 6-11 is a sample of this faux FBI email.[45]

---

[44] www.cnn.com/2021/11/13/politics/fbi-fake-emails-cyber-threat/index.html

[45] https://krebsonsecurity.com/2021/11/hoax-email-blast-abused-poor-coding-in-fbi-website/

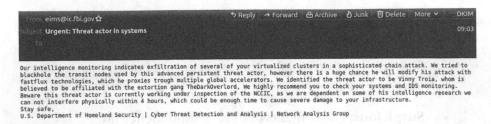

From eims@ic.fbi.gov ☆   ↢ Reply   → Forward   🗄 Archive   ♨ Junk   🗑 Delete   More ∨   DKIM
Subject Urgent: Threat actor in systems   09:03
To

Our intelligence monitoring indicates exfiltration of several of your virtualized clusters in a sophisticated chain attack. We tried to
blackhole the transit nodes used by this advanced persistent threat actor, however there is a huge chance he will modify his attack with
fastflux technologies, which he proxies trough multiple global accelerators. We identified the threat actor to be Vinny Troia, whom is
believed to be affiliated with the extortion gang TheDarkOverlord, We highly recommend you to check your systems and IDS monitoring.
Beware this threat actor is currently working under inspection of the NCCIC, as we are dependent on some of his intelligence research we
can not interfere physically within 4 hours, which could be enough time to cause severe damage to your infrastructure.
Stay safe,
U.S. Department of Homeland Security | Cyber Threat Detection and Analysis | Network Analysis Group

Figure 6-11. *2021 FBI email scam*

To that end, please consider the following training parameters and
potential self-awareness techniques to stop social engineering from
jeopardizing your environment:

- Team members should only trust requests for sensitive
  information from known and trusted team members
  and providers. An email address alone in the "From"
  line is not sufficient to verify the request, nor is an
  email reply. The sender's account or service could be
  compromised. The best option is to learn from two-
  factor authentication techniques and pick up the phone
  or verify the email using another communications
  path. For example, call the party requesting the
  sensitive information or unusual access, and verify
  the request. If the request seems absurd, like granting
  administrative rights or sharing a password, verify that
  this is acceptable according to internal policies or with
  other stakeholders, such as IT or human resources
  (it could be an insider attack). Simple verification
  of the request from an alleged trusted individual,
  like a superior, can go a long way to stopping social
  engineering. In addition, all of this should occur before
  opening any attachments or clicking any links. If the
  email is malicious, the payload and exploit may have

executed before you performed any verification just by clicking or opening the malicious content.

- If the request is coming from an unknown source, but is moderately trusted – such as a cloud service you interact with – there are some simple precautions you can take. First, check all the links in the email and make sure they actually point back to the proper domain. Just hovering over the link on most computers and email programs will reveal the contents. If the request is over the phone, never give out personal information. Remember, they called you. For example, the IRS will never contact you by phone; they only use USPS for official correspondence. If you receive a panic call, don't let yourself fall for the "sky is falling" metaphor. Chicken little learned this lesson a long time ago.

- Teaching how to identify genuine correspondence is rather difficult. Social engineering can take on many forms, from accounts payable to service outages, to faux upgrade requests, to profile verification and updates. Just stating "please verify your email address" or "verify your credit card" only handles a very small subset of social engineering attempts. In addition, if peers receive the same correspondence, it only eliminates spear phishing attempts as the probable attack vector. The best option is to consider if you should be receiving the request in the first place. Is this something you normally do, or is it out of the ordinary to receive it? If it is, default back to trust. Verify the intent before proceeding. This is especially true with the inception of deepfake voice and photos that are nearly impossible to distinguish from real people and images.

- Suspicious correspondence is the easiest way to detect and deflect social engineering attempts. This requires a little detective-style investigation into the correspondence by looking for spelling mistakes, poor grammar, bad formatting, or robotic voices on the phone that could be deepfakes. This is expressly true if the request is from a source you have never interacted with before. This could be a request for a password reset, adding access to a service, or to provide information that otherwise should be secured. If there is any reason to be suspicious, it is best to err on the side of caution: do not open any attachments or files, click any links, or verbally reply. Instead, report the phishing attempt to your information security department. They will help you determine if you should reply or not.

- Curiosity, paired with security overconfidence, is the worst offender, from a social engineering perspective. "I believe I am fully protected by my computer and my company's information technology security resources." That's a false assumption. Modern attacks can circumvent the best systems and application control solutions, even leveraging native OS commands to conduct their attacks. The best defense for a person's curiosity is pure self-restraint. Do not reply to "Can you hear me?" from a strange phone call; do not open attachments, if any of the preceding criteria have been realized; and do not believe nothing can happen to you (Spiderman got lucky with his spider bite, however). The fact is, it can, and your curiosity should not be the cause. Being naïve will make you a victim.

Social engineering is a big security problem, and it gets worse when working with cloud service providers. Threat actors know they can spoof the cloud provider, and trust is only based on the company name, not necessarily the people you would interact with daily.

The hard truth is that no technology is 100% effective against social engineering attacks. Spam filters can strip out most malicious emails, and Robocall Systems can block malicious or suspicious phone calls, but in the end, it is up to end users to not fall for an attack. While endpoint protection solutions can find known or behavior-based malware, nothing can stop the human problem of social engineering, especially if the threat originates from the inside or from an asset on the inside that is being used as a mule. The best defense for social engineering is education and an understanding of how these attacks leverage our own traits to be successful. If we can understand our own flaws and react accordingly, we can minimize the threat actor's ability to compromise assets and gain access to cloud (and on-premise) environments. Finally, remember this is our addition to the OSI model as an eighth layer.

Supply-Chain Attacks

In the last year, we have all been painfully educated on the threats to our supply chains. Whether these attacks affect products like commercial oil and gas, or software solutions we license, a successful cybersecurity attack against our supply chain can have painful real-world ramifications. While the emphasis has been nearly solely focused on upstream supplies, what about attacks on your clients? What happens when the attack affects the clients that your business sells to? What possible effect can that have on your business, and what potential data could they lose that could cause disruption or create risk for you upstream?

As a business, we generally vet the vendors we purchase from using tools like Security Assessment Questionnaires (SAQ) (covered later in the book, and a sample is in Appendix A). However, we rarely vet the clients we sell to as well. If their cybersecurity is poor, their risk could also be your risk. Supply-chain attacks can be a risk in both directions.

First, let's consider what data a client may have from your organization. The most common are

- Contact information for your employees – including names, email addresses, phone numbers, and maybe even employee cellphone numbers

- Banking information, including wiring information for making electronic payments for the products or solutions you sell

- A wide variety of credentials for logging into your client portal and related websites associated with the product or services

- If it is a software solution, license keys to enable the solution

While the vast majority of security professionals would consider this data held and transmitted by your customers to be low risk, there is the potential for some client data regarding your organization to be high risk:

- If the client consumes your personally identifiable information (PII) for additional processing. In other words, they are purchasing your data, and then a breach in their organization of your data could be a very high-risk event. This is common when you have clients purchase the analytics you collect as a part of your normal operations and product usage. This type of attack notably happened with Equifax and T-Mobile in 2014.[46]

- If a client consumes your product and can actively provide customization scripts or code to a forum or online repository, an insider threat or compromised environment could introduce malicious code that others unwillingly consume. This risk affects both upstream and downstream clients in the supply chain.

- If your client has a mutual relationship with your organization in which you buy and sell products or solutions with them, the amount of shared data grows exponentially with the depth of the relationship. This happens many times with technology integrations and partnerships. A compromise on either side could leak all the data mentioned earlier, in addition to sensitive information regarding roadmaps, design plans, and financial information that could stress the relationship and ability to conduct business.

To that end, if your customer is compromised, the recommendations for your business are a slight variation of traditional mitigation options:

- Identify all geolocations in which your client consumes your solution. Depending on the products and solutions you sell, local laws may require you to follow up with government agencies, like the Federal Trade Commission or local police. This is especially true

---

[46] https://www.t-mobile.com/news/press/experian-data-breach-faq

for controlled products like munitions, age-restricted products, and even software that includes strong encryption.

- Notify all employees engaged with the client so they are on alert for phishing and other scams related to the compromised company.

- Depending on the size of your business, traditional fraud alerts and credit freezes may be appropriate to secure your financial information. This is especially true if you allow electronic debits from your accounts.

The simple takeaway from this section is that the supply chain is vulnerable upstream and downstream. Your cybersecurity plan should account for the impact of breaches from either direction. In the worst-case scenarios, it might be time to cease conducting business with that client or supplier. The data they lose could be a game-over event for your business. And remember, your shared relationship for technology and data typically operates through the cloud.

Other Cloud Attack Vectors

There was a time when every company worried about their website being defaced or about whether an asset had a vulnerability. Businesses did not worry about phishing; they worried about spam (trash email). They did not think about malicious auto-updates; they worried if the next update from Windows would crash every computer if a particular antivirus product was on the system. In the last 20 years, cybersecurity has certainly changed; in the last couple years, an evolution has occurred that is more frightening than the prior 20 years combined.

In the past, a threat actor would typically attempt to exploit a flaw for financial gain. They could use ransomware or leverage the breach for data exfiltration and monetization on the dark web. In the last year, attacks have homed in on technology companies themselves, and they are generating news headlines as attackers inflict pain upon clients and vendors alike.

For many organizations, the more technology and cybersecurity-focused a target, the higher the profile when breached. After all, shouldn't a cybersecurity company be the most secure organization?

The fascinating part is that many of these tech-focused organizations targeted in supply-chain attacks have implemented solid cybersecurity practices, such as hardening and monitoring, that are practical for productivity and secure operations. Unfortunately, we have seen that this is not enough. The supply chain is at risk from end to end.

So, it begs the question: how are threat actors now succeeding? The answer is a two-attack vector approach that is relatively new to businesses and a major disruption for the supply chain. Both vectors originate on the Internet and target the cloud.

A supply-chain attack vector is intrinsically basic: attacks to the business itself, the old-school approach of scanning, phishing, and hammering on assets to break in through the front door (the Internet). Some assets operated by an individual in the office or working from home can also be conducted against cloud assets. Every Internet-facing, on-premise asset and the plethora of devices and applications operated by employees, contractors, and vendors are now targets, too.

Over the last 20 years, we have focused on cybersecurity for on-premise attacks, and traditional solutions have high effectiveness in mitigating the threats if they are properly implemented. In the last few years, however, we have shifted these attacks to the vendors who are supplying these solutions.

The other attack vector companies need to consider is the cybersecurity (or lack thereof) of the products they develop internally and the software and solutions they license, including security tools themselves, deployed throughout the enterprise (the USS Yamato NCC 71807 suffered a catastrophic warp core breach from this type of attack in *Star Trek*). This is not a new threat, but these products are becoming a targeted focal point by threat actors. The flaws, vulnerabilities, exploits, and poor configurations present in the solutions companies bring to market are causing a world of pain for their clients and the manufacturers themselves.

While many companies have adopted secure code review, penetration testing of their products and best practices for patch management, threat actors are increasingly tailoring their attacks to target vendors, the supply chain, and to compromise companies that have licensed their solutions. SolarWinds Orion is the most profiled breach based on this attack vector.

Consider a simple worm targeting Android users of WhatsApp.[47] The application itself was identified to have a vulnerability. Malware was designed to use WhatsApp as a mule to propagate the worm. Facebook, the owner of WhatsApp, was not targeted by threat actors, but, rather, the product they produce became the transport vehicle through the cloud for infecting other assets. And beyond the other implications, the revenue impact of an exploited product flaw could be massive. SolarWinds, for instance, saw its stock lose nearly 40% of its value[48] by January 2021.

Even Apple, with all the data privacy and security testing, can still be a victim. For example, iOS 14.4 patches multiple zero-day vulnerabilities[49] that were being exploited in the wild. No one is immune, but we need to take note. Threat actors are no longer just targeting the doors and windows of organizations; they are now targeting the products we manufacture and

---

[47] https://resources.infosecinstitute.com/topic/android-malware-worm-auto-spreads-via-whatsapp-messages/

[48] https://www.barrons.com/articles/the-solarwinds-hack-was-huge-jpmorgan-is-defending-the-stock-51610645288

[49] https://www.zdnet.com/article/apple-fixes-another-three-ios-zero-days-exploited-in-the-wild/

place within our organization to support the business. And threat actors are leveraging supply-chain attacks to infect not just a single end user but also all the clients and users that consume the initial victim's solutions.

Thousands of technology vendors are ramping up their security to ensure this type of attack does not occur within their products. They are verifying build servers, certificates, API logs, and many other potential sources for an indicator of compromise. They are performing monitoring and working to ensure their products are tamper resilient. But like targeting a business, no remediation, mitigation, or product testing will be 100% effective.

As technology vendors, everyone needs to test their products end to end more than ever and find as many design flaws and vulnerabilities before the threat actors do. Organizations and vendors need to fix them promptly and ensure that even their basic design is secure. Otherwise, the entire application could be a house of cards when attacked.

CHAPTER 7

Mitigation Strategies

The more we think about the cloud, the more we learn that the same challenges that existed on-premise now have morphed onto the cloud. Yes, the risk surface has changed. Yes, the exposure has changed. And yes, the ownership and the environment have changed. Yet, we are still talking about privileged management, identity management, vulnerability management, patch management, and credential and secrets security. The disciplines we have worked with for years are the same. However, how we actually implement the controls, provide management, and provide detailed monitoring are different in the cloud. Therefore, it is important to keep in mind the cybersecurity basics; just think about new ways of applying them in the cloud. These mitigation strategies are the most effective for cloud-based attack vectors and are just extensions of what we have been doing for years. The more things change, the more they stay the same.

Privileged Access Workstations

One of the most common methods for protecting the cloud is to secure all administrative access to the cloud computing environments used for management. Typical workstations used by individuals with privileged credentials are appealing targets for threat actors. This is because those credentials can be stolen and then used for attacks and subsequent lateral movement. Since these are real credentials, the attack is much harder to detect. Therefore, the best practice for protecting administration of

© Morey J. Haber, Brian Chappell, Christopher Hills 2022
M. J. Haber et al., *Cloud Attack Vectors*, https://doi.org/10.1007/978-1-4842-8236-6_7

the cloud is to provide a dedicated asset (physical or virtual machine) exclusively for privileged access to the cloud. Such an asset is called a Privileged Access Workstation (PAW).

In a typical environment, an identity (user) is provided a dedicated PAW for cloud administration and unique credentials and/or secrets to perform tasks linked to the asset and user. If access using those secrets is attempted from non-PAW resources or on another PAW, it can be an indicator of compromise.

Operationally, when logging into their PAWs, users still should not have direct access to the cloud. A privileged access management solution should broker the session, monitor activity, and inject managed credentials (to obfuscate them from the user) to enable them to perform their mission securely. When this is set up correctly, all these steps are completely transparent to the end user and only take a few seconds to complete automatically. This approach is a security best practice. Therefore, solutions that provide privileged access management are crucial to managing privileged access through PAWs, especially when connecting to the cloud.

Here are best practices for implementation of a PAW:

- Uses dedicated assets (physical or virtual) that are hardened and monitored for all activity.

- Operates with the concept of least privilege and operationalize application allow and block listing (formerly application white and block listing).

- Is installed on modern hardware that supports TPM (Trusted Platform Module). Preferably 2.0 or higher to support the latest biometrics and encryption.

- Managed for vulnerabilities, and automated for timely patch management.

- Requires MFA for authentication into sensitive resources.

- Operates on a dedicated or trusted network and does not operate on the same network as potentially insecure devices.

- Only uses a wired network connection. Wireless communications of any type are not acceptable for PAWs.

- Uses physical tamper cables to prevent theft of the device, especially if the PAW is a laptop and in a high-traffic area.

While a PAW provides increased security for any cloud administrators, it should never be used for

- Browsing the Internet, regardless of the browser

- Email and messaging applications

- Activity over insecure network connectivity, such as Wi-Fi or cellular

- Use with USB storage media or unauthorized USB peripherals

- Remote access into the PAW from any workstation

- Applications or services that would undermine security best practices or create new vulnerabilities

To streamline this approach and avoid using two physical computers, many organizations leverage virtualization technologies (from VMware, Microsoft, Parallels, Oracle, etc.) that allow a single asset to execute a PAW side by side with the base operating system. The primary system is used for daily productivity tasks, and the other serves as the PAW. However, when using this approach, it is preferred that both daily activity and the PAW be virtualized on a hardened OS to provide better segmentation, but this may not always be practical. The PAW, if nothing else, should be virtualized and isolated from the OS (no clipboard sharing, file transfer, etc.) and not the daily productivity machine.

Access Control Lists

An access control list (ACL) is a security mechanism used to define who or what has access to your assets, buckets, network, storage, etc., and the permissions model for the object. An ACL consists of one or more entries that explicitly allow or deny access based on an account, role, or service in the cloud. An entry gives a specified entity the ability to perform specific actions.

Each entry consists of two pieces of information:

- **Permission**: Which defines what actions can be performed (e.g., read, write, create, delete)

- **Scope**: Which defines who or what can perform the specified actions (e.g., a specific account or role)

For example, suppose you have a storage bucket for which you need to restrict access. There are multiple roles involved with various levels of security and business requirements. One role may allow read access, but the other can have maintenance functions. In this case, your ACL would consist of potentially two entries:

- In one entry, you would give "Read" permission to a scope of authorized accounts that can view the data.

- In the other entry, you would give "Write" and/or "Delete" permissions to the scope of accounts responsible for maintenance.

The end results are a list of ACLs that restrict access on a "need to know" basis for the data contained in the storage bucket. While this example is simplistic for an enterprise cloud-based application, it forms the basis for our ACL discussion and protecting assets in the cloud.

Consider the n-tier web-based cloud architecture in Figure 7-1.

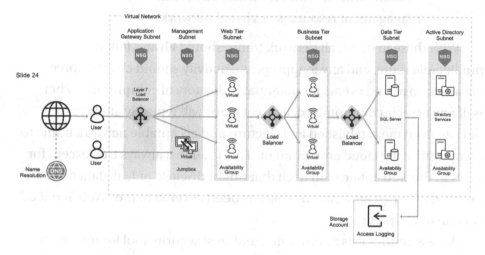

Figure 7-1. *N-tier cloud-based web application*

Access control lists should be present in every connection between tiers and within every Availability Group to prevent inappropriate network and access communications. This includes ACLs for preventing

1. Network traffic from jumping over tiers without communicating through the appropriate assets

2. Connections from the Internet from directly communicating with any layer, besides the load balancer

3. Inappropriate nations or known hostile IP addresses from accessing the application, by adding geolocation (IP and geolocation services) ACLs to the load balancer itself

4. Inappropriate communications within a tier
    to prevent lateral movement or inappropriate
    application-to-application access

5. Communications from any layer attempting
    to communicate with the virtual environment
    management resources or virtual network

With these in mind, all network traffic should always follow a
predictable route, and any inappropriate activity should be monitored
via alerts, logs, and events for potential indicators of compromise. That
is, if any asset is compromised, a threat actor will typically attempt to
deviate from the established architecture and acceptable network traffic to
compromise the cloud environment. This is almost always true except for
flaws in the web application itself that might disclose or leak data due to a
poorly developed application. This has been covered in the "Web Services"
section of Chapter 6.

Access control lists are your first and best security tool for restricting
access in the cloud when access and network traffic should always
follow a predefined route and originate only from specific sources. If you
consider the cloud has no true perimeter, only certain TCP/IP addresses
are exposed to the Internet, and traditional network architectures are
virtualized, ACLs help maintain these conceptual boundaries and allow
complex architectures far beyond what was ever possible on-premise.

Hardening

Harden, harden, harden your assets. If we are not clear on this
recommendation, harden, harden, harden everything in your
cloud environment and everything that is connected and performs
administration. (Batman learned this when fighting Superman.) While
this may seem like the most basic recommendation, improper hardening
accounts for some of the most basic attack vectors in the cloud.

First, let's have a quick refresher on hardening. As covered in Chapter 6, asset hardening refers to the process of reducing weaknesses in your security devices by changing custom and default settings and using tools to provide a stricter security posture. It is a necessary step that must be taken even before assets are placed live on a network and ready for production in the cloud. This eliminates potential runtime issues with hardening and loopholes that can be exploited by threat actors based on services, features, or default configurations present in an operating system, application, or asset.

Next, what does good cloud hardening entail? It is not the same as the controls used for traditional on-premise servers and workstations, since environmental conditions are different. Hardening for virtual machines does mirror on-premise counterparts, but hardening of containers, serverless environments, and virtual infrastructures has different characteristics due to the cloud service provider's actual implementation of technology and lack of end-user physical access, like USB ports and drive bays.

So, how does an end user get started reconciling hardening assets from on-premise to the cloud? Luckily, someone has already done the bulk of the work for you. Consider these hardening standards presented in Table 7-1. (Note, this is only a sampling based on the major cloud service providers covered in this book.)

Table 7-1. *Hardening standards for cloud environments and virtual machines*

Center for Internet Security (CIS): www.cisecurity.org/cis-benchmarks/		
AWS	CIS Benchmarks for Amazon Web Services Foundations	AWS Foundation is a comprehensive set of management and security solutions for cloud and hybrid assets.
	CIS Benchmark for Amazon Web Services Three-tier Web Architecture	The three-tier architecture is the most popular implementation of a multitier architecture and consists of a single presentation tier, logic tier, and data tier.
	CIS Benchmark for AWS End User Compute Services	End-user computing (EUC) refers to computer systems and platforms that help nonprogrammers create applications.
Azure	CIS Benchmarks for Microsoft Azure Foundations	Azure Foundation is a comprehensive set of security, governance, and cost management solutions for Azure. This offering is underpinned by the Microsoft Cloud Adoption Framework for Azure.
	CIS Benchmark for Microsoft Office 365 Foundations	Microsoft 365 is a Software as a Service (SaaS) solution that includes Microsoft Office and other services, such as email and collaboration, from Microsoft's Azure cloud services.

(continued)

Table 7-1. (*continued*)

Center for Internet Security (CIS): `www.cisecurity.org/cis-benchmarks/`		

GCP	CIS Benchmarks for Google Cloud Platform Foundation	The Google Cloud Platform Foundation is a comprehensive set of back-end and consumer solutions for security and management of assets in GCP.
	CIS Benchmark for Google Workspace Foundations	Google Workspace is a collection of cloud computing, productivity, and collaboration tools, software, and products developed and marketed by Google.

NIST 800-144: `https://nvlpubs.nist.gov/nistpubs/Legacy/SP/nistspecialpublication800-144.pdf`
Other Guidelines on Security and Privacy in Public Cloud Computing

NIST 800-53 rev 5: `https://nvlpubs.nist.gov/nistpubs/SpecialPublications/NIST.SP.800-53r5.pdf`
Security and Privacy Controls for Information Systems and Organizations

ISO 27017: `www.itgovernance.co.uk/shop/product/isoiec-27017-2015-standard`
Information Technology – Security Techniques – Code of Practice for Information Security Controls based on ISO/IEC 27002 for Cloud Services Standard

ISO 27018: `www.itgovernance.co.uk/shop/product/isoiec-27018-2019-standard`
Information technology – Security techniques – Code of practice for protection of personally identifiable information (PII) in public clouds acting as PII processors

FedRamp: `www.fedramp.gov`
The Federal Risk and Authorization Management Program (FedRAMP) provides a standardized approach to security authorizations for cloud service offerings used by government entities.

While these represent some of the best third-party hardening recommendations, it is extremely important to note that almost all of the cloud service providers also provide hardening guidelines for their own technology stacks. These guidelines will specify what settings to change, native tools to use, and auditing capabilities to apply for their unique features, per solution.

As an empirical practice, hardening of cloud assets is a collection of tools, techniques, and best practices to reduce weaknesses in technology applications, systems, infrastructure, hypervisor, and other areas that are cloud service provider independent. The goal of asset hardening is to reduce security risk by eliminating potential attack vectors and condensing the system's attack surface. By removing superfluous programs, accounts functions, applications, open ports, permissions, access, etc., threat actors and malware have fewer opportunities to gain a foothold within your cloud environment.

Asset hardening demands a methodical approach to audit, identify, close, and control potential security weaknesses throughout your cloud deployment. There are several types of asset hardening activities in the cloud. Consider this word map in Figure 7-2. We have chosen a word cloud for this illustration because it helps emphasize the differences between on-premise and the cloud. Depending on your cloud implementation, this may help you decide on your hardening priorities (especially when you add risk as the variable that chooses a word's color and size) and help communicate them with team members. One side note: Never underestimate the power of a word cloud when trying to convince teams of your priorities or the importance of a topic. It is a legitimate tool to explain relevance or statistics based on the topic.

Figure 7-2. *Word cloud of hardening in the cloud*

Although the principles of asset hardening are universal, specific tools and techniques do vary depending on the type of hardening you carry out. Asset hardening is needed throughout the technology life cycle, from initial installation through configuration, maintenance, and support to final assessment at end-of-life decommissioning. Systems hardening is also a requirement of compliance initiates, such as PCI DSS, HIPAA, and many others.

The type of cloud hardening you carry out depends on the risks in your existing technology, the available resources, and the priority for making corrections based on risk. Consider these characteristics that are required for hardening in the cloud:

- **Audit**: Carry out a comprehensive audit of your existing cloud technology. Use penetration testing, vulnerability scanning, configuration management, and other security auditing tools to find flaws in the system and prioritize fixes. Conduct system hardening assessments against resources, using industry standards from NIST, Microsoft, CIS, DISA, etc.

- **Strategy**: You do not need to harden all your systems at once, but they should be hardened before going into production. Therefore, create a strategy and plan based on the type of asset and the risks that are identified within your technology ecosystem, and use a phased approach to remediate the most significant flaws to ensure any remaining issues can be addressed in a timely manner or granted an exception based on the risk they represent.

- **Security Updates**: Ensure that you have an automated and comprehensive vulnerability and patch management system in place to identify incorrect asset settings, as well as missing security patches. This will help remediate settings that may weaken your implementation as well as vulnerabilities that can be used in conjunction with an existing weakness that has not been mitigated.

- **Network**: Ensure that cloud-based security controls are properly configured and that all rules are regularly audited, secure remote access points and users, block any unused or unneeded open network ports (ACLs), disable and remove unnecessary protocols and services, and encrypt network traffic.

- **Applications**: Remove any components or functions you do not need, restrict access to applications based on user roles and context (such as with application control), and remove all sample files and default passwords. Application passwords should then be managed via a privileged access management solution that enforces password best practices (password rotation, length, etc.). Hardening of applications should also entail inspecting integrations with other applications and systems and removing, or reducing, unnecessary integration components and privileges.

- **Database:** Create administrative restrictions, such as by controlling privileged access, on what users can do in a database, turning on node checking to verify applications and users, encrypting database information in both transit and at rest, enforcing secure passwords, implementing role-based access control (RBAC) privileges, and remove unused accounts.

- **Virtual Machines (Operating Systems):** Apply operating system updates; remove unnecessary drivers, file sharing, libraries, software, services, and functionality; encrypt local storage; tighten registry and other systems permissions; log all activity, errors, and warnings; and implement privileged user controls. One very important note, operating system hardening that is present on-premise with physical machines is nearly identical for virtual machines in the cloud, except for any hardening that allows communications from the virtual machine to (through) the hypervisor, such as shared files and clipboard. This hardening will come from the hypervisor or cloud service provider's hardening guidelines for their platform. Therefore, you can look

for guidance from the operating system manufacturer/
source, US Department of Defense (DoD), Center of
Internet Security (CIS), etc. The biggest difference
would be any controls that pertain to physical access
hardening.

- **Identity and Account Management**: Enforce least
  privilege by removing unnecessary accounts (such
  as orphaned accounts, default accounts, and unused
  accounts) and privileges throughout your entire cloud
  environment.

Asset hardening requires continuous effort, but the diligence will pay
off in substantive ways across your organization via:

- **Targeted Functionality**: With fewer unneeded
  programs and less functionality present after
  hardening, there is less risk of operational issues,
  misconfigurations, incompatibilities, resource issues,
  and, thus, compromise.

- **Improved Security**: A reduced attack surface translates
  into a lower risk of data breaches, unauthorized access,
  systems compromise, and even malware.

- **Compliance and Auditability**: Fewer running
  processes, services, and accounts, coupled with
  a less complex environment, means auditing the
  environment will usually be more transparent and
  straightforward. Only what is needed is truly executing.

Finally, with any attack vector mitigation, test, test, and test your
hardening. It is not uncommon for hardening to break an application or
disable a service required by a web application in the cloud. It is a bad
idea to harden the environment only after it enters production.

Hardening should be tested throughout development and quality assurance to verify any exceptions and to document the risk of not hardening them. This is not only a good security practice, but many regulatory bodies also require it.

Vulnerability Management

Like everything else we have been discussing, vulnerability management is a security best practice across any environment, but there are key differences and implications to understand when it is being applied in the cloud. This is mainly due to the methods used for a vulnerability assessment. If you are looking for a good definition for vulnerability management and vulnerability assessment, and the security best practices for each, please reference *Asset Attack Vectors*[1] by Haber and Hibbert (2018).

These are the five most popular techniques for performing vulnerability assessments in the cloud:

1. **Network Scanning**: Target an asset based on network address or host name to perform a vulnerability scan.

   a. **Authenticated**: Using appropriate privileged credentials, a network scan authenticates into an asset using remote access to perform a vulnerability assessment.

   b. **Unauthenticated**: Using only network-exposed services, a network scan attempts to identify vulnerabilities based on open ports, running services, TCP fingerprints, exploit code, and services that will output versioning explicitly (like version 4.20) or through the formatting of strings.

---

[1] https://link.springer.com/book/10.1007/978-1-4842-3627-7

235

2. **Agent Technology**: Agent technology is typically small and lightweight software installed with system or root privileges to assess for vulnerabilities across the entire asset and then report the results to a local file or centrally to a vulnerability management system.

3. **Backup or Offline Assessments**: Using templates, image backups, or other offline asset storage, assets are unhardened (remote access enabled and a privileged account enabled or created) in a controlled environment and subject to a vulnerability assessment using authenticated network scanning technology. This provides accurate results, as long as the image being assessed is recent, not modified, and can be powered on during assessments. Duplicating an entire environment is typically done in quality assurance or a lab.

4. **API Side Scanning Technology**: This modern approach to vulnerability assessments uses the API available from a cloud service provider to manage an asset and leverages it to enumerate the file system, processes, and services within an asset for vulnerabilities. This approach is only valid since the hypervisor in a cloud service provider typically has complete asset access via an API to apply vulnerability assessment signatures for positive identification. Since this is an identification process only, API side scanning can use read-only API accounts, as contrasted to network scanning with

authentication that typically needs administrator or root access. Also, API side scanning does not require special remote access services to be enabled.

5. **Binary Inspection**: Outside of code analysis, binary inspection is a newer technique that assesses a compiled binary for vulnerabilities. It can identify binaries that can contain open source vulnerabilities and is designed to target compiled applications obtained from third parties that may be a part of your build process and cloud offering. This technique helps identify vulnerabilities early to expedite remediation plans and hold the source accountable based on the open source they may consume.

What makes these techniques interesting compared to on-premise technology is that Backup Assessments and API side scanning technology were developed specifically for the cloud because

- Network scanning technology using authentication requires a host to be unhardened and allow for remote access in the cloud (which is undesirable).

- Unauthenticated network scanning does not provide sufficient results to determine if an asset is truly vulnerable to a known attack, when exposed to the Internet.

- Outside of a subset of operating systems that can operate in virtual machines (mainstream Windows, Linux, and a few others), agent technology may not be compatible with your cloud-based virtual machines – especially if you use custom builds.

- Agent technology generally has operating systems dependencies that may be a part of your current build process and introduce unnecessary risk and costs when enabled.

- Agent technology typically does not operate well in container or serverless environments.

- Network scanning and agent technologies utilize network traffic and CPU for an asset to identify vulnerabilities. If you have many assets and pay your cloud service provider based on resource consumption, there is likely a significant cost associated with each scan.

- Binary inspection is currently limited to compiled open source technology on Linux and Windows and cannot assess compiled proprietary libraries.

As we have stated, vulnerability management in the cloud is the same as on-premise. The goal is to find the risks, but the techniques for an assessment may be different. Another difference is in MTTR (Mean Time to Repair) or, in this case, Mean Time to Remediate. Since the risk surface is larger in the cloud, especially for Internet-facing assets, high and critically rated vulnerabilities should have a tighter SLA (service-level agreement) for remediation using patch and verification methods.

Finally, as discussed throughout this book, vulnerability and patch management should be your highest priority in the cloud, along with credential and secrets management, to mitigate and remediate cloud attack vectors.

Penetration Testing

While penetration testing (pen testing for short) may not sound like a cloud attack vector mitigation strategy, it plays a crucial role in the security of your cloud applications. By definition, penetration testing is an authorized simulation of a cyberattack on a computer system, cloud assets, or other technology performed to evaluate the overall security of the system and its ability to thwart attacks. Penetration testing should never be confused with a vulnerability assessment since, in lieu of using signatures to detect a vulnerability, penetration testing uses active exploit code to prove that a vulnerability can be leveraged (exploited) in an attack. The process is performed to identify exploitable vulnerabilities, including the potential for unauthorized parties to gain access to the system's features, data, runtime, configuration, and, potentially, lateral movement into assets that are more critical to the organization.

Penetration tests themselves can be conducted live, in production assets, or in a lab to test the system's resiliency. Security issues that the penetration test discovers should be remediated before a production deployment or in accordance with the service-level agreements based on the criticality of the original vulnerability leveraged.

Individuals who conduct penetration testing are classified as ethical hackers or white hats and help determine the risk of a system before a threat actor (black hat) actually finds the weakness first and exploits it.

As a part of your organization's cloud attack vector mitigation strategy, consider the following security best practices around penetration:

- Penetration tests should be conducted periodically. They should occur at least once a year, but preferably much more frequently. Most compliance initiatives require at least one pen test a year, but this is typically insufficient to truly assess a system for risk, especially when changes occur on a more frequent base.

For every organization, the goal should be continuous penetration testing to obtain a real-time assessment of the risks for any environment.

- Penetration tests should be conducted with every major solution release or when significant features or changes to the code base have occurred.

- The penetration test results are highly sensitive and should be handled with care. After all, they provide a blueprint on how to hack your systems.

- Penetration testing results will help support the security controls needed for many cloud compliance initiatives, like SOC and ISO.

- Unless you are in the Fortune 100, penetration tests typically should not be performed by company employees. As a security best practice, license a reputable third-party organization to perform required tests.

- Penetration testing service companies should be changed frequently, about every year or after an assessment of a system is complete, to provide a fresh perspective on the attack vectors and to ensure that testers don't become complacent. And yes, complacency really does happen when ethical hackers are asked to assess the same system repeatedly.

- Most cloud service providers require notification about when a test is going to occur and from what source IP addresses, so the penetration test is not mistaken for an actual attack. Each cloud service provider has a different process for this notification, and the time periods allowed for active testing do vary. Make sure this is well known and communicated before the start of any testing. In some cases, a cloud service provider may consider testing without notification of a material breach of contract.

Penetration testing your cloud systems, applications, and cloud service providers is a critical component of your cloud attack vector protection strategy. The results will help your organization determine how a threat actor may breach your organization and the ability of your assets to notify and thwart a potential attack. The logged results can serve as indicators of compromise for real-world future attacks and symptoms for other related security issues.

Never forget that penetration testing is one of the most valuable tools in your arsenal for proving, in the real world, that your cloud environment has been properly (with reasonable confidence) implemented to safeguard your business, data, and applications.

Patch Management

One commonality between the cloud and on-premises technology is patch management. While there are literally dozens of ways of applying patches to cloud resources – from templates to instances and agents – the simple fact is that vulnerabilities will always be identified, and the best way to remediate them is to apply a security patch via patch management. Patch management solutions are designed to apply security updates and solution patches, regardless of asset type. If it is software, it should be able to be patched. Some solutions provide automatic updates natively, while others require a third-party solution for features and coverage.

Depending on the operating system and implementation, patch management solutions can include:

- **Critical Updates**: A widely released fix for a code-specific (open source) or product-specific, security-related vulnerability. Critical updates are the most severe and should be applied as soon as possible to protect the resource.

- **Definition Updates**: Deployed solutions that need signature or audit updates periodically to perform their intended mission or function. Antivirus definitions and agent-based vulnerability assessment technologies are examples of these types of signature updates.

- **Drivers**: Non-security-related driver updates to fix a bug, improve functionality, or support changes to the device, operating system, or integrations.

- **Security Updates**: A widely released fix for a product-specific, security-related vulnerability that is noncritical. These updates can be rated up to a "High" and should be scheduled for deployment during normal patch or remediation intervals. These updates can affect commercial or open source solutions.

- **Cumulative/Update Rollups**: A cumulative update provides the latest updates for a specific solution, including bug fixes, security updates, and drivers all for a specific point in time. The purpose is to bundle all the updates in a single patch to cover a specific time period or version, for simplification or ease of deployment.

- **General Updates**: General bug fixes and corrections that can be applied and which are not security related. These updates are typically related to performance, new features, or other non-security runtime issues.

- **Upgrades**: Major and minor (based on version number) operating system or application upgrades that can be automated for deployment. In the cloud, these are rarely done in production, but rather to the templates and virtual machines that may be a part of your DevOps pipeline.

To protect your cloud resources, critical updates and security updates contain a plethora of information regarding the patches and their corresponding CVEs, as published by each vendor. Understanding the risk from a vulnerability management scan will help prioritize your patch management initiatives in the cloud. However, knowing how to patch in the cloud becomes a functional difference as compared to on-premise. Here are some patch management considerations for the cloud:

- Patch management solutions on-premise typically require an asset to have an operating system with an agent technology installed to apply a patch. Assets in the cloud may not have agents installed or may not even be capable of having agents installed.

- Patching operating resources in the cloud may not be possible during production, except for virtual machines. This would follow a change control process similar to the process for on-premise. For non-virtual machines, patching the asset in the cloud should be a part of the DevOps pipeline, with redeployment of the solution, if needed.

- When possible, consider using the native patch management features of the cloud service provider for the services they offer. It is in the cloud service provider's best interest to maintain a secure environment. The vast majority of CSPs provide easy-to-use tools to ensure the products they offer are simple to maintain and secure.

- Mitigating controls or virtual patches are possible in the cloud to mitigate a vulnerability for a short period, giving you time to formulate or test a potential patch for your systems. If, for any reason, a critical or high-impact vulnerability patch cannot be applied immediately, consider mitigating controls or a third-party vendor's virtual patch as a stopgap solution. Note: a mitigation is a setting or policy change to lower the risk, whereas a remediation is the actual application of a security patch that fixes the vulnerability.

In the end, patch management in the cloud is the same as patch management on-premise. You must apply patches in a timely fashion and with potentially a high urgency due to the risk surface. The difference in deploying a patch is different due to the lack of patch management agent technology and DevOps pipelines. This means you may not patch in production but release a new or patched version as a part of your DevOps pipeline. Both should be well understood and a part of your strategic plan to remediate the threats from cloud attack vectors. Also, remember to monitor and measure your patch management approach to look for improvements and to optimize how quickly your organization can close a security gap. As stated earlier, good asset management can help to ensure that coverage is truly complete.

IPv6 vs. IPv4

Internet protocol (IP) is a standardized protocol that allows resources to find and connect to each other over a network. IPv4 (version 4) was originally designed in the early 1980s, before the growth and expansion of the Internet that we know today. Note: there is a long history for IPv4 development that is worth reading if you are interested in its original roots in military communications.

As the use of the Internet became commercial and has grown globally, networking experts warned about IPv4's limited capabilities, from the number of possible addresses (32 bits) all the way to its lack of built-in security. As a result, IPv6 (addressable 128 bits) was developed and ratified by the Internet Engineering Task Force (IETF) with the features and solutions the modern Internet requires:

- Improved connectivity, integrity, and security

- The ability to support web-capable devices

- Support for native end-to-end encryption

- Backward compatibility to IPv4

Outside of the limited number of publicly addressable resources available to IPv4, which can be solved in many cases using NAT (Network Address Translation) in the cloud and on-premise, the extended range of addresses improves scalability and also introduces additional security by making host scanning and identification more challenging for threat actors.

To start, IPv6 can run end-to-end encryption natively. While this technology was retrofitted onto IPv4, it remains a discretionary feature and is not always properly implemented. The most common use case for IPv4 encryption and integrity checking is currently used in virtual private networks (VPN) and is now a standard component of IPv6. This makes it available for all connections and supported by all modern, compatible resources. As a simple benefit, IPv6 makes it more challenging to conduct man-in-the-middle attacks, regardless of where it is deployed since encryption is built in virtually, eliminating an entire class of attacks.

IPv6 also provides superior security for name resolution, unlike the DNS attack vector discussion we had earlier. The Secure Neighbor Discovery (SEND) protocol can enable cryptographic confirmation that a host is who it claims to be at the time of connection. This renders Address Resolution Protocol (ARP) poisoning and other naming-based attacks nearly moot and, if nothing else, much more difficult for a threat actor to conduct. In contrast, IPv4 can be manipulated by a threat actor to redirect traffic between two hosts where they can tamper with the packets or at least sniff the communications. IPv6 makes it very difficult for this type of attack to succeed.

Put simply, IPv6 security, when properly implemented, is far more secure than IPv4 and should be your primary protocol when architecting solutions in the cloud, as well as for hybrid implementations. The biggest drawback here is making sure all your assets, including security solutions like firewalls, can communicate correctly using IPv6. Threats targeting hybrid environments that include IPv4 and IPv6 plumbed together do represent a significant risk for an organization. A pure implementation is best, and it is not without its own tools and does have an administrative learning curve.

For organizations considering IPv6 for their cloud environments, please take note of the following best practices:

- As you begin an IPv4 to IPV6 conversion, exercise caution when using tunneling, while both protocols are active. Tunnels do provide connectivity between IPv4 and IPv6 components or enable partial IPv6 in segments of your network that are still based on IPv4, but they can also introduce unnecessary security risks. Keep tunnels to a minimum and use them only where

necessary. When tunneling is enabled, it also makes
network security systems less likely to identify attacks,
due to the routing and encryption of traffic that is
inherently harder to identify.

- Consider the entire environment and architecture.
  A network architecture under IPv6 can be difficult
  to understand and document compared to IPv4.
  Duplicating your existing setup, and just swapping the
  IP address, will not deliver the best results. Therefore,
  redesign your network to optimize the implementation.
  This is especially true when you consider all the
  components affected by IPv6 from the cloud, DMZ,
  LAN, and public-facing addresses (which will need to
  be addressable as IPv4 – normally).

- Confirm that your entire environment is compatible, up
  to date, and that planning for the switch is documented
  and tested. This is not like turning on a light switch.
  This includes a complete asset inventory for the
  cloud and hybrid environment. It is easy to miss a
  network device or security tool that is being used by
  individuals during the process, especially for basics like
  vulnerability and patch management. These will create
  an unnecessary, escalating risk over time. Therefore, do
  not enable IPv6 until you are ready. Test, test, and test
  your IPv6 conversion, unless this is a new installation,
  which is always preferred.

Privileged Access Management (PAM)

Finally, it's time to have a detailed discussion about privileged access management (PAM). Protecting an asset in the cloud entails far more than security patches, proper configurations, and hardening. Consider the damage a single, compromised privileged account could inflict upon your organization from both a monetary perspective and a reputation perspective; Equifax,[2] Duke Energy[3] (based on a third-party software vendor), Yahoo,[4] and Oldsmar Water Treatment,[5] to name just a few, were each severely impacted by breaches that involved the exploitation of inadequately controlled privileged access. The impacts ranged from hits to company stock prices and executive bonuses, to the changing of acquisition terms, to even hindering the ability to do basic business, like accepting payments.

A compromised privileged password does have a monetary value on the dark web for a threat actor to purchase, but it also has a price that can be associated with an organization in terms of risk. What is the value and risk if that password is compromised and its protected contents exposed to the wild? Such an incident can have a significant, negative influence on the overall risk score for the asset and company.

A database of personally identifiable information (PII) is quite valuable, and blueprints or trade secrets have even a higher value if they are sold to the right buyer (or government). My point is simple: privileged

---

[2] https://sevenpillarsinstitute.org/case-study-equifax-data-breach/

[3] https://www.charlotteobserver.com/news/business/article188108864.html

[4] https://money.cnn.com/2017/10/03/technology/business/yahoo-breach-3-billion-accounts/index.html

[5] www.cnn.com/2021/02/08/us/oldsmar-florida-hack-water-poison/index.html

accounts have a value (some have immense value), and the challenge is not just about securing them but also about identifying where they exist in the first place. Our asset management discussion highlighted this in detail. If you can discover where privileged accounts exist, you can measure their risk and then monitor them for appropriate usage. Any inappropriate access can be highlighted, using log management or a SIEM, and properly escalated for investigation, if warranted. This is an integral part of the process and procedures we have been discussing.

Some privileged accounts are worth much more than others, based on the risk they represent and the value of the data they can access. A domain administrator account is of higher value than a local administrator account with a unique password (although that may be good enough to leverage for future lateral movement). The domain administrator account gives a threat actor access to everything, everywhere, in contrast to a unique administrative account that only provides access to a single asset.

Treating every privileged account the same is not a good security practice. You could make the same argument for a database administrative account vs. a restricted account used with ODBC for database reporting. While both accounts are privileged, owning the database is much more valuable than just extracting the data.

What should you do to take protection around credentials and privileges to the next level as a part of your cloud-based cybersecurity strategy? Apply the following best practices:

- Identify crown jewels (sensitive data and systems) within the environment. This will help form the backbone for quantifying risk. If you do not have this currently mapped out, it is an exercise worth pursuing as a part of your data governance and asset management plan.

- Discover all privileged accounts using an asset inventory scanner. You can accomplish either via free solutions or via an enterprise PAM solution. Also, consider your vulnerability management scanner. Many VM scanners can perform account enumeration and identify privileges and groups for an account.

- Map the discovered accounts to crown jewel assets. Based on business functions, this can be done by hostname, subnets, AD queries, zones, or other logical groupings. These should be assigned a criticality in your asset database and linked to your vulnerability management program.

- Measure the risk of the asset. This can be done using basic critical/high/medium/low ratings, but it should also consider the crown jewels present and any other risks, like assessed vulnerabilities. Each of these metrics will help weight the asset score. If you are looking for a standardized starting place, consider CVSS[6] and environmental metrics.

- Finally, overlay the discovered accounts. The risk of the asset will help determine how likely a privileged account is to be compromised (via vulnerabilities and corresponding exploits) and can help prioritize asset remediation outside of the account mapping.

In the real world, a database with sensitive information may have critical vulnerabilities from time to time, specifically in-between patch cycles. This should, however, be as minimal time as possible. The asset may still present a high risk when patch remediation occurs, if the

---

[6]https://nvd.nist.gov/vuln-metrics/cvss

privileged account used for patching is unmanaged. This risk can only be mitigated if the privileges and sessions are monitored and controlled. Criticality can be determined either by the vulnerabilities or the presence of unrestricted, unmanaged, and undelegated privileged access. Therefore, inadequately managed privileged accounts, especially unprotected ones, ones with stale, guessable, or reused passwords, or even default passwords, are just unacceptable in your cloud environments. Thus, implementing and maturing privileged access management plays a foundational role in not only mitigating cloud attack vectors but also unlocking the potential of the cloud.

Vendor Privileged Access Management (VPAM)

One of the most interesting things about information technology is that there are rarely truly original ideas that are game changers for cybersecurity. Often, the next best thing follows the same security best practices we have been engaging with for years, and the new, hot solution is built upon prior art. In fact, one could argue that most modern cybersecurity solutions are simply derivations of previous solutions with incremental improvements in detection, runtime, installation, usage, etc., to solve the same problems that have plagued organizations for years. While some may have innovative approaches that are even patentable, in the end, they are doing the same thing. This is true for antivirus, vulnerability management, intrusion detection, log monitoring, etc.

So when we have a new term like vendor privileged access management (VPAM), we need to look at the root definitions and then understand what the combination and derivate solution really looks like and ultimately why it is different. To begin, let's review a few of the basic definitions that are relevant to VPAM:

- **Vendor**: A person or company offering something for sale, services, software, or tangible product, to another person or entity. In many cases, the offering requires installation, maintenance, or other services to ensure success of the offering over a period of time. A vendor does not need to be the manufacturer of the offering, but it is the entity that is actually performing the sale of the solution. Warranties and liability can vary based on terms and conditions from the vendor and manufacturer. When applied to cybersecurity, the manufacturer typically supplies updates, while the vendor may assist with the installation, if contracted to.

- **Privileged Access Management**: PAM consists of the cybersecurity strategies and technologies for exerting control over the elevated ("privileged") access (local or remote) and permissions for identities, users, accounts, processes, and systems across an environment, whether on-premise or in the cloud. By moderating the appropriate level of privileged access controls, PAM helps entities reduce their attack surface and prevent, or at least mitigate, the damage arising from attacks using accounts with excessive privileges and remote access.

- **Remote Access**: Remote access enables access to an asset, such as a computer, network device, or infrastructure, for a cloud solution from a remote location. This allows an identity to operate remotely, while providing a near seamless experience in using the asset to complete a designated task or mission.

- **Zero Trust**: The underlying philosophy0 behind zero trust is to implement technology based on "never trust, always verify." This concept implies that all identities and assets should never allow authentication unless the context of the request is verified and actively monitored for appropriate behavior during a session. This includes implementing zero-trust security controls, even if access is connected via a trusted network segment or originating from an untrusted environment. The management of policies governing access and the monitoring of behavior are performed in a secure control plane, while access itself is performed in the data plane.

Vendor privileged access management allows for third-party identities/vendors to successfully access your assets remotely using the concepts of least privilege and without the need to ever know the credentials needed for connectivity. In fact, the credentials needed for access are ephemeral, potentially instantiated just in time, and all access is monitored for appropriate behavior.

What makes VPAM different from any other solution is how it is built upon existing technology. It takes vendors' identity (including identities managed externally) and successfully merges the best practices for secure remote access, privileged access management, and zero trust into a single solution. VPAM leverages the best attributes of the cloud to provide the control plane for privileged remote access, and it allows the implementation to occur in the data plane, wherever the organization has assets that need vendor remote access or management. Figure 7-3 illustrates this using a standard reference architecture.

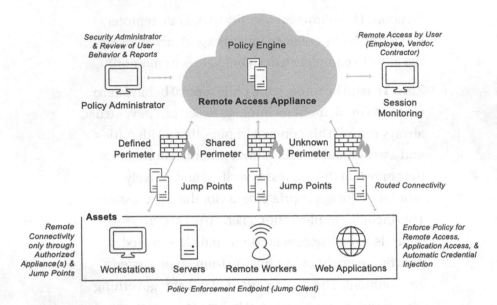

Figure 7-3. *Reference architecture for VPAM*

When you consider modernizing your vendor remote access as the work-from-anywhere (WFA) movement continues, consider VPAM. It is one new solution category that takes the best of breed from many existing solutions and unifies them to solve significant challenges of vendor remote access – especially with regard to privileges. In fact, when using VPAM, entities do not need to bolt together multiple solution providers to achieve the desired results. VPAM vendors can provide vendor privileged remote access out of the box based on a SaaS solution (control plane) and can provide a rapid time for deployment (data plane). And, as a Sci-fi reminder, the prefix code for the USS Reliant (NCC-1864) was simply 16309, a five-digit numerical code to take complete remote of a starship. Vendors should never have such simplified administrative access.

VPAM can be used for vendors, contractors, or remote employees who need access to assets on-premise, in the cloud, or located within hybrid environments.

Multi-factor Authentication (MFA)

While we have been focusing on passwords as the primary form of authentication with credentials (single factor), other authentication techniques are needed to secure the cloud properly. As a security best practice and required by many regulatory authorities, multi-factor authentication (MFA) techniques are the standard to secure access. MFA provides an additional layer (beyond username + password combinations) that makes it more challenging to compromise an identity. Thus, MFA is always recommended when securing sensitive assets.

The premise for MFA (two-factor is a subset category for authentication) is simple. In addition to a traditional username and password credential, a "passcode" or other evidence is needed to validate the user. This is more than just a PIN code; it is best implemented when you have something physical to reference or provide as "proof" for your identity. The delivery and randomization of "proof" varies from technology to technology and from vendor to vendor. This proof typically takes on the form of knowledge (something the user knows that is unique to them), possession (something they physically have that's unique to them), and inherence (something they have in a given state).

The use of multiple authentication factors provides important additional protection around an identity. An unauthorized threat actor is far less likely to supply all the factors required for correct access when MFA is in place. During a session, if at least one of the components is in error, the user's identity is not verified with sufficient confidence (two of three criteria match); in that case, access to the asset being protected by multi-factor authentication is denied.

The authentication factors of an MFA model typically include the following:

- A physical device or software, like a phone app or USB key, that produces a secret passcode, re-randomized regularly.

- A temporary secret code known only to the end user, like a PIN that is transmitted via a communication medium, like email or text at the time of requested authentication.

- A physical characteristic that can be digitally analyzed for uniqueness, like a fingerprint, typing speed, facial recognition, or voice pattern with keywords. These are called biometric authentication technologies.

MFA is an identity-specific layer for authentication. Once validated, the user privileges assigned are no different, unless policies explicitly require multi-factor authentication to obtain step-up privileges. For example, if credentials are compromised in a traditional username and password model, a threat actor could authenticate against any target that will accept them locally or remotely. For multi-factor, even though there is an additional variable required, including physical presence, once you are validated, lateral navigation is still possible from your initial location (barring any segmentation technology or policy) unless you are validated again (step-up) to perform a specific privileged task, like authenticating to another remote asset. The difference is solely your starting point for authentication.

MFA must have all the security conditions met from an entry point, while traditional credentials do not, unless augmented with other security attributes. A threat actor can leverage credentials within a network to laterally move from asset to asset, while changing credentials as needed.

Unless the multi-factor system itself is compromised, or they possess an identity's complete multi-factor challenge and response, the hacker cannot successfully target a multi-factor host for authentication. Hence, there must always be an initial entry point for starting a multi-factor session. Once a session has been initiated, using credentials is the easiest method for a threat actor to continue a privileged attack and accomplish lateral movement.

The continued use of MFA in the cloud is always recommended for step-up authentication, unless you blend it with additional security layers, like Single Sign On (SSO).

Single Sign On (SSO)

Before we dive into Single Sign On, let's expand on basic authentication. As we have stated, authentication models for end users can be single factor (1FA), two-factor (2FA), or multi-factor (MFA discussed previously). Single-factor authentication is typically based on a simple username and password combination. (Yes – we know, we have stated this multiple times, but you will not forget this based on our repetition, or when it appears on a test). Two-factor is based on something you have and something you know. This includes, for instance, a username and password from single factor (something you know) and a mobile phone or two-factor key fob (something you have). Multi-factor authentication is one step above and uses additional attributes, like biometrics, to validate an identity for authentication.

The flaw with all these authentication models is the something that you know part, traditionally a password. It can be shared, stolen, hacked, etc., and it is the biggest risk to a business when it is compromised. In fact, to manage a cloud environment, you would probably have to remember dozens of unique passwords or use a password manager. LastPass,[7] for example, caused a large-scale panic regarding a purportedly massive primary password data breach. Fortunately, the incident turned out not to be true, but it did create fears of similar cloud-based cyberattacks using credentials.[8]

If authentication is for cloud assets, then the implications of an unauthorized identity gaining access could be devastating, especially for clients using this type of service for Internet-facing assets. Therefore, it is important for organizations to mitigate the issue by replacing passwords (something you know) with something you know and that can be changed, but which cannot be shared or as easily hacked as a password.

Next, consider how many passwords you have for work. Most organizations have hundreds of applications, and if you have embraced digital transformation, you now have hundreds or thousands of cloud-based vendors supplying these applications. This potentially means credentials – username (most likely your email address) and a password – for each one. As a security best practice, you should not reuse your password, which means you have potentially hundreds of unique passwords to remember. This is not humanly possible. We previously mentioned password managers and their potential risks, but a better approach is SSO, especially when combined with MFA.

So, what is SSO? Single Sign On is an authentication model that allows a user to authenticate once, to a defined set of assets, without the need to reauthenticate for a specified period of time, as long as they are operating from the same trusted source. When 2FA or MFA is also applied for the validation, there is a high degree of confidence that the identity is who they say they are. When these methods achieve this high confidence, the

---

[7] www.theverge.com/2021/12/28/22857485/lastpass-compromised-breach-scare

[8] www.pcworld.com/article/428084/the-lastpass-security-breach-what-you-need-to-know-do-and-watch-out-for.html

associated applications in the defined set can be accessed, without the user having to remember unique passwords for each one over and over again. This SSO model negates the need for a password manager.

Now apply this SSO model to the cloud and all your users. Notice I did not say identities, since SSO is typically only used for human authentication, and not machine-to-machine authentication. From a trusted workstation, an end user authenticates once and can use all the applications they need until they log out, reboot, change the IP address or geolocation, etc. If their primary password is compromised, then only that password needs to be changed, and not passwords for the potentially hundreds of applications hosted by SSO. In fact, if Single Sign On is implemented correctly within an organization, the same end user cannot (and should not be able to) log directly into an application without using the SSO solution. The SSO user should not even know the passwords for the applications operating under SSO. That is all managed by the SSO solution itself, regardless of whether it is injecting credentials or using SAML.

Single Sign On enables a single place to authenticate for all business applications and a single place for credential management. With this in mind, please consider these dos and don'ts for your SSO implementation into the cloud:

Dos

- Harden your SSO implementation based on the vendor's best practices.

- Enable SSO controls that terminate sessions or automatically log off the user based on asset and user behavioral changes. This includes system reboots, IP address changes, geolocation changes, detected applications, missing security patches, etc.

- Select a vendor for SSO that supports open standards, like SAML, and can accommodate legacy applications based on your business needs.

- All authentication logging for your SSO should be monitored for inappropriate access and potentially authentication attempts occurring simultaneously from different geolocations.

- Consider a screen monitoring (recording) solution as an add-on for SSO, when sensitive systems are accessed, to ensure user behavior is appropriate.

- Identify all applications in scope of your SSO deployment, and ensure they support. SAML or other appropriate technology that is secure.

- Verify that the identity directory services are accurate and up to date.

- Consider user privileges when granting SSO access and honor the principle of least privilege.

- Enforce session timeouts globally or based on the sensitivity of individual applications.

Don'ts

- Don't allow SSO from untrusted or unmanaged workstations. This includes BYOD, unless absolutely needed, since the security state of the device cannot be measured or managed by your information technology and security team.

- Don't implement SSO using only single-factor authentication. That is just a bad idea since a single, compromised password could expose all delegated applications for that user.

- Don't allow SSO, ever, from end-of-life operating systems and devices that cannot have the latest security patches applied.

- Don't allow end users to perform password resets on managed SSO applications.

- Don't allow personally identifiable changes to an end user's profile within an application, like account name and password. Changes of this nature can break SSO integration or be used to compromise an application for additional attack vectors.

- And DON'T use SSO for your most sensitive privileged accounts – keep them separate. Consider using a PAW and manage the workstation and credentials separately. No one should be able to authenticate once and have a wide variety of privileged access.

- Do not allow direct access to an application that can bypass SSO.

While Single Sign On sounds like a solution to solve the majority of your authentication problems for users in the cloud, a poor implementation can make it a bigger risk than without it. When done correctly, SSO forms a foundation for centrally monitoring, managing, logging, and even directory service consolidation, for all end-user access. And note, we have only been discussing end-user access. Remember, SSO does not apply to machine-based identities, and organizations should not include administrative accounts in SSO unless additional security controls are in place. If SSO for administration is needed, consider a privileged access management solution with full session recording and behavioral monitoring.

Identity As a Service (IDaaS)

The discussion on MFA and SSO is all dependent on the fact that we have a valid identity and account relationship. On-premise, for many organizations, identity management starts with Microsoft's Active Directory and is linked with multiple, disparate solutions using identity governance and access (IGA) solutions. In the cloud, the proposition is the same, but just like everything else, it is different enough to have substantive implications.

There is a strong need for identity governance to support cloud-based solutions, but also to be compatible with, or even to replace, on-premise technology. The complexity of having multiple directory services is highly undesirable for any organization. This complexity can create challenges around performing a certification for appropriate access or providing an attestation to prove the scope of access within an organization based on role, application, or even data type is accurate. This is where Identity as a Service (IDaaS) has stepped in. It uses the cloud to solve a fundamental problem in the cloud for identity management and governance.

As an attack vector mitigation strategy, consider having one (or as few as possible) identity directory services for managing all your cloud identities, human or machine. If possible, have them linked, synchronized, or even replace your on-premise directory services. While many readers may understand this immediately, as a best practice, the benefits solve a myriad of challenges in reconciling identities across multiple authorities:

- A single source of authority for all identities used for forensics, indicators of compromise, logging, certificates, and attestations, without the need to try to reconcile the same account across multiple directory services.

- The joiner, mover, or leaver process for identity governance is greatly simplified for recording all changes to an identity throughout its life cycle.

- Identifying rogue, orphaned, or shadow IT identities requires only auditing one directory service (outside of potentially local accounts). This also minimizes the need for any local accounts.

- A consolidated solution can reduce the costs and workforce required to maintain and service multiple directory services.

- If a security incident requires modifications to an identity and its associated accounts, changes are needed only in a single location vs. manual changes across multiple directory services, some of which could be missed.

Managing identities in the cloud is crucial to all remote access, automation, DevOps pipelines, administrative access, maintenance, backups, etc.; any one of these can be abused as an attack vector, as we have been discussing. Therefore, managing identities with a solution in the cloud, one that is made for the cloud, represents the best model and architecture to ensure that the management of identities, and all their associated accounts, does not become an attack vector in itself.

Cloud Infrastructure Entitlement Management (CIEM)

Cloud Infrastructure Entitlement Management (CIEM, but pronounced "Kim" – but not Ensign Harry Kim) is the next generation of solutions for discovering and managing permissions and entitlements, evaluating access, and implementing least privilege in the cloud. The goal of CIEM is to tackle the shortcomings of current identity access management (IAM) solutions, while addressing the need for identity management in cloud-native solutions. While the CIEM concept can be applied to organizations utilizing a single cloud, the primary benefit is to have a standardized approach that extends across multiple cloud and hybrid cloud environments and continuously enforces the principle of least privilege and measures entitlement risk in a uniform manner.

CIEM solutions can address cloud attack vectors by ensuring the principle of least privilege is consistently and rigorously applied across a cloud and multicloud environment. Least privilege in the cloud entails enabling only the necessary privileges, permissions, and entitlements for a user (or machine identity) to perform a specific task. Privileged access should also be ephemeral or finite in nature.

CIEM is a new class of solutions, built entirely in the cloud and for the cloud, allowing organizations to discover, manage, and monitor entitlements in real time and model the behavior of every identity across multiple cloud infrastructures, including hybrid environments. The technology is designed to provide alerts when a risk or inappropriate behavior is identified and to enforce least privilege policies for any cloud infrastructure, with automation to change policies and entitlements. This makes it simple for a solution owner to apply the sample policies across what have traditionally been incompatible cloud resources.

The benefits of CIEM are crucial for any digital transformation project and multicloud environments:

- Provides a consolidated and standardized view for identity management in multicloud environments and allows the granular monitoring and configuration of permissions and entitlements.

- The cloud provides a dynamic infrastructure for assets to be constructed and torn down based on demand and workload. If overly provisioned, the management of identities for these use cases can lead to excessive risk. CIEM provides an automated process to ensure that all access is appropriate, regardless of the state in a workflow.

- Identity access management solutions that cloud providers offer are designed to work only within the provider's own cloud. When organizations use multiple providers, instrumenting policies and runtime to manage them becomes a burden due to the inherent dissimilarities. CIEM solves this problem, logically enumerating the differences and providing a single view of entitlements, with actionable guidance for enforcing least privilege.

- Mismanagement of identities in the cloud can lead to excessive risk. A security incident is bound to happen without a proactive approach to managing cloud identities and their associated entitlements. This is especially true if an identity is over-provisioned. Implementing management and the concept of least privilege for these identities can lower risk for the entire environment.

- When CIEM is used with adjacent privileged access management solutions, the management of secrets, passwords, least privilege, and remote access can all be unified to ensure that any gaps in entitlements or privileges are addressed and access is right-sized to the use cases/needs.

With increasing momentum behind digital transformation strategies, the use of cloud environments has exceeded the basic capabilities of legacy on-premise PAM and IAM solutions. Those solutions were never designed and implemented to manage the cloud nor the dynamic nature of resources in the cloud. CIEM is fast becoming a must-have solution for managing cloud identities, alongside PAM.

Here are some cloud security best practices a CIEM solution can help you address:

- **Account and Entitlements Discovery**: Your CIEM implementation should inventory all identities and entitlements and appropriately classify them. This is performed in real time to adjust for the dynamic nature of cloud environments and the ephemeral properties of resources in the cloud.

- **Multicloud Entitlements Reconciliation**: As workloads expand across cloud environments, organizations must reconcile accounts and entitlements and identify which ones are unique per cloud and which ones are shared, using a uniform model to simplify management.

- **Entitlements Enumeration**: Based on discovery information, entitlements can be reported, queried, audited, and managed by the type of entitlement, permissions, and user. This allows for the pivoting of information to meet objectives and manage identities and entitlements-based classification.

- **Entitlements Optimization**: Based on the real-time discovery, operational usage of entitlements helps classify over-provisioning and identify which identities can be optimized for least privileged access, based on empirical usage.

- **Entitlements Monitoring**: Real-time discovery also affords the ability to identify any changes in identities and entitlements, thus providing alerting and detection of inappropriate changes that could be a liability for the environment, processes, and data.

- **Entitlements Remediation**: Based on all the available data, CIEM can recommend and, in most cases, fully automate the removal of identities and associated entitlements that violate established policies or require remediation to enforce least privilege principles.

Based on capabilities and model, a typical CIEM solution is deployed using the architecture in Figure 7-4.

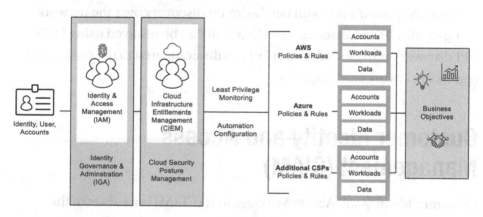

Figure 7-4. *Architecture for a CIEM solution*

The primary CIEM components include:

- API-based connectors to enumerate identities and entitlements per cloud instance and vendor

- Database for storage of current and historical identities, entitlements, and remediation policies

- Policy engine for identifying threats, changes, and inappropriate identity and entitlement creation and assignments

- User interface for managing the solution and aggregating multicloud information into a single view

The primary reason CIEM succeeds over legacy on-premise solutions is predicated on the API-based connectors, which operate in real time. CIEM continuously assesses the state of identities and entitlements, applies them to a policy engine, and supports automation tailored to identify risks in cloud environments. This then allows a user to see attributes for all cloud providers in a single interface using common terminology (much of which has been previously discussed). On-premise technology generally relies on batch-driven discovery over the network using agents, IP addresses, or asset lists that can be resolved using DNS. API discovery provides nearly perfect results compared to the error-filled results of network scanning.

Customer Identity and Access Management (CIAM)

Customer Identity and Access Management (CIAM) is a subset of the larger identity access management (IAM) market and is focused on managing the identities of customers (outside of business) who need access to corporate websites, cloud portals, and online applications. Instead of managing identities and accounts in every instance of a company's software application, the identity is managed in a CIAM service, making reuse of the identity possible. The most significant difference between CIAM and business (internal) IAM is that CIAM targets consumers of the service to manage their own accounts, profile data, and what information can, and should, be shared with other organizations.

In many ways, CIAM begins to fulfill the mission of BYOI (bring your own identity), but only for the consumer world. It is only a matter of time, in our opinion, before this will enter the business world in lieu of filing our banking information and details for employment history.

As a solution, CIAM is how companies give their end consumers access to their digital resources, as well as how they govern, collect, analyze, market, and securely store data for consumers that interact with their services. CIAM is a practical implementation that blends security, customer experience, and analytics to aid consumers and businesses alike. CIAM is designed to protect sensitive data from exploitation or exfiltration to comply with regional data privacy laws.

With the earlier definition in mind, embarking on a CIAM journey using a homegrown solution is typically out of reach for most organizations due to the complexity, data privacy, and security requirements for such a vast process. Therefore, many organizations will license CIAM as a Service to meet their business objectives in the cloud.

When selecting a CIAM vendor, please consider these six foundational requirements:

1. **Scalability**: Traditional cloud or on-premise IAM solutions that can manage thousands of identities associated with employees, contractors, vendors, and machine accounts require role-based access to static lists of resources and applications. In contrast, CIAM may potentially need to scale to millions of identities, based on the consumer implementation. While these requirements may be burstable based on events or seasonal activities, scalability is a requirement of CIAM that natively leverages cloud-based features to operate correctly. Fixed implementations of CIAM generally cannot scale appropriately when high transactional loads are placed on the system.

2. **Single Sign On (SSO)**: SSO allows an identity to authenticate into one application and automatically be authenticated into additional applications based on an inherited trust from the initial application. The most common SSO example is present in Google G Suite. Once authenticated, an identity has access into YouTube, Google Drive, and other Google applications hosted on the Alphabet platform. SSO is a feature for federated identities, and this implementation is designed for consumers to utilize these services transparently, while managing their own account and profile. In effect, they are their own administrators for their information, in contrast to IAM in an organization, which is managed by human resources and the information technology team.

3. **Multi-factor Authentication (MFA)**: MFA is designed to mitigate the risks of single-factor authentication (username and password) by applying an additional attribute to the authentication process. This can be done using various methods, since passwords alone are a prime target for threat actors. Typical CIAM implementations of MFA can use:

   - A one-time SMS PIN sent to the user's mobile device or email

   - A confirmation email with a unique URL or pin

   - A dedicated MFA mobile application, like Microsoft or Google Authenticator

- A biometric credential, like a fingerprint or face recognition leveraging a trusted device's embedded technology

- An automated voice call requiring a response via touchpad or voice to confirm the action.

MFA has become a de facto security standard for almost all sensitive consumer transactions, and it has been commercialized based on its business counterpart. For any CIAM implementation, cloud-based MFA is an absolute requirement. The flexibility to implement MFA based on any of the techniques mentioned earlier will ensure that adoption has limited resistance.

4. **Identity Management**: Managing identities in your solution needs to be centralized, scalable, and have distinct features for self-service by end users (consumers). Centralized identity management eliminates data silos, data duplication, and helps drive compliance by simplifying data mapping and data governance. All information about an identity is in a central location for management, security, auditing, and analytics processing. And, if an identity needs to be deleted, CIAM solutions can appropriately mark it for removal, without the concerns of orphan information. This is a huge concern for security requirements like GDPR (covered in the following).

5. **Security and Compliance**: Data privacy laws like GDPR and CCPA are fundamentally changing how organizations collect, store, process, and share personally identifiable information. These legal

obligations have a substantial impact on how you implement and manage your CIAM solution. As discussed, centralized identity management provides a foundation for understanding where all of a user's sensitive information resides. Based on the individual requirement, security and compliance can be managed by:

- Allowing organizations to provide users, upon request, with copies of their data.

- Allowing organizations to provide users, upon request, with audit records of how their data is being used.

- Ensuring initiatives like MFA are being implemented against the appropriate identity and not another record, location, or directory service for the same identity.

- Implementing "reasonable" and/or "appropriate" security measures to safeguard all identities.

- Ensuring all identity information is appropriately stored and encrypted, since it is centralized.

- Auditing access to all identity-related information for forensics and other compliance initiatives, like PCI and HIPAA.

- A properly implemented CIAM solution will help meet all of these objectives present in many local compliance initiatives.

6. **Data Analytics**: One of the primary objectives of CIAM is to provide a consolidated analytics view of usage and behaviors based on federated (and

sometimes unfederated – guest users that are not centrally managed) identities. This single view of consumers provides myriad business advantages and also aids organizations to meet auditing requirements for data privacy due to centralization and confidence in the security model. Automation and analytics can help drive a customized experience, allow for targeted marketing, drive higher retention rates, and provide business insight into critical consumer trends. If properly analyzed and correlated against other variables outside of the organization, this data can be a significant competitive advantage.

Ergo (and not Star Lord's father Ego), a well-implemented CIAM solution can achieve the goal of centralized, data-rich consumer profiles that function as a single source of truth about identities and their behavior for consumption by third parties.

Cloud Security Posture Management (CSPM)

Cloud Security Posture Management (CSPM) is a product and market segment designed to identify cloud configuration anomalies and compliance risks associated with cloud deployments, regardless of type. By design, CSPM solutions are designed to be real time (or as near real time as possible) to continuously monitor cloud infrastructure for risks, threats, and indicators of compromise based on misconfigurations, vulnerabilities, and inappropriate hardening. As discussed, these are three critical areas to manage to mitigate cloud attack vectors. Therefore, the primary goal is to enforce your organization's policy for risk tolerance for these three security disciplines.

CSPM as a solution category was originally branded by Gartner,[9] a leading IT research and advisory firm. CSPM solutions are implemented using agent and agentless technology (cloud APIs) to compare a cloud environment against policies and rules for best practices and known security risks. If a threat is identified, some solutions have automation to mitigate the risks automatically, while others focus on alerting and documentation for manual intervention.

While it is considered more advanced to use Robotic Process Automation (RPA) to remediate a potential issue, false positives, denial of service, account lockouts, or other undesirable effects can occur if remediation interferes with the normal workload. This is where risk tolerance becomes an important factor in the decision for notification, automatic remediation, or a hybrid model requiring manual approval before automation.

Environments that have adopted CSPM typically embrace a cloud-first strategy and want to enforce compliance regulations and security best practices in hybrid cloud and multicloud environments. This makes them ideal for any cloud deployment. With this flexibility, several key features distinguish CSPM from other cloud security solutions:

- Automatically detects and remediates cloud misconfigurations in real time (or near real time)

- Provides a catalog and reference inventory of best practices for different cloud service providers and their services, including how they should be hardened using native recommendations or third-party recommendations, like from the Center of Internet Security (CIS)

---

[9] https://orca.security/resources/blog/cspm-2021-gartner-cool-vendor/

- Provides a reference map of current runtime and dormant configuration to established compliance frameworks and data privacy regulations

- Provides monitoring for storage buckets, encryption, account permissions, and entitlements for the entire instance and reports back findings based on compliance violations and actual risk

- Inspects the environment in real time (or near real time) for publicly disclosed vulnerabilities with operating systems, applications, or infrastructure

- Performs file integrity monitoring of sensitive files to ensure they are not tampered with or exfiltrated

- Operates and supports multiple cloud service providers, including all the major vendors listed in Chapter 5

CSPM tools play an essential role in securing a cloud environment by reducing the potential attack vectors that a threat actor can exploit. It is also important to note that some of these tools can be specific to a cloud service provider and, thus, will not operate across other cloud environments unless the solution provider has explicitly added support. So, for instance, some tools may be limited to being able to detect anomalies in an AWS or Azure cloud, but not in a GCP environment.

As a mitigation strategy for cloud attack vectors, all organizations should consider some form of CSPM solution above and beyond their traditional security tools. This is one place where the best practices have stayed the same, but the tool has evolved to solve the problem.

Cloud Workload Protection Platform (CWPP)

Cloud Workload Protection Platform (CWPP) is another solution category coined by Gartner.[10] It is a workload-centric security solution that focuses on the protection requirements of workloads in the cloud and automation present in modern enterprise cloud and multicloud environments.

As we have discussed in length, cloud workloads have evolved past physical servers and virtual machines to containers and even serverless processes and code. Figure 7-5 helps illustrate the current state compared to the previous state of on-premise data centers with physical services.

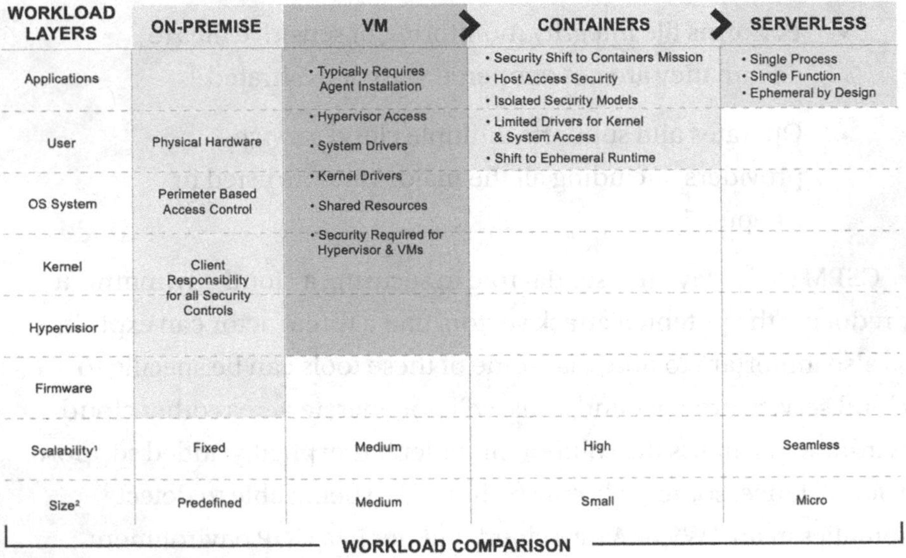

WORKLOAD LAYERS	ON-PREMISE	VM	>	CONTAINERS	>	SERVERLESS
Applications		• Typically Requires Agent Installation		• Security Shift to Containers Mission • Host Access Security • Isolated Security Models		• Single Process • Single Function • Ephemeral by Design
User	Physical Hardware	• Hypervisor Access • System Drivers		• Limited Drivers for Kernel & System Access • Shift to Ephemeral Runtime		
OS System	Perimeter Based Access Control	• Kernel Drivers • Shared Resources				
Kernel	Client Responsibility for all Security Controls	• Security Required for Hypervisor & VMs				
Hypervisior						
Firmware						
Scalability¹	Fixed	Medium		High		Seamless
Size²	Predefined	Medium		Small		Micro

WORKLOAD COMPARISON

Figure 7-5. *Evolution of computing resources from on-premise to cloud and serverless environments*

---

[10] https://www.gartner.com/reviews/market/cloud-workload-protection-platforms

These workloads provide the foundation for operating systems, networks, and storage of the data that deliver applications as part of a larger resource. The more things change, the more they stay the same. Monitoring a single process on-premise using a network management solution, or an application performance solution is the same as monitoring for processes or functions in the cloud for serverless environments. Only the runtime environment has changed as we focus on smaller, more specific tasks that lend themselves as a component to the overall resource. It is important to note that, as we discuss this in the context of the cloud, workloads technically could reside in the cloud, on-premises, or be architected using a hybrid model. Only the cloud portion can be managed with CWPP, unless a particular vendor's solution can accommodate this diversity in use cases. This requirement is a must have for some organizations, but clearly not for everyone.

For organizations considering moving workloads to the cloud, consider these potential roadblocks that would prevent a migration and have implications for modernizing workload monitoring.

Enterprises typically have one (or multiple) legacy applications and infrastructure that prevent a complete movement of functionality to the cloud due to hardware, software, or other runtime infrastructure requirements – including security.

Shadow IT is not only a challenge on-premise; it can happen in the cloud and can become exaggerated in multicloud environments. Understanding where and how a workload is processed end to end, including shadow IT, is critical for successful monitoring and movement to the cloud. Unfortunately, the old story of a server sitting under someone's desk still does happen.

Custom applications developed line by line in-house are now the exception. Tools like GitHub have made source code reusable and shareable among teams and the public community at large. Using automation, like DevOps and its cycle of "continuous innovation and continuous development" (CI/CD), has helped make the cloud a rapid vehicle for application development and adoption. Older, non-Agile development methodologies, like Waterfall, do not support these methods and are contrary to best practices for code development and support in a cloud environment. Organizations may need to rethink how they develop and publish code before embracing the cloud for workloads.

Security. Mic drop. Okay, that is a little dramatic, but the security for on-premise solutions that rely on firewalls and access control lists does not translate well to the public cloud. The risk can be contained on-premise, but in the public cloud, the exposure can be to the entire Internet. When considering moving workloads to the cloud and the solutions used for monitoring and maintaining them, do not forget about security. It should be your first thought, not your afterthought. This includes all the traditional security best practices, from vulnerability and patch management through anti-malware and identity management.

A comprehensive CWPP solution should give you the ability to discover workloads that have been deployed, whether they are on-premise, hybrid, public, private, or multicloud environments.

Finally, depending on the resources being monitored, a workload may be persistent, nonpersistent, or ephemeral. While a physical server is typically installed and configured for years, virtual machines may reside in any state from powered off, powered on, or even rolled back via snapshots based on use cases like quality assurance, security, or corruption. VMs can be instance templates, or they can even have a shared base operating system that needs to be managed, and that can affect the runtimes of dozens of other virtual machines.

With the trend to apply protection to shrinking workloads that focus on the process or function, workload management needs to resolve and isolate dependencies that affect monitoring itself and be aware that they exist. As a result, CWPP should not be thought of as another endpoint protection platform or network monitoring solution. CWPP specifically focuses on protecting workloads regardless of type, location, cloud, and mission. Thus, it is another valid cloud-based mitigation strategy.

Cloud-Native Application Protection Platform (CNAPP)

Nearly the last acronym, we promise, and it is an easy one. CNAPP (or CNAP, depending on whom you ask about the final "P"; some definitions drop it from the acronym) is a combination of CSPM and CWPP in a single solution. If you consider the capabilities of CWPP and CSPM and their overlapping technology, the combination creates a more robust solution that scans workloads and configurations (vulnerabilities and hardening, too) in development and protects workloads at runtime. It makes natural sense to combine the two disciplines, but as we have learned so far, things are not always that simple in the cloud.

So when should your environment consider CNAPP over CSPM and CWPP? From a technology perspective, CNAPP is a better choice, but from a business and role-based access perspective, it might be better to keep them separate, especially if:

- A stand alone vendor has features that are unique to their offering, as compared to a combined offering.

- Role-based access, from development to runtime, requires segregation of duties that can be blurred in a single solution from a management, monitoring, or data bleed perspective.

- Platform support is not available in a combined solution, but it is available in a stand-alone solution.

- Other solutions based on cloud vulnerability management and configuration monitoring provide sufficient overlap to select only a CWPP solution.

As native cloud-based security solutions mature, expect the lines to blur between them even more. CNAPP is one of the first categories to undergo this transition, and we expect disciplines like vulnerability management and compliance reporting to soon become commodities in CSPM, as compared to their stand-alone on-premise counterparts. It ultimately will be up to your organization to choose whether a merged solution is the best fit or a stand-alone one. In our opinion, this is akin to antivirus solutions and anti-spyware solutions merging over a decade ago to become anti-malware and endpoint protection platforms.

Cloud Access Security Broker (CASB)

A Cloud Access Security Broker (CASB) is typically a cloud-hosted solution (some vendors still use on-premise versions, but that is a fading trend) that provides a connection barrier and broker between users and cloud service providers. The basic design addresses security gaps for any XaaS deployment and connections into an on-premise environment. A CASB also allows organizations to extend and implement their security policies from on-premises infrastructure and apply them to the cloud. This ensures visibility and continuity based on existing controls and develops new policies that are cloud specific.

CASBs have become a critical part of enterprise security, allowing businesses to safely use the cloud, while protecting sensitive corporate workloads and data. This allows a CASB to serve as a policy enforcement center, consolidating multiple types of security policy enforcement engines and applying them to any assets in the cloud. A typical CASB deployment is also asset agnostic and supports everything from BYOD to servers regardless of whether they are managed or not by the business.

While CASB technology was one of the first solutions to address cloud attack vectors, its mission follows security best practices and helps reinforce that the more things change, the more they stay the same. Consider these typical features usually found in a CASB solution:

- Cloud governance and risk assessment based on asset and identity interaction

- Data loss prevention including the inappropriate exfiltration of data

- Control over native features of cloud services, like collaboration and sharing that are standard features for some solutions

- Threat prevention based on network traffic patterns

- User Behavior Analytics (UBA) to identify and block inappropriate actions

- Configuration monitoring and auditing for the entire system

- Malware detection and intrusion prevention

- Data encryption and key management of all communication pathways

- SSO and IAM integration to facilitate appropriate authentication

- Contextual access control and least privilege access

As digital transformation continues to dominate business initiatives, supporting visibility and control in these environments is crucial to meeting compliance requirements, protecting your assets from cloud attack vectors, and allowing your trusted identities to safely use cloud services – without introducing more risks to your organization.

Artificial Intelligence (AI)

Artificial intelligence (AI) and, to a lesser extent, machine learning (ML) have become increasingly prevalent as a solution to solve complex information security problems. AI is an approach that allows assets to acquire intelligence in a way that is similar to how living organisms learn to use algorithms. It is important to note that we did not state humans, in this definition, since the learning patterns of insects and rodents have also been duplicated with artificial intelligence, and the results have been quite useful.

AI technology can learn from repeated interactions with situations and events to develop correlations and predictions about current and future behavior. Artificial intelligence algorithms can discern information from a data series, without dependence on a previously determined relationship or characteristics. Training occurs as it does with living organisms, and relationships are further strengthened by repetition and reinforcement. This approach has grown in practical terms, with the increase in computing power available in the cloud, multitenant correlated datasets, and allowing the aggregation, ingestion, and analysis of very large datasets and events from similar data sources. In this way, artificial intelligence enables a level of reasoning that mimics a living brain, since the ability to analyze data at this volume and speed is impractical for living tissue.

To be clear, AI should not be confused with machine learning. Machine learning is actually a subset of AI, where the algorithms have been predefined for a specific data type and expected output. Machine learning is best characterized as fixed algorithms within artificial intelligence that can learn and postulate, while true AI is a step above that develops new algorithms to analyze data. AI is more analogous to a human learning when a new behavior is needed without a previous frame of reference. Therefore, artificial intelligence is more associated with the interpretation of information that is learned to drive conclusions or make decisions, while, to work effectively, machine learning must already have an awareness of the scope of data being processed. Because of this relationship, many machine learning implementations are part of, or afterthoughts, when an artificial intelligence application project has been fully understood and the results can be modeled for better efficiency.

Due to the considerable volume of data created by modern information networks, artificial intelligence can be a useful way to supplement human analysis of security events and identify indicators of compromise. This value is self-evident due to the inability of humans to interpret raw security event data, which can easily overwhelm even advanced security tools when there is a high quantity of data. AI can help security analysts by detecting when a cloud attack has occurred, evaluating identity behavior, assessing vulnerabilities and exposures, and correlating the information from known, and potentially unknown, attack strategies. This analysis is particularly useful in situations where behaviors can be unpredictable, identities and process ephemeral, and where targeted rules defined in policies are problematic in determining if an event was malicious or not.

Artificial intelligence can be used to assess anomalies and build a foundation for these situations. The results can be correlated by other external sources but will serve as a contextually relevant tool to assess what threat actors have potentially impacted an organization and to what degree. AI is useful because it can create initial relationships and then strengthen or weaken those relationships based on continuous analysis.

If we consider that carbon-based (yes - another Star Trek reference to humans) security analysts also have varying levels of effectiveness in their roles, consider these potential outcomes of using AI to improve cloud security:

- AI can help reduce the datasets in a critical situation to a more manageable level simply by filtering out noise. A security analyst can then better focus on the problem, not on unrelated events.

- AI can reduce stress and mistakes in crisis situations, where the heat of the moment can limit visibility, dull senses, impair the ability to interpret information, and lead to false conclusions.

283

- AI can minimize the repetitive work that frequently reduces the effectiveness of a security analyst.

- AI can significantly reduce analyst burnout due to the need to make decisions based on correlated data in events, logs, and alerts with attack patterns.

- AI can be implemented initially to detect advanced persistent threats as a part of threat-hunting exercises, and it can operate unsupervised in controlled circumstances. This releases the security analyst to handle more appropriate tasks and to act as the final arbiter of processed decisions, as opposed to hunting for a threat that might not even exist.

- As the implementation matures, AI can be relied on to handle entire classes of security events that previously relied on human intervention. The human element is critical for oversight, but the mundane component could potentially be eliminated.

- Security organizations can also utilize AI to quickly identify lateral movement actions hidden within network traffic based on modeled network behavior. This is critical in modeling network traffic in and out of cloud environments for appropriate behavior and access.

Artificial intelligence is a useful tool to supplement security best practices in the cloud, but it should not be treated as the only method of detection, prevention, and response. Nothing will completely replace the need for the security basics, security analysts, and forensic information that are needed to dig deep or to hunt for adversaries. One thing that remains certain is that AI will continue to evolve. Once the security basics have matured, AI should be considered a mitigation technology within your cloud strategy.

Single Tenant vs. Multitenant

Today, there are many cloud-native, built and optimized for the cloud, Software-as-a-Service (SaaS) solutions from which to choose. Yet, many competing solutions continue to bear the mantle of "cloud based," even though they really represent just a lift and shift of their traditional software solution to the cloud. This latter rebranding and stretching of the meaning of cloud is referred to as "cloud washing."

When it comes down to it, if the price is right, the uptime measures up against a service-level agreement, and the solution is secure, does it matter if the solution is truly "cloud based" in the strictest sense? Does it really matter if the solution is cloud native and multitenant or a re-engineered version to work in the cloud as a single tenant?

Let's step back a moment and review the definitions of single tenant and multitenant from our earlier chapters:

- A **single-tenant solution** refers to installing an application that does not share back-end or database resources with another operating instance. The runtime and data are dedicated to a single company, department, or organization. A role-based access model is used to control permissions and isolate datasets.

- A **multitenant solution** shares common resources, including, potentially, a back-end database that provides a logical separation of data and permissions to isolate information, configurations, and runtime from other logical groups of users and companies. Multitenancy provides a method to scale the solution efficiently. If multitenancy is properly implemented, resources can be shared while preventing data bleeding from one tenant to another and still providing data and operational segmentation.

Traditional, on-premise technologies are normally considered single-tenant solutions, while cloud-based solutions are generally considered multitenant. However, these are perceptions, not hard rules, and often, these definitions are blurred in an organization's actual usage of cloud applications. For instance, when you subscribe to a SaaS multitenant solution, the shared resources behind your subscription are utilized by multiple other organizations, but your custom coding and implementation may be a single tenant representing a hybrid tenant environment.

With this reminder, let's look at the benefits and security trade-offs of single-tenant vs. multitenant SaaS solutions. Embracing a multitenant SaaS solutions means your company must forgo the following three security best practices:

- **Change Control**: A multitenant SaaS vendor controls when your version is upgraded and patched. They will provide a maintenance window for the upgrade. You will be forced to accept the changes – even if it is not within a desirable time frame for your business. If the upgrade introduces unwanted change (bug or incompatibility), there is no way to roll back the changes since multiple organizations leverage the same multitenant shared resources.

- **Security**: With any multitenant solution, there is always a risk of data bleed or a vulnerability that spreads between organizations sharing resources. This can even be true with a simple back-end misconfiguration or an unsecure third-party add-on that undermines the security of the multitenant model. In essence, these types of negative cloud security events are outside the SaaS customer's control.

- **Customization**: Beyond a few multitenant SaaS vendors that have designed customization directly into their platform to create hybrid tenant environments, most multitenant solutions do not allow extensive customization to meet individual business requirements due to the number of shared resources they consume. While this may also be perceived as an advantage to avoid customized obsolesce, it can cause distribution and unnecessary rework when APIs or features become deprecated as the service releases newer versions.

Foregoing these security practices is a trade-off that organizations must weigh in lieu of maintaining the hardware, operating system, maintenance, and security patches for the solution as compared to an on-premise instance or a private cloud deployment.

Now, let's look at how the same security practices play out in a single-tenant SaaS solution:

- **Change Control**: In a single-tenant SaaS model, the end user can decide when to upgrade to a new version. They may also choose to skip a version altogether. A common risk here is waiting too long to upgrade and potentially operating with an end-of-support or end-of-life version. A SaaS-based single-tenant version needs to be managed within your current change control procedures and policy. This requires effort not normally associated with a SaaS solution – even if the upgrade is fully automated.

- **Security**: Your SaaS-based single tenant is your own. Any misconfigurations or missing security patches that need to be manually authorized can introduce unnecessary risk. While it is a SaaS-based solution, you still have the change control responsibilities of patching and maintenance, just like full versions, even though the vendor will fully automate their installation. Again, while this is probably fully automated, the organization will need to maintain this, just like any other application for patch management. And, since the solution is a single tenant, there is a very low risk of data bleed, unless the hosting company itself becomes compromised.

- **Customization**: A single-tenant SaaS solution allows for the most customization possible since any changes will not affect any other tenants or organizations. However, there is a risk that compatibility with future versions might break when the version is upgraded. Luckily, since you can control the version, you can test customization before any upgrade and stay on an older version until you are ready.

So, what else is different between a single-tenant and multitenant SaaS solution? If the cost to the end user is acceptable, the choice of multitenant vs. single tenant is really just a trade-off between change control and acceptable security risk. If you always want to be on the latest version, either model is acceptable. You just have to manage the change control yourself.

If you want to customize the SaaS solution, the SaaS solution's capabilities should be given the most importance as the tenancy model. Hybrid tenancy-based solutions are a good solution for this requirement.

And finally, consider security. All SaaS solutions should allow automatic security patching, but the difference defers back to your change control requirements.

Ultimately, it is up to you to decide if change control, security, and customization are that important when choosing a SaaS solution. While the vendor's runtime cost should include lower multitenant solutions, well-designed single-tenant solutions can be just as cost-effective for them and for you.

Cyber Insurance

To start, cyber insurance is not a primary cloud attack vector mitigation strategy. In fact, it is not even a secondary mitigation strategy. It is, however, a required mitigation solution based on common contractual requirements. Often, as part of a contract, organizations must demonstrate that they have a financial backstop if an incident does occur. Organizations that rely on cyber insurance to provide compensation are deficient in basic security controls and may even be denied coverage if violations are found in their security implementations.

To meet contractual requirements around cyber insurance and satisfy cloud-based cybersecurity controls, consider these common cyber insurance questions in Table 7-2 and what controls can be implemented to ensure it is a viable cloud mitigation strategy (keep in mind it is not your first or second layer of defense).

Table 7-2. *Common cyber insurance questions regarding your organization's risk mitigation strategy*

Common Questions for Cyber Insurance Eligibility Requirements	Cloud Attack Vector Mitigation Strategies	Technology in the Cloud and for Hybrid Environments
Do your users have local admin rights on their laptop/desktop?	Removes all admin rights and elevates access as needed to applications based on the proper content and only for the duration needed. This is one of the most powerful ways to reduce the attack surface and defend against both external and internal threats originating from endpoints.	• Endpoint privilege management
Can you confirm human and nonhuman accounts abide by least privilege at all times?	Enforces least privilege and application control across all human/nonhuman identities and accounts across any time of endpoint or other asset. This massively reduces the attack surface and can even help protect organizations against tricky, fileless threats and zero days.	• Endpoint privilege management • Privileged password management
What protections are in place to protect remote access to the cloud or corporate network?	Secures remote access to corporate network, applications, and assets and makes all connections outbound using a dedicated remote access solution or VPN. The implementation should monitor and manage all privileged remote sessions from vendors and employees and also vault credentials, auto-injecting into sessions without revealing to the end users.	• Secure remote access • Virtual private network (VPN) • Zero-trust network access

Do you manage privileged accounts using tooling or software solutions?	This is a best practice fit for privileged access management (PAM) solutions. PAM solutions can manage every privileged user, session, and asset across the enterprise – whether cloud, on-premises, or in a hybrid environment.	• Privileged access management • Enterprise password management solutions
Do you use multi-factor authentication for remote network access originating from outside your network by employees and third parties (e.g., VPN, remote desktop)?	Provide a solution with built-in multi-factor authentication for remote access, as well as the ability to seamlessly integrate with third-party MFA tools. MFA provides an extra layer to ensure that access is only given to the correct identity.	• Secure remote access • Virtual private network (VPN) • Zero-trust network access
Do you utilize any unsupported operating systems or platforms? If so, what compensating controls are in place for these systems and supporting platforms?	Restricts privileges to the minimum necessary to help limit any potential misuse of systems or platforms that are end of life. Any implementation should enforce segmentation/microsegmentation to broadly isolate unsupported and risky platforms from other networked assets to help contain spread of potential breaches or abuse.	• Privileged password management • Endpoint privilege management • Secure remote access • Virtual private network (VPN) • Zero-trust network access

(continued)

Table 7-2. (*continued*)

Common Questions for Cyber Insurance Eligibility Requirements	Cloud Attack Vector Mitigation Strategies	Technology in the Cloud and for Hybrid Environments
Have you reviewed your environment for the indicators of compromise (IoC) to confirm that none were found?	Security solutions should be able to capture sessions, including keystroke logs, screen recording, commands typed/executed, and more that can help pinpoint breaches and the internal pathways of threat actors. The goal is to identify IoCs that suggest lateral movement or potentially inappropriate privilege escalation, either from commands or rogue user behavior. Finally, file integrity monitoring illuminates any suspicious changes affecting critical application or operating system files.	• Privileged password management • Endpoint privilege management • Secure remote access • Virtual private network (VPN) • Zero-trust network access
Please describe any steps that you take to detect and prevent ransomware attacks	An organization's security posture should prevent and mitigate ransomware and malware from landing and expanding by implementing robust security over remote access, onboarding and managing privileged credentials, and enforcing least privilege and application control. These security controls also should thwart any ransomware, malware, or human operator from achieving lateral movement and privilege escalation to progress the attack, keeping them marooned at the initial point of compromise.	• Privileged password management • Endpoint privilege management • Secure remote access • Virtual private network (VPN) • Zero-trust network access

Monitoring Technology

One of the oppositions to new technology placed on an endpoint is the need for an agent. In fact, for years, one of the biggest objections by companies has been the need for agent technology at all. Time and time again, end users resist adding to their endpoint agent stack due to bloat, incompatibilities, resource consumption, and additional management overhead. In recent years, vendor consolidation and multidiscipline agents have reduced this friction. Yet, agent technology remains one of the least desirable ways to deploy and manage an endpoint.

Now, consider the cloud. Security problems in the cloud can be solved with agent technology when we cloud wash our solutions. However, as we embrace modern cloud implementations with containers, microservices, serverless processes, and ephemeral assets, we find that agent technology is difficult, if not impossible, to deploy and maintain. In fact, performing basic disciplines, like privileged access management (PAM), vulnerability management, file integrity management, and anti-malware protection, requires agents – especially when authenticated access is neither available nor desirable due to security best practices for asset hardening.

The simple factor of enabling SMB, SSH, or even WMI to allow authenticated access in the cloud is a security risk. Therefore, end users were left with agent technology to solve the problem, even when the cloud implementation is best optimized without them. This held true until recently.

Consider what the cloud excels at – automation. Cloud service providers (CSP) have created robust application programming interfaces (APIs) to enable automation and to enable machine-to-machine connectivity. These APIs allow for everything from asset creation through deletion and even running commands and monitoring processes within assets. The APIs accomplish all of this without using agents.

Modern security solutions can now inspect assets during runtime and determine characteristics – just like an authenticated scan or if an agent is running locally all through the hypervisors API. One such technology is called API scanning. API-based scanning technology leverages the CSP API to enumerate the file system, processes, and services within an asset for vulnerabilities, malware, asset discovery, and account management. This approach succeeds where agents are less desirable since the hypervisor has complete asset access (via the API) to enumerate any contents operating virtually. API-based scanning requires a translation layer to perform complex functions via the API and map the results into a typical asset inventory, file system list, and runtime anomalies, like malware, that we see from traditional solutions. Since this is an identification process only, API side scanning can use a read-only API account (operating use best practices like least privilege) compared to network scanning, with authentication that typically needs administrator or root access.

API scanning does not require any remote access protocols, thus reducing the asset's risk surface. This approach is the first step in removing agent technology from the cloud. API-based scanning technology also optimizes runtime in the cloud and costs based on consumption-based pricing.

Now consider that all assets in the cloud are some form of endpoint. While we normally think of endpoints as laptops and desktops used by end users, endpoints in the cloud are more akin to servers operating in a third-party data center where you do not own or manage the infrastructure. While cloud assets may be segmented, like on-premise, exposing any unnecessary open ports is generally a bad idea – even if the cloud implementation is private. This leads us to a discussion on risk assessment. To perform vital asset and security management functions in the cloud, we need to ask: Which technologies are the highest risk for cloud asset and security management? Consider Table 7-3, security technology in the cloud.

Table 7-3. *Security technology in the cloud*

Technology	Risk	Maturity	Description
Network scanning	High	Mature	Network scanning requires authenticated remote access into an asset, typically with administrator or remote privileges. As a best practice, each asset should have unique, ephemeral credentials managed by a privileged access management solution. This type of implementation is typically complex and error prone in very large environments, while requiring a secondary interface that is private or management only to process scanning requests.
Agent technology	Medium	Mature	While agent technology poses a much lower risk than network scanning, the installation typically uses system, administrative, or root privileges to operate. Its risk is mitigated since it generally does not have any open listening ports or require remote access. The risk, however, is the management of the agent itself and attacks based on the supply chain, mixed matched versions, and potential incompatibilities with the host.
API scanning	Low	Emerging	All access to the asset is API based via the cloud service provider. Access is granted as read only. It does not require any code to be deployed to the asset to perform the desired functions. There are no exposed listening ports, and the API can be hardened to only allow access from the trusted vendor.

As one would expect, API scanning is an emerging technology based on the capabilities available from cloud service providers. As they continue to provide additional automation, new APIs are being created to streamline services. When utilized by third-party vendors, the APIs can be implemented to provide new functionality. In many cases, this functionality can replace legacy network scanning and agent technology-based solutions. This may ultimately spell the demise of agent technology in the cloud, something many security professionals and information technology administrators eagerly await.

CHAPTER 8

Regulatory Compliance

A threat actor does not care about the law, compliance, regulations, or security best practices. In fact, they are hopeful that your cloud environment is deficient on many of these concepts and recommendations to help facilitate the success of their malicious activity. While regulatory compliance is designed to provide legally binding guidelines for industries and governments, they do not provide the necessary means to stay secure, and do not think for one moment that a cloud service provider will do it for you out of the box. That just does not happen – compliance does not equal security. Regulatory compliance measures are enforced guidance toward good cybersecurity hygiene, but implementing them without good processes, people, training, automation, and diligence will leave you susceptible to a breach. Therefore, when reviewing regulatory compliance initiatives, consider the following for your cloud deployments:

- How they apply to your organization based on laws, sensitive information, contracts, industry, and, especially, geography (country and region)?

- What overlaps exist between them, and what processes can satisfy multiple requirements?

- Be sure to adopt the strictest guidance for your initiatives. The strictest and most comprehensive requirement should always win since it will exceed any looser requirements.

Scoping is, therefore, as critical as the region your cloud service provider hosts your instances and data. Just applying general rules to sensitive systems is not enough to achieve good security. And how you demonstrate compliance and security to regulatory agencies, local governments, and customers can mean all the difference between securing new business and revenue versus a game-over security incident.

To that end, keep in mind that any regulatory compliance requirements are the absolute minimum your organization should be doing. If you are not meeting the minimums, or have lapses in the requirements, you are the low-hanging fruit a threat actor seeks.

So, how do you get started with a good regulatory compliance program? It starts with asking the right questions.

Security Assessment Questionnaires (SAQ)

Security questionnaires are a list of business and technical questions that organizations compile to determine if a vendor's security and compliance posture is satisfactory before engaging in a business relationship or licensing their solution. Distributing security questionnaires to vendors, partners, and answering them for clients is considered a cybersecurity best practice across most industries today.

The contents, format, and questions may differ between organizations, but all Security Assessment Questionnaires are designed to determine if a business partner can be trusted to protect sensitive customer information adequately. As guidance, almost all SAQs contain the following topics that can be mapped to the industry-leading regulatory frameworks for cloud security, including NIST, ISO, and CIS:

- Application and Interface Security

- Audit Assurance and Compliance

- Business Continuity Management and Operational Resilience

- Datacenter Security

- Encryption and Key Management

- Governance and Risk Management

- Identity and Access Management

- Infrastructure Security

- Hiring and Personnel Policies

- Security Incident Management

- Supply Chain Management, Transparency, and Accountability

- Threat and Vulnerability Management

As you may have realized, many of these topics have been covered throughout this book. The questions themselves can be Boolean (yes/no), verbose (requiring a detailed explanation), or complex (requiring proof or collateral for answer). While the latter is rare, it will occur when working with the highly secure environments that are involved in financial transactions and government agencies. One word of caution for anyone creating or answering an SAQ: the results you enter are typically legally binding. Therefore, you must answer honestly. If you have lied or exaggerated on an answer, your organization could be liable if a breach occurs, and you could even be denied cyber insurance!

Consider these eight recommendations for your SAQ:

1. Only list questions that apply to your organization and the data you are trying to protect. Avoid asking questions just for the sake of knowing the answer if they are not relevant. SAQs are not RFPs (Request for Proposal) and should be as targeted as possible.

2. Use the same SAQ across all vendors, clients, and other business partners. Consistency will help a ton in vetting the answers and identifying gaps.

3. Create a centralized database for all the answers so they can be searched and cross-referenced over time and per business partner. This will also help you if you need to query your vendor base, should a particular threat arise for which you need an answer.

4. If a particular answer does not come back satisfactorily, or an entire SAQ does not pass your scoring criteria (next recommendation), design and implement a remediation plan for the vendor, and even consider replacing the vendor.

5. Develop a scoring mechanism for each question and potentially a point system for each answer. Some questions will be critical, like having a vulnerability management program, while others might be less severe.

6. When building your questionnaire, consider how certifications like SOC will address the vast majority of questions without requiring submission of both an SAQ and a SOC certification report.

7. When possible, map any questions to the source framework or controls for relevance, as well as to subsequent updates, as the frameworks evolve. This will simplify future audits by having a mapping already prepared by question, security control, and audit.

8. Depending on your business vertical, consider adding questions that will help prove your own regulatory compliance for initiatives like HIPAA, PCI, and SOX. These are specific questions focused on credit card payments and the storage of PII (personally identifiable information).

Security Assessment Questionnaires are a critical tool for doing business in the cloud. If your organization has not already implemented a program around them, you should consider it for future services that will be provided in the cloud. As a reference, a sample SAQ is available for review in Appendix A.

System and Organization Controls (SOC)

System and Organization Controls (SOC)[1] started with their inception back in 2002 under the Sarbanes-Oxley Act, as audit reports originally focused on the financial industry. The initial offering was designed to ensure public companies were responsible for their financials and to standardize reporting. The audits are performed by Certified Public Accountants, who are endorsed by the American Institute of Certified Public Accountants (AICPA).[2] In short, SOC Reports provide a level of confidence in those

---

[1] https://www.infosecurity-magazine.com/opinions/soc-audit-reports/
[2] https://www.aicpa.org/home

seeking to leverage opportunities with a company as a vendor or service provider. These reports help establish credibility using a foundation for financials and best practices for business operations. Similar to providing your driver's license with a vehicle endorsement, an officer can easily see, without knowing you, that you are "certified" to drive the vehicle; your driver's license is the first step in that endorsement.

SOC Reports have evolved into four different types that cover much more than just financial diligence:

- **SOC 1**: The original SOC Report – focuses on the financials of an organization.

- **SOC 2**: Focuses on the operational risk of a company by examining service and security controls for the business and technology operations.

- **SOC 3**: Only available if the company has already obtained SOC 2 certification as SOC 3 c is a redacted version of SOC 2 that covers all the same areas at a generalized level. It is meant to be used for public consumption and is often delivered without an NDA (non-disclosure agreement).

- **SOC for Cybersecurity**: An emerging report created in response to increased cyberattacks. This one focuses on an organization's risk management program.

For cloud attack vectors, we can skip SOC 1 and proceed to SOC 2. So, what makes up a SOC 2?

A SOC 2 Report, also known as an audit report, is focused on the Trust Services Criteria (TSC). The Trust Services Criteria is made up of five categories: privacy, security, confidentiality, processing integrity, and availability.

- **Privacy**: Personally identifiable information (PII) is used, retained, collected, disclosed, and disposed of in accordance with policy.

- **Security**: Systems and data are protected against unauthorized access, disclosure, and damage that could compromise or affect the system's ability to meet its objectives.

- **Confidentiality**: Information deemed confidential is protected and appropriately secured.

- **Processing Integrity**: System processing is accurate, valid, complete, and timely, and customer data remains correct through any data processing.

- **Availability**: Information and systems are available for operation and use for company and client objectives based on measurable controls.

Each of these trust categories has predefined criteria that apply to infrastructure, software, personnel, procedures, and data. Every report has security as part of its common criteria. Organizations can choose which of the other trust services they'd like to include in the audit. There are 61 criteria and approximately 300 points of focus for Trust Services.

In reality, a SOC 2 report can play a pivotal role for both a company seeking to obtain SOC 2 certification by establishing policies and procedures for operations and a prospecting client looking to get oversight into an organization. As cybercrime continues to ramp up, customers, clients, and prospecting clients are increasing their due diligence to ensure that a business relationship is trustworthy, competent, and is factoring in security with the appropriate amount of seriousness. Breaking down reporting typology even further, SOC 2 reports can be divided into two categories: Type I report and Type II reports.

- **Type I** reports confirm that the controls of an organization exist at a *specific point in time*. Companies obtaining their SOC 2 certification for the first time typically go through a SOC 2 Type I Audit. During this audit, an auditor will validate and report on the company's description of the controls, along with the sustainability of those controls.

- **Type II** reports include the same validation of controls as in Type I; however, an additional section discusses the operating effectiveness of having those controls put into place. Unlike a SOC Type I Audit, which validates the controls at a specific point in time, a SOC 2 Type II Audit validates the controls over a predefined time frame, with six months being the AICPA suggested minimum to prove normal operations.

Organizations seeking to license cloud technology should always look for vendors with SOC 2 Type II reports to validate their offering. For businesses operating in the cloud, this should be a minimum goal.

SOC 3 reports are similar to SOC 2 Type II, but are not as detailed or comprehensive as the SOC 2 Type II in the final report. However, the source material is the same for SOC 3 and SOC 2 Type II reports. A SOC 3 report is designed for companies that need to limit the amount of detail that is contained in the report so they can leverage it for public distribution.

In cases where SOC 1 and SOC 2 reports are available from companies, some type of non-disclosure agreement (NDA) is typically required between parties due to the confidential nature of the report and the findings that detail the internal operations of an organization and any potential exceptions or control gaps. This is not the case with a SOC 3 report. Instead, most companies might choose to host a SOC 3 report on their public-facing website and have it available for download.

Please understand, a SOC 3 is NOT a replacement for a SOC 1 or SOC 2 report. However, if you are looking to interview a company and understand what type of practices they have, then the SOC 3 is a great report to review and is satisfactory for most organizations, creating high-level visibility without signed confidentiality agreements.

Next, let us discuss SOC for Cybersecurity. In April of 2017, the American Institute of Certified Public Accountants (AICPA) created a cybersecurity risk management report framework to help organizations communicate the effectiveness of their cybersecurity risk management programs. Unlike SOC 1 reports, which focus on financials, and unlike SOC 2 reports, which focus on service providers, the SOC for Cybersecurity is intended for all other organizations that didn't meet the criteria as a "Service Organization." This ultimately helped pave the path for companies to prove that their risk management program and approach to cybersecurity can be validated.

When it comes to examining SOC audit reports related to the cloud, cloud solution vendors, and cloud service providers, it's best to understand the differences in reports and how they could play a critical part in providing assurances that the company you are interviewing, examining, or buying from holds security as a priority. When you get a SOC report, ensure that you read through it and understand the areas covered. Knowing a company is SOC certified is great, but reading through the SOC audit report will help you understand the organization's security posture and any security controls you may need to adopt or add yourself.

Cloud Security Alliance (CSA)

Some of you might not be familiar with the Cloud Security Alliance.[3]
For those of you familiar with the CSA, great (it is similar to the United
Federation of Planets[4])! For everyone else, don't worry; they're not
another Rebel Alliance[5] that stands bravely against the evil of the Galactic
Empire, never backing down despite overwhelming odds. (Seriously, we
are trying to make regulatory compliance fun – really). Rather, the CSA is
a nonprofit organization formed to promote the use of best practices for
providing security assurance within cloud computing. The organization
also provides education on the uses of cloud computing to help secure all
other forms of interconnected computing. The Cloud Security Alliance is
a consortium comprised of subject matter experts from a wide variety of
disciplines. These experts are united in their objectives to

- Promote a common level of understanding between
  the consumers and providers of cloud computing
  regarding the necessary security requirements and
  attestation of assurance.

- Promote independent research into best practices for
  cloud computing security.

- Launch awareness campaigns and educational
  programs on the appropriate uses of cloud computing
  and cloud security solutions.

- Create consensus lists of issues and guidance for cloud
  security assurance.

---

[3] https://cloudsecurityalliance.org/
[4] https://memory-alpha.fandom.com/wiki/United_Federation_of_Planets
[5] https://www.starwars.com/databank/rebel-alliance

The Cloud Security Alliance was founded in 2008 and has grown to 80,000 plus members worldwide. CSA was propelled to the spotlight in 2011 when the Presidential Administration selected the CSA Summit as its platform for debuting the federal government's cloud computing strategy. The CSA has over 25 active working groups that focus on cloud standards, certification, education and training, guidance and tools, global reach, and innovation driving.

In our opinion, if you are working in the cloud and are not a CSA member, you probably should be. If possible, get involved! The rebellion needs you, and many of their initiatives are outlined in the next few sections.

Cloud Security Alliance Cloud Controls Matrix (CMM)

The CSA Cloud Controls Matrix[6] is a cybersecurity control framework for cloud computing. It is a document that lists 16 domains covering all key aspects of cloud technology. Each domain is broken up into 133 control objectives. It can be used as a tool to proactively assess cloud implementations by providing guidance and direction on which security controls should be implemented and which actor within the cloud supply chain should be implementing them. The control framework aligns with the CSA Security Guidance Version 4 and is currently considered a de facto standard for cloud security assurance and compliance.

The controls in the CSA CCM are mapped and align with industry-accepted security standards, control frameworks, and regulations. Because the CSA CCM maturity is an ongoing effort, the current Version 4 includes previous versions and is a compounded effort. Therefore, Version 4 currently has the following mappings:

---

[6] https://cloudsecurityalliance.org/research/cloud-controls-matrix/

- ISO/IEC 27001/27002/27017/27018

- CMM Version 3

- CIS Control Version 8

And additional mappings for

- AICPA TSC

- PCI DSS

- NIST 800-53 Rev 5

It is important to note the list continues to evolve and is updated based on the state of cloud security.

Next, let us take a look at Version 3. This includes

- ISO 27001/27002/27017/27018

- NIST SP 800-53

- AICPA TSC

- German BSI C5

- PCI DSS

- ISACA COBIT

- NERC CIP

- FedRAMP

- CIS

This mapping is important because of the cumulative nature of the standards and the inclusion of previous specifications. The CSA CMM is a guide that lists the controls an organization can use as a framework to comply with regulations. Since each control maps to several industry-accepted standards, frameworks, and regulations, fulfilling the CSA CMM controls also fulfills the accompanying standards and regulations. This allows you to select which components exceed your goals and follow standards for compliance or regulation as a best practice.

It is important to note that each control in the CSA CMM specifies who should fulfill the control, either the cloud service provider or the customer. It also specifies the cloud model type, IaaS, PaaS, SaaS, or cloud environment – private, public, or hybrid – and the applicable controls. The CSA CMM also defines the roles and responsibilities between the cloud service provider and the cloud customer by separating which control guidance is relevant to each party as a best practice. Many times, this may appear in contractual requirements in business relationships. This introduces an obvious question of how to map the CSA CCM to a legal contract or a Request for Proposal (RFP).

The CSA has a Consensus Assessment Initiative Questionnaire (CAIQ)[7] (covered in detail in the next section), which is a survey assessing the security capabilities of a cloud service provider. It was developed to create a commonly accepted industry standard to document the security controls across cloud application offerings by service providers.

In terms of the CSA CCM, the CSA CAIQ is a companion to the CCM that provides a set of "Yes or No" type questions a cloud customer or auditor may ask a cloud provider. Based on the security controls in the CSA CCM, the questions can be used to document which security controls exist within a service provider's offering. Oftentimes, organizations will use the CSA CAIQ instead of trying to create their own line of questioning. Additionally, you might see the CAIQ questions used to build a Request for Proposal or bound to a contract for organizations to use and ensure proper security coverage, roles, and responsibilities.

---

[7]https://cloudsecurityalliance.org/artifacts/consensus-assessments-initiative-questionnaire-v3-1/

Today, the latest version of the CSA CCM introduces some changes to the previous structure of the framework, with a new domain dedicated to logging and monitoring, as well as modifications to some existing ones. The current list of domains covered by CSA CMM Version 4 contains:

- Application and Interface Security

- Audit and Assurance

- Business Continuity Management and Operational Resilience

- Change Control and Configuration Management

- Data Security and Privacy – DSP (old DSI)

- Datacenter Security

- Cryptography, Encryption, and Key Management

- Governance, Risk Management, and Compliance

- Human Resources Security

- Identity and Access Management

- Infrastructure and Access Management

- Infrastructure and Virtualization

- Interoperability and Portability

- Universal Endpoint Management

- Security Incident Management, E-Discovery, and Cloud Forensics

- Supply Chain Management, Transparency, and Accountability

- Threat and Vulnerability Management

- Logging and Monitoring

The CSA encourages organizations to use the CMM as a companion to the CSA Security Guidance document because it allows users to identify security controls and understand how they should be applied.

Cloud Security Alliance Consensus Assessment Initiative Questionnaire (CAIQ)

In the previous section, we covered the CSA CMM and mentioned that the CMM should accompany the CAIQ. While we briefly mentioned what the CAIQ is, we wanted to dive deeper into what makes up the CAIQ. Understanding the CAIQ and its development will help you understand how to use it better as a companion with the CSA CMM.

The CSA CAIQ is an industry-accepted way to document which security controls exist within a service provider's offering across their applications. This is done by providing transparency around their security controls. The CSA CAIQ is made up of the "Yes and No" questions a customer or auditor might ask to obtain a sense of confidence that the application is secure or meets their standards. It can also provide insight and reveal some risk areas that organizations might not wish to accept. Ultimately, it becomes a tool for customers who are seeking validation that service providers are doing their due diligence to protect the customers' interests.

Threat actors are getting wealthy by preying on the ill prepared, and they are exploiting those unidentified risks present in an organization. We need to make it harder for threat actors and do our part along the way with due diligence on both sides of the fence, as both a customer and a service provider.

Center for Internet Security (CIS) Controls

The Center for Internet Security (CIS)[8] was created in 2001 by the FBI[9] and SANS Institute,[10] and it publicized the Top 20 Critical Controls for cybersecurity. Over time, these controls evolved into what some of you might recognize as the SANS Top 20. The effort and burden of improving and maintaining the guidelines were transferred in 2015 to the Center for Internet Security in order to simplify, consolidate, and avoid duplication of effort between organizations. The name was eventually shortened and has been adopted as CIS Controls. In 2021, the 20 major areas were consolidated into 18 with the release of Version 8. We will cover both Versions 7 and 8 and highlight the differences because major organizations have not adopted the latest version yet.

As a matter of record, CIS is a community-driven nonprofit, responsible for the CIS Controls and CIS Benchmarks. They are globally recognized for their best practices for securing IT systems and data. CIS is also home to the Multi-State Information Sharing and Analysis Center (MS-ISAC),[11] which is the trusted resource for cyber threat prevention, protection, response, and recovery for the United States, local governments, and for territorial government entities. In addition, they are home to the Elections Infrastructure Information Sharing and Analysis Center (EI-ISAC),[12] which supports the rapidly changing cybersecurity needs of the US elections offices and electronic voting initiatives.

---

[8] https://www.cisecurity.org
[9] www.fbi.gov/
[10] https://www.sans.org/
[11] www.cisecurity.org/ms-isac/
[12] www.cisecurity.org/ei-isac/

CIS Controls

The CIS Controls are a set of actions that have been prioritized and separated into three categories: basic, foundational, and organizational. They represent a series of best practices, which provide a defense-in-depth approach to mitigate the most common cyberattacks on systems, assets, data, and networks. These controls are maintained by a community of information technology experts who can apply their first-hand knowledge as cyber defenders to help create these globally accepted best practices. These experts who contribute to the CIS Controls come from a diverse background of industry verticals, including retail, government, education, healthcare, financial services, and many others.

There is no shortage of information available for security professionals to make smart and effective security decisions to secure their assets, data, and cloud environments. As one can imagine, with the abundance of security information, technology options, security tools, and opinions, a clear path for securing an organization becomes foggy. To add insult to injury, the pandemic has propelled companies in numerous directions, creating more security risks, spurring cloud adoption and digital transformation to increase at dizzying rates, and making business decisions without security at the forefront.

So, how can the cybersecurity community, as well as other industries, sectors, and coalitions, band together to establish a priority of action, help support each other, and keep the knowledge of security current in the face of this evolving problem of cybercrime, compromise, and breach? This is where the heart and soul of CIS Controls live. This is why restating the threats and problems in the world is so important. There are solutions.

CIS Controls are constantly living and breathing through updates, community feedback, and modifications, and they present the best practices today to handle all the challenges we have discussed. As a result, CIS Controls have been accepted by an international community of individuals for:

- Sharing insight into attacks and attackers, identification of root causes, and translating indicators of compromise into classes of actionable defense

- Documenting stories of adoption and sharing tools to solve problems based on empirical, as well as theoretical, results

- Tracking the evolution of threats, the capabilities of adversaries, and current attack vectors of intrusions

- Mapping the CIS Controls to regulatory and compliance frameworks and bringing collective priority and focus to them for easier consumption

- Identifying common problems (like initial assessment and implementation roadmaps) and solving them as a community, expanding shared knowledge of what works and what does not.

These items help ensure that CIS Controls are not just another framework with a never-ending list of things to do and secure. Instead, the CIS Controls are prioritized and focused actions that have the support of the community, which enables them to be usable, scalable, implementable, and to help achieve compliance.

CIS Controls Methodology and Contributors

Due to the CIS Controls being community driven, experts from every industry vertical, from analysts to users, to auditors, all help contribute to the success of CIS Controls. The CIS Controls are not limited to blocking the initial compromise of an asset, but they also address the detection of already-compromised assets, preventing or disrupting continued threat actions. The defenses identified through these controls help reduce the initial attack surface by hardening configurations, identifying compromised assets, disrupting threat actor behavior, and providing continuous defense, along with a response capability that can be maintained and improved. To make this a reality, there are five critical tenets of an effective cyber defense system, as defined by CIS Controls:

1. **Offense Informs Defense**: Use knowledge of actual attacks that have compromised systems to provide the foundation to continually learn from these events and build effective, practical defenses. Include only controls that have been proven in stopping known, real-world attacks.

2. **Prioritization**: Invest first in controls that will provide the greatest risk reduction and protection against the most dangerous threat actors and that can be feasibly implemented in your computing environment. The CIS Implementation Groups discussed in the following are a great place for organizations to start identifying relevant sub-controls.

3. **Measurements and Metrics**: Establish common metrics to provide a shared language for executives, IT specialists, auditors, and security officials to measure the effectiveness of security measures within an organization so that required adjustments can be identified and implemented quickly.

4. **Continuous Diagnostics and Mitigation**: Carry out continuous measurement to test and validate the effectiveness of current security measures and to help drive the prioritization of next steps.

5. **Automation**: Automate defenses so that organizations can achieve reliable, scalable, and continuous measurements of their adherence to the controls and related metrics.

CIS Implementation Groups

CIS Controls have been divided up into three different implementation groups. The idea behind these groups is to prioritize the implementation of the CIS Controls based on risk profile and the resources an enterprise has available to them in order to implement the framework. Each Implementation Group (IG) identifies a set of safeguards (formerly CIS Sub-controls) that need to be implemented. Each IG has self-assessed categories for an organization based on relevant cybersecurity attributes. Currently, there are a total of 153 safeguards in the latest version of CIS Controls, which we will cover later in this section.

Ideally, each enterprise should start with IG1, which is defined as the "Essential Cyber Hygiene" and is the foundational set of cyber defense safeguards that every enterprise should apply to protect against the most common attacks. From there, IG2 acts like a super setup on the IG1 Safeguards, with additional controls, and IG3 is comprised of all 153 controls and safeguards for the largest of entities. In addition, CIS encourages organizations to classify themselves within one of the three Implementation Groups to decide which applies to their organization. For example, consider these self-classifications:

- **Family-Owned Business**: Less than ten employees. Self-classify as IG1

- **Regional Organization Providing Services**: Self-classify as IG2

- **Large Enterprise with Thousands of Employees**: Self-classify as IG3

Ultimately, organizations can then focus on implementing the safeguards for their IG once the classification has been decided. There are three main characteristics organizations use to identify their category within CIS:

1. **Data sensitivity and criticality of services offered by the organization**. Organizations providing services that must be available for any reason. For example, public safety, critical infrastructure, or working with data that must be protected under a further restricted set of requirements (federal legislation) need to implement more advanced cybersecurity controls than those that do not.

2. **Expected level of technical expertise exhibited by staff or on contract**. Cybersecurity knowledge and experience are difficult to obtain, yet are necessary to implement many of the detailed cybersecurity mitigations outlined within the CIS Controls. Many of the CIS Controls require minimum core IT competencies, whereas others necessitate in-depth cybersecurity skills and knowledge for successful implementation.

3. **Resources available and dedicated toward cybersecurity activities**. Time, money, and personnel are all necessary to implement many of the best practices contained within the CIS Controls. Enterprises that can dedicate these resources toward cybersecurity can mount a more sophisticated defense against today's adversaries. While there are open source tools available that

assist an organization's implementation, they may
come at the cost of additional management and
deployment overhead that needs to be considered.

CIS also highly encourages organizations to perform a risk assessment
using a methodology such as CIS RAM.[13] CIS RAM (Risk Assessment
Method) is an information security risk assessment method that helps
organizations implement and assess their security posture against the CIS
Controls. This will allow organizations to be informed about which CIS
Safeguards they should be implementing and why.

Ultimately, the Implementation Groups (IGs) are not absolute;
according to CIS, they are intended to provide a rough measure that
organizations can use to prioritize their cybersecurity efforts and provide
guidance on how to get there.

Defining Implementation Groups

- **Implementation Group 1**: An IG1 organization is a
small-to-medium-sized entity with limited IT and
cybersecurity expertise to dedicate to protecting IT
assets and personnel. The principal concern of these
organizations is to keep the business operational
because they have limited tolerance for downtime.
The sensitivity of the data they are trying to protect
is low and principally surrounds employee and
financial information. However, some small-to-
medium-sized organizations may be responsible
for protecting sensitive data and, therefore, will fall
into a higher group. Sub-controls selected for IG1

---

[13] https://www.cisecurity.org/white-papers/cis-ram-risk-assessment-
method/

should be implementable with limited cybersecurity expertise and aimed to thwart general, non-targeted attacks. These sub-controls will also typically be designed to work in conjunction with small or home office commercial-off-the-shelf (COTS) hardware and software.

- **Implementation Group 2**: An IG2 organization employs individuals responsible for managing and protecting an entity's information technology infrastructure. These organizations support multiple departments with differing risk profiles based on job function and mission. Small organizational units may have regulatory compliance burdens that fall into this classification. IG2 organizations often store and process sensitive client or company information and can withstand short service interruptions. A major concern is the loss of public confidence if a breach occurs. Sub-controls selected for IG2 help security teams cope with increased operational complexity. Some sub-controls will depend on enterprise-grade technology and specialized expertise to properly install and configure.

- **Implementation Group 3**: An IG3 organization employs security experts specializing in the different facets of cybersecurity (risk management, penetration testing, application security). IG3 systems and data contain sensitive information or functions subject to strict regulatory and compliance oversight. An IG3 organization must address the availability of services and the confidentiality and integrity of sensitive data. Successful attacks can cause significant harm to the public welfare. Sub-controls selected for IG3 must abate targeted attacks from a sophisticated adversary and reduce the impact of zero-day attacks. While this approach provides generalized guidance for prioritizing usage of the CIS Controls, this should not replace an organization's need to understand its own organizational risk posture. Organizations should still seek to conduct their own duty of care analysis and tailor their implementation of the CIS Controls based on what is appropriate and reasonable given their resources, mission, and risks. Using these types of methods, such as those described in CIS RAM, organizations of different Implementation Groups can make risk-informed decisions about which sub-controls in their group they may not want to implement and which higher groups they should strive for. The intention is to help organizations focus their efforts based on the available resources and integrate the new CIS Controls into any pre-existing risk management process.

CIS Controls, Version 7

Before we dive into CIS Controls Version 8, I want to make sure you understand the 20 CIS Controls covered in Version 7. After we cover the updated 18 CIS Controls in Version 8, we will cover the differences and which controls were modified and combined to make up the 18 CIS Controls of Version 8. As mentioned earlier, when we discussed Implementation Groups, the controls are broken down into three groups called basic, foundational, and organizational categories.

Basic

1. **Inventory of Hardware**: The purpose of inventorying hardware is to ensure accountability for authorized devices on the network, ensuring they are tracked, inventoried for accuracy, and corrected as inaccuracies are discovered. Additionally, this control should prevent hardware assets that are NOT authorized or approved from gaining any access. This control is broken down into eight additional sub-controls, ranging from 1.1 through 1.8. Two of these sub-controls apply to IG1, five apply to IG2, and all eight apply to IG3. Understanding the graduation between the IGs and what applies to your organization will help you mature your security posture as your business grows.

2. **Inventory of Software**: A software inventory ensures accountability that only authorized software is being used. All software should be inventoried, tracked, and updated so that the inventory remains accurate. This also addresses the issue of unmanaged or unauthorized software on assets (shadow IT) that should not be installed in the environment. Inventory of software is broken down into ten sub-controls. Three apply to IG1, five apply to IG2, and, of course, all ten apply to IG3.

3. **Continuous Vulnerability Management**: When you think of vulnerability management and the continuous evaluation of threats (batch-driven and job-scheduled vs. continuous real-time or near-real-time assessments), the purpose is to minimize the

risk surface for threat actors through vulnerabilities that are identified on assets. In addition, the ability to classify these vulnerabilities and remediate them will help reduce overall risk. Hopefully, you have memorized this conclusion. Continuous vulnerability management is broken down into seven sub-controls. Two apply to IG1, and all seven apply to IG2 and IG3.

4. **Control of Administrative Privileges**: The controlled use of administrative privileges addresses the highest provisioned accounts for rights, permissions, and entitlements on assets, including networks, in the cloud, and applications. It covers the ability to control, track, prevent, and fix the entitlements related to privileged access to enforce least privilege. The controlled use of administrative privileges contains nine sub-controls. Two are assigned to IG1, eight are assigned to IG2, and all nine are assigned to IG3.

5. **Secure Configuration**: Secure configuration targets mobile devices, servers, workstations, virtual machines, and other endpoints for the configuration of hardware and software. This covers the ability to actively manage the security configurations. Like other controls, this covers the ability to track, report, and fix errors as they are discovered. This control is designed to help reduce a threat actor's surface to exploit the vulnerable services and settings. This control contains five sub-controls. Only one is covered by IG1, and all five are required in IG2 and IG3.

6. **Maintenance and Analysis of Logs**: This control
   pertains to all types of audit logs events and the
   ability to collect, manage, and analyze them. It is
   used to help detect, understand, and recover from
   an attack, as well as provide information for threat
   hunting, indicators of compromise, and evidence
   of compromise. This control has eight sub-controls.
   Only one sub-control is covered in IG1. Seven sub-
   controls in IG2, and all eight in IG3.

Foundational

1. **Email and Browser Protections**: This control aims
   to reduce the risk from a threat actor leveraging the
   ability to manipulate interactions with web browsers
   and email systems. This control is broken down
   into ten sub-controls. Of the ten controls, two are
   assigned to IG1. Nine are assigned to IG2, and all
   ten are assigned to IG3. If you consider that email
   and phishing are the number one attack vector for
   endpoints, organizations should consider adopting
   as many of the controls in this IG category as
   possible.

2. **Malware Defenses**: Malware can cripple any
   organization; this control aims to minimize the
   malware spread by controlling the installation and
   execution at multiple points in an organization. It
   also addresses the ability to rapidly update defenses,
   data collection, and take corrective action. This
   control contains eight sub-controls, three of which
   are covered under IG1 and all eight are covered in
   IG2 or IG3.

3. **Limitation of Ports and Protocols**: The ability to control and limit the use of network ports, protocols, and services is imperative to reducing risk in an organization from threat actors, especially in the cloud. This control focuses on managing ports, protocols, and services on all types of networks and connected assets. Being able to account for and correct anomalies is key to the success of this control. This control covers five sub-controls: one in IG1, four in IG2, and all five in IG3.

4. **Data Recovery**: The ability to back up and recover data in a timely fashion is critical to operations and services delivered on-premise and in the cloud. Unfortunately, this discipline is often overlooked until it is too late. This control focuses on the processes and tools needed to properly back up targeted information and recover data within an acceptable time frame. The control contains five sub-controls, four of which are in IG1 and all five are covered in IG2 and IG3.

5. **Secure Configuration of Network Devices**: Similar to control five, this control targets network devices, including firewalls, routers, and switches. This control addresses the security configuration of network infrastructure devices (including software-defined networks) and the ability to track, report, and repair them so that the attack surface can be minimized for a threat actor looking to exploit vulnerable services and settings. This control has seven sub-controls. One is covered in IG1, and all seven are covered in IG2 and IG3.

6. **Boundary Defense**: This control targets the flow of data and focuses on limiting security and log data that could damage the organization if transferred across networks that have different trust and that are not properly encrypted and secured. This control has twelve sub-controls. Two are covered in IG1 and there are eight in IG2, while all twelve are covered in IG3.

7. **Data Protection**: Being able to protect data, no matter where it is located, is key for any business, regardless of where the assets reside. This control addresses the processes and tools required to prevent data loss, addresses the effects of data that has been exfiltrated, and ensures the privacy and integrity of sensitive information. This control has nine sub-controls. Three are covered in IG1, five are in IG2, and all nine are covered in IG3.

8. **Controlled Access Based on Need to Know**: The foundation of security and privacy goes back to the premise of "need to know." This control breaks down the "need to know" aspect into classifications. Organizations must have the ability to track, control, prevent, and correct access to resources based on their classification and need. The goal is to limit the exposure of information, resources, and systems to only those that need it. This is another way of implementing least privilege. This control has nine sub-controls. There is only one in IG1, five in IG2, and all nine are covered in IG3.

9. **Wireless Access Control**: Today, there are more wireless connected devices ever before. The ability to secure the connectivity of wireless devices (regardless of wireless medium) is critical. This control covers the processes and tools required to manage wireless networks, access points, protocols (cellular, Wi-Fi, Bluetooth, etc.), and wireless client systems. This control is broken down into ten sub-controls. Only two sub-controls are in IG1. There are seven in IG2 and all ten in IG3.

10. **Account Monitoring and Control**: The ability to properly discover and manage accounts is important in every organization. (This is another one of those statements that we will continue to repeat until readers scream "Uncle.") If not managed properly, they pose one of the biggest cyber risks organizations confront. This control targets the life cycle of system and application accounts. The life cycle includes the complete joiner, mover, and leaver (create, use, and delete) process for identities and accounts. Proper monitoring and control over these accounts will drastically reduce the risk of getting compromised. This control contains thirteen sub-controls. There are seven covered in IG1, twelve covered in IG2, and all thirteen are covered in IG3.

Organizational

One thing to note about these last four controls is that they are geared toward people and processes. While each control still contains some technical aspects, these last 4 recommended controls differ from the previous 16 in terms of characteristics.

1. **Security Awareness Training**: Every successful organization has an effective security awareness program. In some cases, it is a lifeline and extension of the company, since most organizations believe security starts with the end user. This control focuses on identifying the specific knowledge, skills, and abilities needed to support an organization's security defense. It includes developing and executing a plan that is strategically geared toward security awareness and training. It is also geared toward identifying and remediating security gaps through policy and organizational planning. For many organizations, this entails continuous security awareness, in lieu of once a year cybersecurity training. This control contains nine sub-controls. Six sub-controls are addressed in IG1, while all nine are covered in IG2 and IG3.

2. **Application Security**: When it comes to applications and software security, ensuring that the applications are developed without vulnerabilities or poor security practices is critical to minimizing security risks and removing the ability for a threat actor to leverage vulnerabilities against an organization. This control focuses on the management and life cycle of all software, both acquired and developed in-house. This control has 11 sub-controls. There are no sub-controls addressed in IG1, and in IG2 and IG3, all 11 sub-controls apply. For any organization that develops software for internal use or for sale, they should consider this control, even if they have self-classified as IG1.

3. **Incident Management**: An organization's ability to recover from an incident and reduce the effects of a disruption or outage is critical in any security plan. This control covers an organization's ability to detect, contain, and limit the effectiveness and damage of an attack. It also includes their ability to eradicate an attacker's presence and to restore the integrity of the systems and network. This control contains eight sub-controls. There are four sub-controls covered in IG1, seven in IG2, and all eight are in IG3.

4. **Penetration Testing (Pen Test)**: The ability to understand an organization's defensive strength requires putting an organization to the test. The goal is to find the weaknesses in defenses and build a plan that will help the organization address them. This is typically done using paid services (by ethical hackers – good guys) to attack the organization by applying techniques similar to those of a threat actor trying to breach the organization via public-facing resources or assets in the cloud. This process will lead to the identification and correction of a weak or vulnerable defensive strategy. Annual penetration testing, at a minimum, is required by most regulatory compliance initiatives, and for software and hardware vendors (especially in the cloud), pen testing is one of the best techniques to help identify mistakes in the product offerings that could be exploited. This control contains eight sub-controls. There are no sub-controls covered in IG1, seven are covered in IG2, and all eight are covered in IG3.

CIS Controls, Version 8

CIS Controls Version 7 underwent a rather extensive overhaul in the creation of Version 8. Due to the significant rise in cyberattacks, the community at CIS Controls released Version 8 to emphasize the basics and focus on what really makes an empirical difference. They not only updated the controls, but they simplified them to streamline adoption of the CIS Controls and maximize security results.

The original 20 CIS Controls have been reduced to 18 in Version 8. In addition, the sub-controls outlined in Version 7 have been reduced and renamed to safeguards. While restating each sub-control or safeguard in this section doesn't really make sense, since they are the same, if you need a listing of Version 8 controls, they can be found on the CIS website. What we cover next is the differences between Version 7 and Version 8. If you are familiar with the sub-controls in Version 7, when you dive into Version 8, you will easily recognize the "safeguards" as compared to the sub-control and the fact that some of them have been simplified and reordered. And remember, Version 8 is brand-new, and organizations are early in phasing in its adoption.

To begin with CIS Controls Version 8, the Implementation Groups (IGs) remain the same. Each IG group represents a recommended implementation of CIS Controls used to build upon with subsequent IG groups. For instance, to implement IG2 Safeguards, you need to implement IG1 Safeguards first. These IG groups are meant to be cumulative, which IG3 covers all safeguards. In Version 8, IG1 includes 56 safeguards, IG2 includes an additional 74, and IG3 covers an additional 23, bringing the total safeguards to 153. CIS Controls Version 8 were founded on the design principle:

Offense informs Defense.

The CIS Controls are identified and prioritized based on data and knowledge of a threat actor's behavior and what will stop their activity:

- **Focus**

  - Help organizations address the most critical things needed to stop a threat actor.

  - Avoid the temptation to solve each and every security issue.

- **Feasible**

  - All safeguards must be specific and practical to implement.

- **Measurable**

  - All CIS Controls, specifically in IG1, must be measurable.

  - Simplified language, removal of ambiguous terminology, and avoidance of inconsistent interpretation.

  - Thresholds on some safeguards.

- **Align**

  - Peaceful co-existence with other governance, regulations, frameworks, structures, and process management schemes.

  - Cooperation and reference to other independent standards and security recommendations where they exist, for example, NIST, CSA, OWASP, MITRE.

Due to the significant changes in technology, ecosystems, security, and strategy adoptions, such as cloud and multicloud, mobility, virtualization, and even remote working, the threat landscape has evolved significantly.

The CIS Controls community has taken the approach from the perspective of a threat actor in just about every discussion. While previous versions focused on fixed boundaries and isolated security implementations, Version 8 focuses less on these principles; this is reflected in the safeguards. In addition, Version 8 brings forward a glossary of terms to reduce any confusion. As mentioned earlier, some of the CIS Controls and original sub-controls (Version 7) have been combined and reduced to help reflect the evolution of technology. If anyone is looking for a starting place to mitigate cloud attack vectors, CIS Controls are a great place to start for guidance, best practices, and proven results.

CIS Controls, Version 7 and 8 Compared

While we have chosen not to document Version 8 in its entirety due to duplication of controls, Version 7 does contain two more control groups that have been merged and augmented in the newest version. Version 8 technically has three CIS Controls that were deleted (by title):

- **Control 9**: Limitation of ports and protocols

- **Control 12**: Boundary defense

- **Control 15**: Wireless access control

While this may seem confusing, reconciling the two versions really helps understand the duplication of effort. The following CIS Controls were changed in Version 8 compared to Version 7 in Figure 8-1.

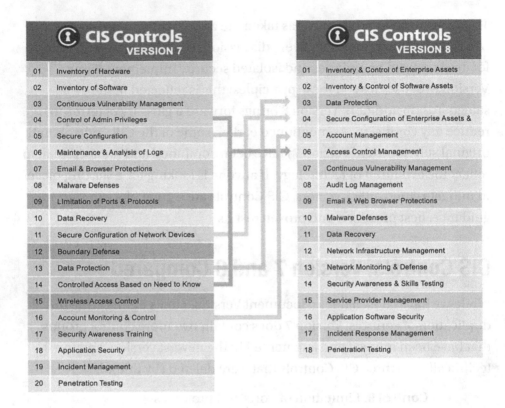

	CIS Controls VERSION 7			CIS Controls VERSION 8
01	Inventory of Hardware		01	Inventory & Control of Enterprise Assets
02	Inventory of Software		02	Inventory & Control of Software Assets
03	Continuous Vulnerability Management		03	Data Protection
04	Control of Admin Privileges		04	Secure Configuration of Enterprise Assets &
05	Secure Configuration		05	Account Management
06	Maintenance & Analysis of Logs		06	Access Control Management
07	Email & Browser Protections		07	Continuous Vulnerability Management
08	Malware Defenses		08	Audit Log Management
09	LImitation of Ports & Protocols		09	Email & Web Browser Protections
10	Data Recovery		10	Malware Defenses
11	Secure Configuration of Network Devices		11	Data Recovery
12	Boundary Defense		12	Network Infrastructure Management
13	Data Protection		13	Network Monitoring & Defense
14	Controlled Access Based on Need to Know		14	Security Awareness & Skills Testing
15	Wireless Access Control		15	Service Provider Management
16	Account Monitoring & Control		16	Application Software Security
17	Security Awareness Training		17	Incident Response Management
18	Application Security		18	Penetration Testing
19	Incident Management			
20	Penetration Testing			

Figure 8-1. *CIS Controls, Versions 7 and 8 compared*

In addition to these changes, CIS Controls Version 8 also gained Control 15, Service Provider Management, specifically for the cloud. This control addresses the need to develop a process to evaluate service providers who are responsible and hold sensitive data or who are liable for an enterprise's critical information technology platforms or processes. The goal is to ensure these providers appropriately protect the data and platforms.

At the end of the day, if you are not leveraging the information available to you and your organization to make better security decisions to reduce risk and make it harder for those threat actors to take advantage of your business, you are doing yourself and your company an injustice. In today's world of opportunistic threat actors, if you leave a vulnerability or misconfiguration exposed for your assets, threat actors will absolutely use them against you to compromise your organization. Do not think you are not a target or immune from them, the moment you become complacent is the moment you have empowered the threat actor to take advantage of you. Please take the time to do your part and embrace these controls and potentially become a part of the community that helps create them for others.

PCI DSS

When it comes to credit card processing, PCI DSS is the de facto of standard for card and payment security. For those of you who might not be familiar with its specifications, we will break it down into a dozen requirements that make up PCI DSS, how it applies to organizations based on transactional volume, and, as silly as it sounds, the acronym, which is very important. PCI DSS stands for Payment Card Industry Data Security Standards[14] which is a set of security standards designed to ensure businesses that accept, transmit, store, and process credit card information securely maintain each of these transactions. Leading banks and credit card companies support this standard. It is not a government organization.

The Payment Card Industry Security Standard Council (PCI SSC) was launched in September of 2006 to administer maturity of the Payment Card Industry Security Standards, with a goal of improving payment account security through the transaction process. The PCI DSS is managed and overseen by the PCI SSC, an independent body consisting of credit card brands Discover, Visa, Visa Europe, UnionPay, Mastercard, American Express, and JBC International. As a side note, the payment brands mentioned and their acquirers (banks) are responsible for enforcing the compliance standard, not the PCI council.

---

[14] www.pcisecuritystandards.org

When you think about how the world has evolved since the pandemic, businesses and people have changed their purchasing behaviors. Businesses are relying more on cloud services and diversifying their cloud strategy among multiple cloud providers to provide the most seamless approach for their employees and customers.

We have seen a major evolution in telecommuting and the remote workforce. Many businesses did not believe their employees could be productive as a remote workforce, so management has been surprised to witness productivity levels maintained and, in many cases, even increased. Unfortunately, all this disruption to the business and workforce due to the pandemic has left a vast threat landscape for threat actors to capitalize on.

Given the increase in digital transactions, higher volumes of online purchases, and supply-chain shortages, security needs to be at the forefront of all e-commerce in the cloud. Money continues to drive cybercrime, whether in the form of ransomware or monetizing data exfiltrated from organizations. Protecting our way of life, since most of us do not use or carry cash anymore, we need to ensure when we make a purchase, no matter how big or small, that our data is protected and the business is taking the proper steps to ensure the transaction is secure.

Let us be honest, the last thing anyone is going to do before they whip out their credit card is check and make sure the merchant is up to par on their security standards. It is an unfortunate truth, since your browser has a padlock in the URL indicating a secure transaction that your session is perfectly safe. Therefore, as we continue to make our way through the roaring 2020s, we know that our world has changed, our workforce has changed, and more online payments are being made than ever before. This section is about how these purchases are secured and verified in the cloud for businesses. And remember, we still use our credit cards in brick-and-mortar stores, too. Those transactions are also processed in or through the cloud.

PCI Compliance Levels

All merchants will fall into one of the four merchant levels based on transaction volume over 12 months. Transaction volume is based on a merchant's aggregate number of transactions (including credit, debit, and prepaid). These are commonly in the specification referred to as "Doing Business As" (DBA). In cases where a merchant corporation has more than one DBA, PCI acquirers must consider the aggregate volume of transactions stored, processed, or transmitted by the corporate entity to determine the validation level. If data is not aggregated, such that the corporate entity does not store, process, or transmit cardholder data on behalf of multiple DBAs, acquirers will continue to consider the DBA's individual transaction volume to determine the validation level. The following are the PCI merchant levels based on transaction volume:

1. Any merchant, regardless of acceptance channel, processing over 6M transactions per year. Any merchant that PCI, at its sole discretion, determines should meet the level 1 merchant requirements to minimize risk to the system.

2. Any merchant, regardless of acceptance channel, processing 1M to 6M transactions per year.

3. Any merchant processing 20,000 to 1M e-commerce transactions per year.

4. Any merchant processing fewer than 20,000 e-commerce transactions per year, and all other merchants, regardless of acceptance channel, processing up to 1M Visa transactions per year.

Something interesting to note here is that any merchant that has suffered a breach that resulted in any amount of account data being compromised may be escalated to a higher validation level. For example, a level 4 small business suffers a data breach in which their customer data is stolen or compromised. The business could be forced to operate as a level 3 moving forward, meaning there are more standards that they will have to meet and comply with despite their size. Failure to comply with standards could result in the major payment brands fining the bank $5,000 to $100,000 per month for violations and the potential to be denied the ability to process credit card data.

To implement the PCI DSS specification, a continuous three-step process is recommended:

- **Access**: Identifying cardholder data, taking an inventory of information technology assets and business processes for payment card processing, and analyzing them for vulnerabilities.

- **Remediate**: Fixing vulnerabilities and eliminating the storage of cardholder data, unless absolutely necessary.

- **Report**: Compiling and submitting required reports to the appropriate acquiring bank and card brands.

And not surprising, these three steps follow the best practices we have outlined throughout this book.

PCI Assessment

When assessing compliance, the PCI council has an approved list of qualified data security firms to perform an on-site assessment. The assessor will follow these guidelines during their assessment:

- Verify all technical information given by merchant or service provider is current and accurate.

- Use independent judgment to confirm the standard has been met and that best intentions are being followed.

- Provide support and guidance during the compliance process for any improvements.

- Be on site for the duration of the assessment (as required and if possible).

- Adhere to the PCI Data Security Standard assessment procedures as a guideline for rules of engagement.

- Validate the scope of the assessment and assets, policies, procedures, environment, and people in scope.

- Evaluate compensating controls for any findings.

- Produce a final report on compliance and recommendations.

In addition, the PCI Security Standard Council maintains a list of approved scanning organizations that perform services to determine whether or not a customer meets the external risk requirements. It is important to note that organizations are certified to perform these services regardless of the tools they use and not the vendors themselves that produce security solutions. However, some vulnerability management vendors do offer these services.

Reports are the official method by which merchants or other entities communicate their compliance status with the PCI Data Security Standards to their respective qualified financial institutions or payment card brands. In addition, there may be a requirement for quarterly submission of a network scanning report, and individual payment card brands may also require submission of other documentation. Depending on the individual payment card brand requirements, merchants and service providers may need to submit a Self-Assessment Questionnaire as a part of their annual review.

PCI Security Standards

Payment Card Industry Standards are broken down into three categories:

- **Manufacturers**: PCI PTS (PIN Entry Devices)

- **Software Developers**: PCI PA-DSS (Payment Applications)

- **Merchants and Providers**: PCI DSS (Secure Environments)

While each of these addresses different aspects, all are related to the protection of cardholder payment data. For this section, we will focus on the "Merchants and Providers" category, which applies the PCI DSS Standards for ensuring the environments in which they operate are secure. The PCI DSS Security Standards are defined by 12 requirements, with multiple sub-requirements. Let's discuss what these 12 requirements mean for any business:

1. **Protect your system with network security controls**. When securing an organization, making sure you build and maintain a secure network is a foundational must. For example, firewalls are devices used to control computer traffic allowed between an entity's networks (internal) and untrusted networks (external), as well as traffic into and out of more sensitive areas within an entity's trusted networks (on-premise or in the cloud). The cardholder data environment is an example of a more sensitive area within an entity's trusted network. A firewall examines all network traffic and blocks those transmissions that do not meet the specified security criteria. All systems must be protected from unauthorized access from untrusted

networks, whether entering the system via the
Internet as e-commerce, employee Internet access
through desktop browsers, employee email access,
dedicated connections such as business-to-business
connections, via wireless networks, or via other
sources. Often, seemingly insignificant paths to and
from untrusted networks can provide unprotected
pathways into key systems. Firewalls are a key
protection mechanism for any environment, and the
cloud is no different. Other system components may
provide firewall functionality, as long as they meet
the minimum firewall requirements, as defined in
requirement 1. This is just one example of a secure
network design that merchants need to implement.

2. **Configure passwords and settings**. Most people
   know that vendor-supplied defaults for system
   passwords should be changed. You would be
   surprised how many either forget, do not realize
   there are default accounts, or don't know about the
   system being online and accessible. While some
   of you might be saying, "how do they not know?",
   consider some of the cyber breaches we have
   previously discussed. If the victims knew they were
   susceptible, don't you think they would have done
   something to avoid the eventual outcome? Most
   would have; others will just deny they knew about
   it. Malicious individuals (external and internal
   to an entity) often use vendor default passwords
   and other vendor default settings to compromise
   systems. These passwords and settings are well
   known by hacker communities and are often easily

determined via public information. Therefore, secure configurations that include password, credential, application configuration, and hardening management are a part of the requirements.

3. **Protect stored account data**. We all know account data in the wrong hands can turn into a very ugly and costly mess for individuals and can possibly result in identity theft. It is no surprise that ensuring your organization protects account data is a requirement. Protection methods, such as encryption, truncation, masking, and hashing, are critical components of account data protection. If an intruder circumvents other security controls and gains access to encrypted data, without the proper cryptographic keys, the data is unreadable and unusable. Other effective methods of protecting stored data should also be considered. For example, methods of minimizing risk include not storing cardholder data unless absolutely necessary, truncating account data if the full Primary Account Number (PAN) is not needed, and not sending unprotected PANs using end-user messaging technologies, such as email and text messaging, or documenting the PAN on paper or other insecure media.

4. **Strong cryptography to protect transmission of account data across open, public networks**. If we send sensitive data, we should protect its transmission from unwanted interception and subsequent compromise. Ensuring cardholder data is encrypted across open, public networks is

a must. Sensitive information must be encrypted during transmission over networks that are easily accessed by malicious individuals. Misconfigured wireless networks and vulnerabilities in legacy encryption and authentication protocols continue to be targets of malicious individuals who exploit these vulnerabilities to gain privileged access to cardholder data environments. This is why requirement 4 covers strong cryptography to protect transmissions of cardholder data.

5. **Use and regularly update anti-malware software**. As for requirement 5, if you are not using solutions to detect and remove malicious code (malware) already, you need to revisit your cybersecurity basics. There is no good scenario in which assets are placed in production without some form of active anti-malware protection regardless of mission. (Insert your favorite science fiction movie that uses a computer virus to advance the plotline, and we hope you are getting our warped sense of humor now).

6. **Regularly update and patch systems**. It goes without saying, developing and maintaining secure systems and applications is crucial in the fight against threat actors and taking away opportunities for them to leverage systems and applications against us. Unscrupulous individuals use security vulnerabilities to gain access to assets and data. Many of these vulnerabilities are fixable via vendor-provided security patches, and others must be identified and remediated, such as if you

develop your own software. In the cloud, this may be your responsibility or the cloud provider's. It is very important to know whose role this is. Ergo, all systems must have all appropriate software patches to protect against the exploitation and compromise of cardholder data by threat actors and malicious software. This is why requirement 6 covers developing and maintaining secure systems and software.

7. **Restrict access to cardholder data to business need to know**. When it comes to privacy and keeping things a secret, it's best to only tell the people that "need to know" vs. allowing anyone to expose a secret. That is, in fact, the opposite of a secret. When it comes to requirement 7, it is no different. Restricting access to cardholder data by business "need to know" is critical to ensuring the cardholder data remains protected. To ensure critical data can only be accessed by authorized personnel, systems and processes must be in place to limit access based on need to know and according to job responsibilities. "Need to know" is when access rights are granted to only the least amount of data and privileges necessary to perform a job.

8. **Assign a unique ID to each person with computer access**. Given the amount of identity theft that occurs both physically and digitally, making sure businesses identify and authenticate access to system components is key to protecting data. Requirement 8 covers this aspect for identifying and authenticating. Assigning a unique identification

(ID) to each identity with access ensures that everyone is uniquely accountable for their actions. When such accountability is in place, actions taken on critical data and systems are performed by, and can be traced to, known and authorized users and processes. The effectiveness of a password is largely determined by the design and implementation of the authentication system. As an example, how many authentication attempts can be made by a user when MFA has been configured compared to the account lockout setting for single-factor authentication? The security and transmission of secrets is incredibly important, but what happens if they are misused is equally important to consider.

9. **Restrict physical access to workplace and cardholder data**. It goes without saying, if you restrict data on a need-to-know model, why shouldn't you restrict physical access to data? This is what requirement 9 covers, restricting physical access to cardholder data. Any physical access to data or systems that house cardholder data provides the opportunity for individuals to access devices or data and to remove systems or hard copies and should be appropriately restricted. For the purposes of requirement 9, "onsite personnel" refers to full-time and part-time employees, temporary employees, contractors, and consultants who are physically present on the entity's premises. A "visitor" refers to a vendor, guest of any on-site personnel, service workers, or anyone who needs to enter the facility for a short duration, usually not

more than one day. "Media" refers to all paper and
electronic media containing cardholder data. At
the end of the day, all physical access to a trusted
network needs to be restricted and monitored on-
premise. For the cloud, this becomes more difficult,
and organizations will need a certification from the
cloud service provider that they are adhering to this
requirement.

10. **Implement logging and log management**. The
key to effective monitoring is having the ability to
detect an anomaly when it occurs, based on the
aggregation of all log data. These anomalies can
vary, from basic behavior and access to extensive
intrusion detection. The purpose in requirement
10 is to track and monitor all access to network
resources and cardholder data via logs. Logging
mechanisms, and the ability to track user activities,
are critical in preventing, detecting, and minimizing
the impact of a data compromise. Thus, logging
should be enabled and aggregated for every asset.

11. **Conduct vulnerability scans and penetration
tests**. Unfortunately, there is no way to validate
systems and processes unless they are regularly
assessed for vulnerabilities and tested for exploits.
Performing regular assessments on your security
systems and processes will allow you to find gaps
and address items that arise due to changes. This
is why requirement 11 covers regularly testing
assets, security, and processes. Vulnerabilities are
being discovered continually by threat actors and
researchers. Often, vulnerabilities are introduced

inadvertently via system changes. System
components, audit logs, applications, operating
systems, and custom software should be assessed
frequently and remediated in a timely manner.

12. **Documentation and risk assessment**. Last, but not
least, requirement 12 involves a company's ability
to maintain a policy that addresses information
security for all personnel. Having a documented
policy that is adhered to in an organization is
important. A strong security policy sets the security
tone for the entire entity and informs personnel
of what is expected of them based on roles and
responsibilities. All personnel should be aware
of the sensitivity of data and their responsibilities
for protecting it. For the purposes of requirement
12, "personnel" refers to full-time and part-time
employees, temporary employees, contractors, and
consultants who are "resident" on the entity's site or
who otherwise have access to the cardholder data
environment.

Finally, an interesting note about PCI DSS is that it also contains
additional requirements for shared hosting providers. If you were to go
back and review requirement 12 in depth, it states that all service providers
with access to cardholder data (including shared hosting providers) must
adhere to PCI DSS. In addition, if you reference requirement 2, it states that
all shared hosting providers must protect each entity's hosted environment
and data. Therefore, shared hosting providers must additionally comply
with the requirements covered in the Appendix of PCI DSS and in the
cloud. This implies that services in the cloud will be shared with multiple
organizations by a single cloud service provider instance.

PCI DSS Summary

Depending on the market your business is in and whether or not cardholder data is part of your responsibility, it's safe to say that there are merits when you apply the PCI DSS Standards. For any consumer who uses credit cards regularly and does not carry cash, understanding the requirements set forth by PCI council gives a sense of security when applied to the merchants we transact with on a daily basis. While nothing is 100% when it comes to security, knowing that businesses are taking security seriously and following standards like PCI DSS to help disrupt a threat actor's ability to prey on unsuspecting cardholders and merchants is comfort in today's economy.

While PCI DSS is a model framework for security, they integrate best practices from years of experience honed by security experts from around the world. To wrap up this section, consider these final recommendations for payment card merchants:

- Buy and use only approved PIN entry devices at your points of sale (POS).

- Buy and use only validated payment software for your point-of-sale (POS) systems or website shopping cart.

- Do not store *any* sensitive cardholder data in computers or on paper that is out of scope for payment processing.

- Segment your network, use firewalls, and control access into your trusted networks that contain cardholder data and process transactions.

- Make sure all wireless networks are properly secured and have updated encryption.

- Use strong passwords, along with multi-factor authentication. Single-factor authentication is never acceptable in a PCI environment or in scope for transactions.

- Be sure to change default passwords on hardware and software, and disable all unnecessary accounts.

- Regularly check PIN entry devices and PCs to make sure that rogue software or "skimming" devices are not installed.

- Regularly train and educate your employees about security and protecting cardholder data.

ISO

When it comes to ISO, many of us recognize the acronym, but not all of us can identify what it stands for: ISO is the International Organization for Standardization.[15] ISO is made up of 165 members representing ISO in their respective countries, with only one member per country. ISO currently has 802 technical committees and subcommittees that take care of standard development and revisions. For the purposes of this book, the ISO 27000 series is all related to information security. The series aspect of the ISO 27000 standard was conceived and announced back in 2005, with some of the constituent standards predating the official announcement.

The specification started as the Seeds of Standards, created by the UK Government's DTI (Department of Trade and Industry[16]). Their Commercial Computer Security Centre (known as the CCSC) was

---

[15] www.iso.org/home.html

[16] https://www.gov.uk/world/organisations/
department-for-international-trade-in-the-usa

charged with several major tasks in this area. One of these tasks was to create a security evaluation criteria for information technology security products, while another was to create a code of good security practices for information security.

The first of these tasks led to the creation of what was known as the ITSEC.[17] The second task led to the publication of a document called DISC PD0003 (where DISC is not an abbreviation for the starship named Discovery), which followed further development by the now defunct Manchester-based NCC (National Computing Centre[18]), and a consortium of user organizations. PD0003 was organized into ten sections, each of them outlining numerous objectives and controls. Despite being published in the early 1990s, its format and content still very much resemble the current ISO 27002 standard. The PD0003 document continued to develop under the custodianship of BIS (Bureau of Indian Standards[19]), and eventually became a formal standard, known as BS7799 in 1995.

Historically, development continued down two paths. BIS developed another standard detailing Information Security Management System (ISMS). It was published in 1998 as BS7799-2 and eventually would become known as ISO 27001. The original BS7799-1 turned into ISO 17799 in December of 2000. Since then, the momentum behind the standards drastically increased. In June of 2005, following several working group meetings, a new version of ISO 17799 was published. In late 2007, it was decided that, to align with the ISO series numbering system, ISO 17799 would be renamed to ISO 27002.

One thing you might find interesting about the ISO standards is that they are not available for free to the public for consumption. An end user or organization must purchase the ISO standard and its accompanying

---

[17] https://www.iitsec.org/
[18] https://www.liquisearch.com/national_computing_centre/failure
[19] www.bis.gov.in/

reference document to view and implement the contents. This allows the ISO to track ownership and generate revenue for the creation of future standards and support.

Understanding ISO 27001

Since its conversion from BS7799-2 standard, ISO 27001 has become the de facto specification for ISMS (Information Security Management System). ISO 27001 enhanced the content of BS7799-2 and aligned it with other standards developed by competing organizations. The objective of ISO 27001 is to provide requirements for establishing, implementing, maintaining, and continuously improving an Information Security Management System (ISMS). Should you choose this as a guideline and adopt this as your standard, it should be a strategic decision with executive sponsorship. Adoption of ISO 27001 will not be successful without a complete organizational commitment. In addition, the design and implementation of an organization's ISMS is influenced by the organization's needs, objectives, security requirements, organizational processes, and the size of the organization.

The original 2005 version of the standard heavily relied on a model called "Plan-Do-Check-Act." However, in the 2013 update to the standard, there was more emphasis placed on measuring and evaluating how well an organization's ISMS is performing than on the complete life cycle. To that end, most organizations have several information security controls. However, without an ISMS, controls tend to be somewhat disorganized and disjointed, having often been implemented as point solutions to specific situations or simply as a matter of convention. Security controls in operation typically address certain aspects of information technology or data security specifically, leaving noninformation technology assets (such as paperwork and proprietary knowledge) less protected for the entire organization. Moreover, business continuity planning and physical security may be managed independently compared to information security. Human resource practices may make little reference to the need to define and assign information security roles and responsibilities throughout the organization.

With these in mind, ISO 27001 includes the following three recommendations:

- Systematically examine the organization's information security risks, taking account of the threats, vulnerabilities, and impacts.

- Design and implement a coherent and comprehensive suite of information security controls and/or other forms of risk treatment (such as risk avoidance or risk transfer) to address those risks that are deemed unacceptable.

- Adopt an overarching management process to ensure that the information security controls continue to meet the organization's needs on an ongoing basis.

ISO 27001 is designed to cover much more than just information technology; it also includes controls that will be tested as part of certification. Which controls will be tested is dependent on the certification auditor and applicability. This can include any controls that the organization has deemed to be within the scope of the ISMS. Testing can be to any depth or extent, as assessed by the auditor, or scope, as stated by the organization. This is important since management determines the scope of the ISMS for certification purposes and may limit it to, say, a single business unit, location, or even departments with the business. The ISO 27001 certificate does not necessarily mean the remainder of the organization, outside the scoped area, has an adequate approach to information security management. Other standards in the ISO 27000 family of standards provide additional guidance on certain aspects of designing, implementing, and operating an ISMS, for example, on information security risk management (ISO 27005).

In regard to certification, an ISMS may be certified compliant with ISO 27001 by a number of Accredited Registrars. Certification against any of the recognized national variants of ISO 27001 (like JIS Q 27001, the Japanese version) by an accredited certification body is functionally equivalent to certification against ISO/IEC 27001 itself.

The ISO/IEC 27001 certification, like other ISO management system certifications, usually involves a three-stage external audit process defined by the ISO/IEC 17021 and ISO/IEC 27006 standards. This is done in two stages, with a follow-up, continuous process:

- **Stage 1** is a preliminary, informal review of the ISMS, for example, checking the existence and completeness of key documentation, such as the organization's information security policy, Statement of Applicability (SoA), and Risk Treatment Plan (RTP). This stage serves to familiarize the auditors with the organization and vice versa.

- **Stage 2** is a more detailed and formal compliance audit, independently testing the ISMS against the requirements specified in ISO 27001. The auditors will seek evidence to confirm that the management system has been properly designed and implemented and is, in fact, in operation (e.g., by confirming that a security committee or similar management body meets regularly to oversee the ISMS). Certification audits are usually conducted by ISO 27001 Lead Auditors. Passing this stage results in the ISMS being certified compliant with ISO 27001.

- **Ongoing** involves follow-up reviews or audits to confirm that the organization remains in compliance with the standard. Certification maintenance requires periodic reassessment audits to confirm that the ISMS continues to operate as specified and intended. These should happen at least annually, but (by agreement with management) are often conducted more frequently, particularly while the ISMS is still maturing.

Understanding ISO 27002

If you have been following along, then you already have the backstory and history on ISO 27002. Originating from the ISO 17799 standard, it is a code of practice for information security. It outlines numerous potential controls and control mechanisms, which you can choose to implement, subject to the guidance within the ISO 27001 standard. The actual controls listed in the standard are intended to address the specific requirements identified via formal risk assessment. The standard is also intended to provide a guide for the development of organizational security standards and effective security management practices. The goal is to help build confidence in inter-organization activities.

ISO 27002 currently contains 14 sections for consideration:

- Security Policy

- Organization of Information Security

- Human Resources Security

- Asset Management

- Access Control

- Cryptography

- Physical and Environmental Security

- Operations Security

- Communications Security

- Information Systems Acquisition, Development, and Maintenance

- Supplier Relationships

- Information Security Incident Management

- Information Security Aspects of Business Continuity

- Compliance

It is also worth noting that, over the years, several industry-specific versions of ISO 27002 have been developed targeting vertical industries. These industry-specific versions include healthcare, manufacturing, and financial.

Comparing ISO 27001 vs. ISO 27002

Some of you might be scratching or beating your head on the table right now. Don't worry, we did too when we first encountered GRC (governance, risk, and compliance). It took some time for us to wrap our heads around all the standards, frameworks, controls, and guidelines. To the information technology neophyte, it can get overwhelming, fast. Thankfully, we had some help and mentoring along the way to ease our transitions into the checks and balances (just like government) GRC provides.

When organizations decide to implement an ISMS, they often wonder what the difference is between ISO 27001 and ISO 27002. To put it simply, ISO 27001 holds the requirements of the Information Security Management System Standard, and ISO 27002 gives guidelines and best practices intended for organizations who are becoming certified or who are implementing their own security processes and controls. ISO 27002 is more focused on specific examples and guidelines, providing a code of practice for use by individuals within an organization.

353

You cannot get certified against ISO 27002 because it is not a management system standard. Instead, it was established based on various guidelines and principles for initiating, implementing, improving, and maintaining information security management within an organization. The actual controls in the standard address specific requirements through a formal risk assessment, as mentioned earlier. The standard consists of specific guidelines for the developments in organizational security standards and effective security management practices that are useful in building confidence within inter-organizational activities.

There are a dozen other standards in the ISO 27000 series, which are all designed to assist companies in securing their organizational information. These include ISO 27005, for organizations looking for more detail on how to carry out risk assessment and risk treatment, and ISO 27004, which provides guidelines intended to help organizations with monitoring, measurement, analysis, and evaluation of their information security performance and the effectiveness of their ISMS.

Every standard from the ISO 27000 series is designed with a specific focus in mind, but if you want to build the foundations of information security in your organization and devise its framework, you should start with ISO 27001. ISO 27002 is designed to be a tool to help organizations with the implementation of ISO 27001 or for organizations who want to implement their own management guidelines and controls surrounding information security.

In the next section, we will highlight a few other ISO standards that will help you mitigate cloud attack vectors.

ISO 27017

The modern-day cloud service offering can be a complex task to comprehend everything that is involved when it comes to selecting a secure cloud service. It is a daunting task that keeps many of us up late at night wondering if we made the right choice or if we will be woken in the middle of the night for a security incident beyond our control.

ISO 27017 is part of the Information Technology Standards. It focuses on security techniques and the code of practice for information security controls, which is based on ISO 27002 for cloud services. It provides guidelines for information security controls that are applicable to the provisioning and use of cloud services. If you are currently following ISO 27002, it will provide additional implementation guidance for those controls. It also has additional controls that specifically relate to cloud services. ISO 27017 covers additional implementation guidance for the controls specified in ISO 27002 and several additional controls related to cloud services that address the following:

- Who is responsible for what, between the cloud service provider and the cloud customer

- The removal or return of assets at the end of a contract

- Protection and separation of the customer's virtual environment

- Virtual machine configuration

- Administrative operations and procedures associated with the cloud environment

- Cloud customer monitoring of activity

- Virtual and cloud network environment alignment

At a high level, ISO 27017 standard is structured to include 18 sections and a dedicated Annex section. The 18 sections are

1. Scope

2. Normative References

3. Definitions and Abbreviations

4. Cloud Sector-Specific Concepts

5. Information Security Policies

6.   Organization of Information Security

7.   Human Resource Security

8.   Asset Management

9.   Access Control

10. Cryptography

11. Physical and Environmental Security

12. Operations Security

13. Communications Security

14. System Acquisition, Development, and Maintenance

15. Supplier Relationships

16. Information Security Incident Management

17. Information Security Aspects of Business Continuity Management

18. Compliance

There are two additional sections in the standard, referred to as Annex A and Annex B. The Annex A section is an integral part of the standard's recommendation. It covers the relationship between cloud service customers and cloud service providers and the shared role and responsibilities within the cloud computing environment. Having defined roles helps to eliminate confusion and identifies who is responsible and accountable. Annex A also discusses responsibility for assets and the removal of cloud service customer assets. Another key area in Annex A is Access Control of cloud service customer data in shared virtual environments. It discusses the segregation in virtual cloud computing and virtual machine hardening. Ensuring the virtual instances are secure and the customer data is protected is key in stopping the threat actors who try to leverage weak security hardening practices to compromise systems. As with any good security program, operational procedures and defined responsibilities are also key, which is covered in Annex A. Visibility into systems through logging and monitoring is also a critical part in any security standard. Annex A also details the monitoring of cloud services and network security management.

Finally, Annex B references security risks related to cloud computing, but it is not referred to as an integral part of the standard; it only provides recommendations.

ISO 27018

Like ISO 27017, ISO 27018 is part of the Information Technology Standards that focuses on security techniques directly related to the code of practice for protection of personally identifiable information (PII) in public clouds acting as PII processors. The standard establishes commonly accepted control objectives, controls, and guidelines for implementing measures to protect personally identifiable information (PII) in line with the privacy principles in ISO/IEC 29100 for the public cloud computing environment. In particular, this document specifies guidelines based on ISO/IEC 27002, taking into consideration the regulatory requirements for the protection of PII, which can be applicable within the context of the information security risk environment(s) of a provider of public cloud services.

ISO 27018 is applicable to all types and sizes of organizations, including public and private companies, government entities, and not-for-profit organizations, which provide information processing services as PII processors via cloud computing under contract to other organizations. The requirements that are outlined in the ISO 27018 standard can also be relevant to organizations acting as PII controllers. However, PII controllers can be subject to additional PII protection legislation, regulations, and obligations – this doesn't apply to PII processors.

Cloud service providers who process PII under contract to their customers need to operate their services in ways that allow both parties to meet the requirements of applicable legislation and regulations covering the protection of PII. The requirements and the way the requirements are divided between the cloud service provider and its customers vary according to legal jurisdiction and according to the terms of the contract between the cloud service provider and the customer. Legislation that governs how PII is allowed to be processed (collected, used, transferred, and disposed of) is sometimes referred to as data protection legislation; PII is sometimes referred to as personal data or personal information. The obligations falling on a PII processor vary from jurisdiction to jurisdiction, which makes it challenging for businesses that are providing cloud computing services to operate multinationally.

As a matter of definition, a public cloud service provider is a "PII processor" when it processes PII for, and according to the instructions of, a cloud service customer. The cloud service customer, who has the contractual relationship with the public cloud PII processor, can range from a natural person, a "PII principal," processing their own PII in the cloud, to an organization, a "PII controller," processing PII relating to many PII principals. The cloud service customer can authorize one or more cloud service users associated with it to use the services made available under its contract with the public cloud PII processor. Note that the cloud service customer has authority over the processing and use of the data. A cloud service customer who is also a PII controller can be subject to a wider set of obligations governing the protection of PII than the public cloud PII processor. Maintaining the distinction between PII controller and PII processor relies on the public cloud PII processor having no data processing objectives other than those set by the cloud service customer, with respect to the PII it processes and the operations necessary to achieve the cloud service customer's objectives.

The intention of this standard, when used in conjunction with the information security objectives and controls in ISO/IEC 27002, is to create a common set of security categories and controls that can be implemented by a public cloud computing service provider acting as a PII processor. It has the following objectives:

- To help the public cloud service provider comply with applicable obligations when acting as a PII processor, whether such obligations fall on the PII processor directly or through contract.

- To enable the public cloud PII processor to be transparent in relevant matters so that cloud service customers can select well-governed cloud-based PII processing services.

- To assist the cloud service customer and the public cloud PII processor in entering into a contractual agreement.

- To provide cloud service customers with a mechanism for exercising audit and compliance rights and responsibilities. This is especially true where audits of data hosted in a multi-party, virtualized server (cloud) environment can be impractical and can increase risks due to third-party physical and logical network security controls.

This standard can assist by providing a common compliance framework for public cloud service providers and for those that operate in a multinational market.

As you can see, dealing with PII and the process of PII can get very complicated on both sides. From the business side, it's a matter of understanding what is required to properly protect the PII data and ensure, when processing PII data, that it is secure and not susceptible to compromise. As a customer, we rely on businesses and organizations and trust they are properly handling our information. When evaluating your cloud service providers and what standard they follow, consider how they will ultimately protect your sensitive information, including PII.

Comparing ISO 27017 and ISO 27018

ISO 27017 and ISO 27018, both based on ISO 27001, have been adapted to the specific requirements of cloud service providers. ISO 27017 is primarily concerned with the relationship between providers and their customers. As part of the ISO 27017 audit, hired experts can help you identify key security elements that improve the quality and reliability of your cloud services. ISO 27018 specifically addresses the requirements of data protection law. The focus here is mainly on the processing of personal data within the cloud.

If you are evaluating your options as a business for which standard or compliance framework to follow for cloud, PII, or the processing of PII, make sure you look at these in the ISO series of standards. Make sure when you are dealing with PII that you evaluate and interrogate the businesses that would be handling and/or processing your PII data to understand what standards or framework they are following. If they claim to follow an ISO Standard, make sure you ask for a copy of their ISO Standard certification as proof. Following a standard vs. being certified in the standard are two different things. While there are still many other frameworks, standards, and regulatory compliance guidelines, ensure you do your homework and understand what the organization follows for their security standards. Ensuring your business is properly aligned will help you mitigate cloud attacks.

NIST

The National Institute of Standards and Technology (NIST[20]) was
established in 1901 and is currently a department within the US
Department of Commerce. NIST is one of the oldest physical science
laboratories in the United States. Initially, the US Congress established
the agency to improve US industrial competitiveness due to challenges in
the US Customary System (US units of measure such as feet and pounds)
that were viewed as inferior compared to the capabilities present from the
United Kingdom, Germany, and other nations at that time.

Today, NIST provides specifications, standardization, and
recommended controls for the electric power grids, electronic health
records, atomic clocks, advanced nanomaterials, and electronic and
technology security. Essentially, any products and services that rely in
some way on technology are in scope for National Institute of Standards
and Technology recommendations.

When it comes to attack vectors affecting the cloud, NIST has created
a wide variety of standardizations that help address modern technology
problems. The most important ones are reviewed next.

NIST 800-53: Security and Privacy Controls for Information Systems and Organizations

NIST 800-53, Security and Privacy Controls for Information Systems and
Organizations, is arguably the backbone and basis for almost all modern
on-premise and cloud-based security frameworks. NIST 800-53 establishes
security controls and privacy controls for virtually any organization
looking to improve their risk management posture. While originally
developed for federal information systems and organizations providing

---

[20] https://www.nist.gov/

services to the federal government and required by Executive Order 13800, the NIST recommendations and scope have become best practices for virtually any organization operating on-premise or in the cloud. NIST SP 800-53 is designed to provide security controls for operations, assets, identities, and organizations to protect against a diverse set of cyber risks that are quantifiable based on the current risk landscape.

The NIST controls are designed to be flexible and customizable to aid organizations in implementation based on the organization's choices in technology and other mitigating controls. NIST SP 800-53 provides a foundation for other initiatives like FISMA, FedRAMP, PCI, SOX, HIPAA, GLBA, etc., but should never be the only framework to consider. It is a foundation.

NIST SP 800-53 applies the categorization method from the Federal Information Processing Standard (FIPS),[21] breaking assets into three risk-based classes:

1. Low impact

2. Moderate impact

3. High impact

NIST SP 800-53 also includes the notion of security control baselines as a starting point for the security control selection process under these classes. This can help with prioritization and has similar examples and expected baselines to the CIS Controls. The security controls described in NIST SP 800-53 are organized into 18 families. Each family contains security controls related to the specific family topic and areas of governance. Security controls may involve aspects of policy, oversight, supervision, manual processes, actions by identities, or automation by humans and machines related to that family. The 18 security control families are:

---

[21] https://www.nist.gov/itl/current-fips

1. Access Control (AC)

2. Awareness and Training (AT)

3. Audit and Accountability (AU)

4. Security Assessments and Authorization (CA)

5. Configuration Management (CM)

6. Contingency Planning (CP)

7. Identification and Authentication (IA)

8. Incident Response (IR)

9. Maintenance (MA)

10. Media Protection (MP)

11. Physical and Environmental Protection (PE)

12. Planning (PL)

13. Personnel Security (PS)

14. Risk Assessment (RA)

15. Systems and Services Acquisition (SA)

16. System and Communications Protection (SC)

17. System and Information Integrity (SI)

18. Program Management (PM)

Finally, as with many similar regulations and guidelines, NIST 800-53 is a living and evolving framework that has been subject to major revisions over time. The latest revision to NIST 800-53, at the time of writing, is SP 800-53 Version 5.1. The biggest changes in the latest release promote NIST 800-53 for all organizations and assets, and not just federal systems. The latest update includes a proactive and systematic approach to make a comprehensive set of security controls available to all public and private sector organizations. This includes any asset in the cloud, on-premise, or in a hybrid environment, regardless of type – from virtual machine to physical device and IoT.

NIST 800-61: Computer Security Incident Handling Guide

NIST 800-61, Computer Security Incident Handling Guides, assists organizations in establishing computer security incident response procedures, workflows, and documentation for managing security-related incidents efficiently and effectively and in a predictable and legally responsible manner. Similar to other NIST publications, NIST 800-61 defines four phases of an incident response life cycle:

- **Preparation**: Allows an organization and its incident response team to prepare for incident handling and, if possible, to address the probability of the incident occurring.

- **Detection and Analysis**: The incident response team analyzes symptoms that might indicate a security incident and decides whether it indeed is a situation that warrants continued pursuit.

- **Containment, Eradication, and Recovery**: This is the period in which incident response team tries to contain the problem and, if necessary, recover from it by restoring any affected resources, data, and processes.

- **Post-Incident Activity**: The cybersecurity incident and all relevant incident handling procedures are scrutinized for continuous improvement. This includes two goals: to reduce the probability of similar incidents recurring and to improve incident handling procedures.

If you are reading this book and have any responsibility for incident response, consider these questions:

- Has your incident response team been spending enough time reviewing both open and closed incidents?

- Has your incident response team been providing self-improvement recommendations based on output from an incident response?

- Has your incident response team been correlating indicators of compromise with actual incidents and providing feedback for better detection?

Based on these answers, your organization may need to consider embracing NIST 800-61 as a guideline for incident response and compliance programs. Managing threats in the cloud and on-premise follows the same philosophy. However, as we have discussed many times, the more things change, the more they stay the same. The incident management process is the same in the cloud, but the tools, environment, and mitigations will all be different. NIST 800-61 helps establish that the process for incident management is the same, regardless of your organization's choices in technology.

NIST 800-207: Zero-Trust Architecture

While there is an entire section covering zero trust as an architectural mitigation strategy for cloud deployments based on the philosophy of a common office environment (COE), the definition of zero trust is one that is hotly debated among security professionals and vendors. Luckily, NIST has cut through all the noise and developed NIST 800-207 to establish a much-needed definition and baseline for Zero-Trust Architectures (ZTAs).

By definition, a zero-trust security model advocates for the creation of zones and segmentation to control sensitive IT resources. This also entails the deployment of technology to monitor and manage data between zones and, more importantly, authentication within a zone(s), while monitoring behavior. This encompasses users, applications, and other nonhuman authentication requests. In addition, the zero-trust model redefines the architecture of a trusted network inside a logical and software-defined perimeter. This can be on–premise or in the cloud. Only trusted resources should interact based on a dynamic authentication model within that construct.

Zero trust is becoming increasingly more relevant today as technologies and processes, like the cloud, virtualization, DevOps, edge computing, edge security, personification, and OT/IoT, have either blurred or dissolved the idea of a traditional firewall and network-zoned perimeter.

While zero trust has become a trendy catchword in IT, it's important to call out that, in practice, this model is very specific about how things should be designed and operated. Zero trust may not work for every environment. In practice, it is best suited for new or refreshed deployments or to strictly control user access to sensitive resources, especially when they are connecting remotely. To that end, there are four architectures in NIST 800-207 that help define whether your environment can meet the scrutiny of following zero trust:

1. **Device Agent/Gateway-Based Deployment**: Isolation of access to data is strictly controlled by agent communication through an established network path and gateway

2. **Enclave-Based Deployment**: Access to secure resources is contained with an established perimeter – called a resource enclave – and access to the enclave is controlled with agent and gateway technology.

3. **Resource Portal-Based Deployment**: A secure portal, presumably web or application based, brokers all communication based on policy, and all access is monitored for appropriate behavior.

4. **Device Application Sandboxing**: An application itself operates in a sandbox so all activity can be monitored and protected from external threats.

Today, there is no certification to prove that your applications and assets are zero trust compliant. Despite Executive Orders from the President of the United States promoting zero trust, any implementations are just an architecture and opinion as to whether they meet objectives or the theoretical designs presented in NIST 800-207. However, current work is being done on NIST 1800-35a to define Zero Trust Architectures, but, as of the writing of this book, it is still very early stages.

Similar to CIS and FedRAMP, we expect there to eventually be a formal certification for applications and architectures to prove they meet the foundational requirements for zero trust. Right now, we are just in the early stages of the definition and the hype in the vendor marketplace.

FedRAMP

The Federal Risk and Authorization Management Program (FedRAMP[22]) was founded in 2011 to provide a cost-effective, risk-based framework for the implementation and adoption of cloud services by the US federal government. FedRAMP provides agencies with a framework, guidelines, audits, and controls to determine which modern cloud technologies are secure for federal consumption and how to maintain them for the safety, security, and privacy of federal information. The primary mission

---

[22]www.fedramp.gov

is to establish FedRAMP as a government-wide program that promotes the adoption of secure cloud services across the federal government by providing a standardized approach for all agencies to implement and measure against. FedRAMP aims to:

- Increase the adoption of secure, cloud-based technologies within federal government agencies

- Provide a consistent and measurable framework by which federal government agencies secure, authorize, monitor, and manage cloud-based technologies and their associated vendors

- Improve government and vendor relationships through a vehicle of trust for solution consumption

- Minimize effort or the duplicate testing of a solution for better adoption across multiple agencies

- Optimize cost, when multiple federal agencies are using the same cloud-based technology

- Provide centralized oversight for federal agencies adopting cloud-based technology and a single catalog for future adoption

For an organization to become FedRAMP certified, the company and their cloud-based solutions must follow the procedure illustrated in Figure 8-2, FedRAMP authorization process.

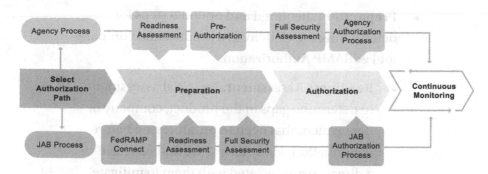

Figure 8-2. *FedRAMP authorization process*

The FedRAMP authorization process requires the engagement of the company providing the solutions, the cloud service provider, the requesting federal agency, an assessor, and a Third-Party Assessment Organization (commonly referred to as a 3PAO). For reference, the 3PAO cannot be the same company providing the readiness assessment or other tasks in the workflow. Also, for the sake of this section, this has been simplified; the actual process is literally a book in itself, and the cost to an organization to obtain and maintain that process can easily hit millions of dollars.

So, what is involved in a FedRAMP Assessment and Certification? There are two different methods the government provides for authorization: Agency Process and JAB (Joint Authorization Board) Process. Based on our collective experience, most organizations will choose the Agency Process over the JAB Process. Both processes use strict security controls derived from NIST 800-53, ISO, SOC, etc., to provide the framework to assess and measure the company, products, and deployment for viability and security.

1. **Agency Process**: A federal agency will sponsor the authorization of the solution and, with the company and assessors, validate the security in a cloud service provider.

369

- **Preparation**: Required and optional steps for determining the viability of a product and company for FedRAMP Authorization.

    - **Readiness Assessment**: An initial assessment to determine gaps in the product, company or deployment that need to be addressed before continuation. Many times, the findings have a direct cost associated with them to mitigate and may require a business justification to continue pursuing FedRAMP authorization. This step is technically optional; however, most organizations choose to perform this work to gauge overall readiness and cost.

    - **Pre-authorization**: A formal review of partnership, commitment, and engagement by all parties. A designation is placed on the FedRAMP marketplace (catalog) indicating the solution is "Ready" for the next steps.

- **Authorization**: The formal authorization process including audits, assessments, and documentation of controls.

    - **Full Security Assessment**: A full security assessment of all controls and mitigation plans for any deficiencies. Note: The federal government has a ton of acronyms here from SSP (System Security Plan), SAP (Security Assessment Plan), and POA&M (Plan of Action and Milestones), to document this process.

- **Agency Authorization Process**: Complete documentation with evidence of all controls that is reviewed by the sponsoring agency and submitted to the FedRAMP PMO (Program Management Office) for review. Once approved, the solution is authorized for sales, usage, and to proceed with continuous monitoring.

2. **JAB Process**: Unlike the agency process, no organization is sponsoring the product's usage. Instead, the Department of Defense (DoD), Department of Homeland Security (DHS), and General Services Administration (GSA) sponsor the submission. However, JAB only allows approximately 12 products per year to use this process, and as a governing body, it selects which ones should be allowed to enter. Therefore, there is no guarantee that if your organization selects the JAB Process for FedRAMP authorization, you will even be selected.

   - **Preparation**: A formal process to determine the readiness of the product and company for authorization. There are no optional steps in the process.

     - **FedRAMP Connect**: Acceptance and queuing of the project within the JAB and FedRAMP PMO.

     - **Readiness Assessment**: Preliminary assessment of the company and products to operate in a secure cloud service provider environment. This includes the FedRAMP marketplace (catalog) designation of "Ready."

- **Full Security Assessment**: A complete readiness assessment of all controls and documentation of any deficiencies that require mitigation.

- **Authorization**: Formal authorization process working with designated government agencies.

  - **JAB Authorization Process**: In lieu of a federal agency sponsor, the designated government agencies will perform the complete review and, after a successful completion, will designate the product "Authorized." This process differs from an agency approach by having stricter timelines defined to ensure completion, vs. getting hung up in government red tape and conflicting agency priorities.

Once either process is selected, the success rate for actual authorization (ATO – Authority to Operate) can vary based on client commitment, product design, technical debt, federal agency willingness, cost overruns, etc. After authorization, the solution must be strictly monitored and maintained for usage. This is the continuous monitoring portion of the process and generally involves having dedicated staff and other FedRAMP authorized solutions for security management, auditing, reporting, logging, and support that can add significant overhead costs for sales to federal agencies.

All in all, FedRAMP certification is required as an approach for servicing most federal government agencies, but the security of the solution being offered must meet strict, continuous controls from design and development to deployment and maintenance. Thus, FedRAMP might not be suitable for many organizations.

Finally, violations in the continuous monitoring process after authorization can have dire consequences for the product and company. Consequences could range from delisting to being eliminated from future federal agency considerations. It is in the best interest of the organization to maintain continuous monitoring per the FedRAMP specifications, maintain good FedRAMP PMO communications, and be completely transparent and honest about their solution.

CHAPTER 9

Architectures

Throughout time, there have been some awe-inspiring examples of architecture. From the Sydney Opera House to the Taj Mahal to the Empire State Building. However, when we think of cloud architectures to support video streaming, social media, and even business applications, we think of the business names (Amazon, Netflix, Twitter, Salesforce, ServiceNow, etc.) and not the underlying plumbing that makes them viable. In fact, much of the plumbing to make the cloud successful is proprietary.

While we can debate three-tier web service architectures, the benefits of single tenancy vs. multitenancy, containers vs. virtual machines, the simple truth is that an argument can be made for any type of cloud architecture over another based on the mission of the business. There is no right or wrong answer. However, there are architectures that are more secure, that cost less to operate, and, in the end, that are easier to maintain. Therefore, in lieu of trying to battle it out based on business objective, we have chosen to discuss architectural themes that are important with regard to security and mitigation of cloud attack vectors. Some of these architectures are new, some stretch goals, and some are not even possible, depending on whether you have developed something from scratch or have cloud washed your services. Consider them as the best strategic approaches to architecture we can recommend.

© Morey J. Haber, Brian Chappell, Christopher Hills 2022
M. J. Haber et al., *Cloud Attack Vectors*, https://doi.org/10.1007/978-1-4842-8236-6_9

Zero Trust

Zero trust is not a new concept, but rather a combination of established security best practices applied together to strengthen on-premise and cloud security. One critical fact is that zero trust is not a product but rather a solutions map into guidelines set forth in the NIST Special Publication (SP) 800-207. Zero-Trust Architecture[1] (being developed by NIST under 1800-35a) defines the core concepts as follows:

- **Zero trust (ZT)** is the term for an evolving set of cybersecurity paradigms that move defenses from static, network-based perimeters to focus on users, assets, and resources.

- **Zero-trust architecture (ZTA)** uses zero-trust principles to plan industrial and enterprise infrastructure and workflows.

Zero trust assumes there is no implicit trust granted to assets or user accounts based solely on their physical or network location (local area networks vs. the Internet) or based on asset ownership (enterprise or personally owned). Authentication and authorization (both subject and device) are discrete functions performed before a session with an enterprise resource is established.

The zero-trust principles and framework are a response to enterprise network trends that include remote users, bring your own device (BYOD), cloud computing, and other assets that are no longer necessarily located within an enterprise-owned network boundary. Zero trust focuses on protecting resources (assets, services, workflows, network accounts, etc.), not network segments, as the network location is no longer seen as the prime component to the security posture of the resource. This is contrary

---

[1] https://www.nccoe.nist.gov/sites/default/files/2022-06/zta-nist-sp-1800-35a-preliminary-draft.pdf

to the network segmentation and firewall discussions we have previously had as a part of some compliance initiatives.

According to NIST, "A zero trust architecture (ZTA) is an enterprise cybersecurity architecture that is based on zero trust principles and designed to prevent data breaches and limit internal lateral movement." The NIST SP 800-207 publication discusses ZTA, its logical components, possible deployment scenarios, and threats. The NIST Special Publication also presents a general road map for organizations wishing to migrate to a zero-trust approach and discusses relevant federal policies that may impact or influence a ZTA. With this in mind, there are seven tenets that define a successful zero-trust implementation, as shown in Table 9-1.

Table 9-1. *Seven tenants of zero trust*

Seven Tenets of Zero Trust

1. All data sources and computing services are considered assets. (Note: NIST refers to these as resources and is another contradiction in terminology.)	5. The enterprise monitors and measures the integrity and security posture of all owned and associated assets.
2. All communication is secured, regardless of network location.	6. All resource authentication and authorization are dynamic and strictly enforced before access is allowed.
3. Access to individual enterprise resources is granted on a per session basis.	7. The enterprise collects as much information as possible about the current state of assets, network infrastructure, and communications and uses it to improve its security posture.
4. Access to resources is determined by dynamic policy, including the observable state of client identity, application/service, and the requesting asset, and may include other behavioral and environmental attributes.	

Zero trust is about knowing who is doing what within your network and ensuring that, in the event of anomalous activity, you can control and limit any threats to the network. Applying the granularity of access, including privileged access to achieve zero-trust objectives, ensures all access is appropriate, managed, and documented, regardless of how the perimeter has been redefined. Zero trust should never introduce a burden to the end user or administrator. Finally, zero trust needs to be applied everywhere, from cloud to endpoint, in order to be successful. This is why defining a common office environment (COE) for zero trust is critically important for mitigating cloud attack vectors.

For information technology professionals and facility administrators, a common office environment (COE) is a term that governs the common features, technology, consumables, and security present in an office environment. This can include everything from desks, staplers, printers, cameras, paper, pens, computers, and software. The range of items will vary per company and vertical, but the terminology is very important as we continue to embark on digital transformations and work-from-anywhere initiatives.

When we consider that an office is not the only location to conduct work, we quickly realize that our COE for desktops and monitors has changed. Many organizations have embraced laptops, notebooks, and tablets as the computing technology of choice to support a COE, but the security and operational software has seen a much more pronounced change. This is simply due to the ability to stay "nearly" always connected and that trusted work and workloads need to operate outside of the traditional office perimeter. Our primary security controls of firewalls, intrusion prevention, network segmentation, and wired network security are no longer the primary method of managing technology in a COE. Organizations must adapt their security controls to home networks and even public Wi-Fi.

So, how does this affect the COE? Probably in ways that you are only now considering as permanent changes. First, what is the best way to provide technology management for users in our new COE? As the COVID-19 pandemic continues to impact organizations, organizations have shifted management technologies to the cloud to facilitate always-on management of devices. This eliminates the need to utilize VPN for every remote employee, the redesign of security management solutions to make them available via a DMZ, or high-risk Internet-exposed services, like remote access. The simple fact is that our new COE has embraced the cloud for device and identity management, and that gives us our first step: management of any asset regardless of its location.

A modern COE embraces the cloud and now leaves us with a second consideration, how to make it actually work? For starters, consider the primary seven tenants of zero trust again from Table 9-1. In our new COE, this translates into a few characteristics our technology management model should now facilitate:

- We have a broad new category called assets. All technology is logically grouped underneath. This follows an ITIL and asset management approach by classifying hardware, software, applications, and other technology into appropriate logical groups that can be managed and measured for risk. This hierarchy is important since the risk to software impacts the device and, therefore, impacts any user operating the device. Risk calculations needed for other portions of zero trust honor this inheritance model.

- Regardless of their location, all communication is always secured and encrypted. The model for communications and appropriate network security should always be in a high security state, and it does not change based on location or network.

379

- Access to any other resource is granted per session and is not persistent. Session access is always continuously evaluated to ensure appropriate intent. Most of the time, this is based on behavioral modeling.

- Devices are hardened, patched, and verified to be in a persistent secure state to resist attacks. Changes in security posture or missing security patches should influence the risk model used for authentication.

- Authentication and authorization are continuously assessed and changes in characteristics should dynamically alter policy and even session activity, if the results are considered undesirable.

- To make all appropriate decisions mentioned previously, data from accounts, applications, the environment, device, etc., all should be collected and analyzed to help calculate a risk score used for authentication and appropriate behavior. This collection and modeling should be done as close to real time as possible to minimize threats.

Our new COE for technology (and security) management in the cloud is ideal to model after zero trust. And, based on the cloud technology and management of resources, some solutions, products, and even tools will adapt more easily than others to this model. For example, a cloud-based solution that does not use local agents on the endpoints will be more difficult to monitor for appropriate behavior, to ensure secure communications, and to provide authorization, at a granular level. This will fall short compared to something that is implemented with agents that can extend functionality to cover the tenants of zero trust.

In addition, not all cloud solutions are built with security in mind. Communications, log storage, and even honoring least privilege can hinder a solution's ability to meet all of the tenets for security best practices. This includes the capability to handle on-premise workloads, from the cloud, and support users and operations wherever they may reside. These controls adhere to the foundational definition of zero trust to remove the perimeter and network security controls from being the primary method used to secure resources.

Consider how the seven tenets of zero trust from NIST 800-207 map to enterprise technology used in a COE. This is illustrated in Table 9-2.

Table 9-2. *Sections of NIST 800-207 Zero Trust mapped to enterprise technology*

Section(s)(NIST 800-207)	Enterprise Technology Requirements for Zero Trust							
	Secure Privileged Accounts	Least Privilege	Application Control	Remote Access	Network Devices and IoT	Virtualization and Cloud	DevOps	Third-Party Integrations
2.1 Tenets of Zero Trust								
1. All data sources and computing services are considered assets.	X	X						
2. All communication is secured regardless of network location.								
3. Access to individual enterprise resources is granted on a per session basis.				X	X	X	X	X
4. Access to resources is determined by dynamic policy.								
5. The enterprise monitors and measures the integrity and security posture of all owned and associated assets.								
6. All resource authentication and authorization are dynamic and strictly enforced before access is allowed.								
7. The enterprise collects as much information as possible about the current state of assets, network infrastructure, and communications and uses it to improve its security posture.								

2.2 Zero-Trust View of a Network

1. The entire enterprise private network is not considered an implicit trust zone.   X   X   X   X   X

2. Devices on the network may not be owned or configurable by the enterprise.   X   X   X

3. No asset is inherently trusted.

4. Not all enterprise resources are on enterprise-owned infrastructure.

5. Remote enterprise subjects and assets cannot fully trust their local network connection.

6. Assets and workflows moving between enterprise and non-enterprise infrastructure should have a consistent security policy and posture.

(continued)

Table 9-2. (*continued*)

Section(s)(NIST 800-207)	Enterprise Technology Requirements for Zero Trust							
	Secure Privileged Accounts	Least Privilege	Application Control	Remote Access	Network Devices and IoT	Virtualization and Cloud	DevOps	Third-Party Integrations
Section 3. Logical Components of Zero-Trust Architecture documents the logical components, or building blocks, of ZT. It is possible that unique implementations compose ZTA components differently yet serve the same logical functionality. • Core components: Policy engine (PE), policy administrator (PA), policy enforcement point (PEP) • Additional components: Continuous Diagnostics and Mitigation (CDM) System, Industry Compliance System, Threat Intelligence Feed(s), Network and System Activity Logs, Data Access Policies, Enterprise Public Key Infrastructure (PKI), ID Management System, Security Information and Events Management (SIEM) System	X	X		X	X	X		

(continued)

Section 3.1. Variations of Zero-Trust Architecture Approaches	X	X		X	X
3.1.1 ZTA Using Enhanced Identity Governance					
3.1.2 ZTA Using Microsegmentation					
3.1.3 ZTA Using Network Infrastructure and Software-Defined Perimeters					
Section 3.2. Deployed Variations of the Abstract Architecture	X	X	X		
3.2.1 Device Agent/Gateway Deployment					
3.2.2 Enclave-Based Deployment					
3.2.3 Resource Portal-Based Deployment					
3.2.4 Device Application Sandboxing					
Section 3.3. Trust Algorithm	X	X	X	X	X
• Access request					
• Subject database and history					
• Asset database					
• Resource policy requirements					
• Threat intelligence and logs					
3.3.1 Trust Algorithm Variations					
• Criteria vs. score based					
• Singular vs. contextual					

Table 9-2. (*continued*)

Section(s)(NIST 800-207)	Enterprise Technology Requirements for Zero Trust							
	Secure Privileged Accounts	Least Privilege	Application Control	Remote Access	Network Devices and IoT	Virtualization and Cloud	DevOps	Third-Party Integrations
Section 3.4. Network/Environment Components	X	X	X	X		X		
There should be a separation (logical or possibly physical) of the communication flow used to perform the actual work of the organization.								
Network requirements to support ZTA								
• Enterprise assets have basic network connectivity.								
• The enterprise must be able to distinguish between what assets are owned/managed by the enterprise and devices' current security posture.								
• The enterprise can observe all network traffic.								
• Enterprise resources should not be reachable without accessing a PEP.								
• Data plane and control plane are logically separate.								

- Enterprise assets can reach the PEP component.
- The PEP is the only component that accesses the policy administrator as part of a business flow.
- Remote enterprise assets should be able to access enterprise resources without needing to traverse enterprise network infrastructure first.
- The infrastructure used to support ZTA access decision process should be made scalable to account for changes in process load.
- Enterprise assets may not be able to reach certain PEPs due to policy or observable factors.

(continued)

Table 9-2. (*continued*)

Section(s)(NIST 800-207)	Enterprise Technology Requirements for Zero Trust							
	Secure Privileged Accounts	Least Privilege	Application Control	Remote Access	Network Devices and IoT	Virtualization and Cloud	DevOps	Third-Party Integrations
Section 4. Deployment Scenarios/Use Cases Lists some possible use cases where a ZTA may make enterprise environments more secure and less prone to successful exploitation. These include enterprises with remote employees, cloud services, and guest networks.	X	X	X	X	X	X	X	X
4.1 Enterprise with Satellite Facilities								
4.2 Multicloud/Cloud-to-Cloud Enterprise								
4.3 Enterprise with Contracted Services								
4.4 Collaboration Across Enterprise Boundaries								
4.5 Enterprise with Public- or Customer-Facing Services								

Section 5. Threats Associated with Zero-Trust Architecture   X   X   X   X   X   X   X

Discusses threats to an enterprise using a ZTA. Many of these threats are similar to any architected networks but may require different mitigation techniques.

5.1 Subversion of ZTA Decision Process

5.2 Denial of Service or Network Disruption

5.3 Stolen Credentials/Insider Threat

5.4 Visibility on the Network

5.5 Storage of System and Network Information

5.6 Reliance on Proprietary Data Formats or Solutions

5.7 Use of Non-person Entities (NPE) in ZTA Administration

(continud)

389

Table 9-2. (*continued*)

Section(s)(NIST 800-207)	Enterprise Technology Requirements for Zero Trust							
	Secure Privileged Accounts	Least Privilege	Application Control	Remote Access	Network Devices and IoT	Virtualization and Cloud	DevOps	Third-Party Integrations
Section 6. Zero-Trust Architecture and Possible Interactions with Existing Federal Guidance	X	X	X	X	X	X	X	X
Discusses how ZTA tenets fit into and/or complement existing guidance for federal agencies.								
6.1 ZTA and NIST RISK Management Framework								
6.2 Zero Trust and NIST Privacy Framework								
6.3 ZTA and Federal Identity, Credential, and Access Management Architecture								
6.4 ZTA and Trusted Internet Connections 3.0								
6.5 ZTA and EINSTEIN (NCPS – Nation Cybersecurity Protection System)								
6.6 ZTA and DHS Continuous Diagnostics and Mitigations (CDM) Program								
6.7 ZTA, Cloud Smart, and Federal Data Strategy								

A COE is a valuable model to establish a baseline for the operations in an office environment and for employees working remotely. In the last two years, the COE for every business has changed significantly due to the pandemic and initiatives like digital transformation. Establishing the cloud as a baseline for any new technology to be deployed is a sound decision that can accommodate workers who are operating from anywhere. When coupled with zero trust, individual use cases and solutions can excel in security and the management paradigms they provide. Consider zero trust as an architecture to solve many of the security concerns you may have in the cloud – not only for business applications but also to securely support the end user.

Cloud-Native

Moving to the cloud can entail a lift-and-shift effort that migrates existing on-premise solutions to the cloud, which, as we have described earlier, is referred to as "cloud washing." Cloud-washed products are not optimized to take advantage of modern cloud architectures, services, and resources, and they certainly are not optimized for consumption-based cost modeling. In many cases, cloud-washed deployments suffer from scalability, security, and fault-tolerance issues, since the cloud lacks the components that would have made them successful on-premise. To solve these problems, some organizations choose to (re)write their applications from scratch or develop new, cloud-native technology that is built in the cloud, for the cloud.

Cloud-native computing is an approach in software architecture and development that utilizes the unique traits and services in the cloud to develop, deploy, and execute scalable applications in modern, dynamic environments, such as public and private clouds. This approach utilizes many of the concepts we have been discussing, such as containers, microservices, serverless functions, and immutable infrastructure. These techniques enable loosely coupled systems that are resilient, manageable, and discernible. Combined with automation and DevOps, cloud-native technology allows developers to make high-impact changes frequently and predictably using development philosophies, like Agile and Scrum, as opposed to legacy approaches, like Waterfall.

The million-dollar question for cloud-native technology as an attack vector mitigation strategy lies within the first few sentences of this section. If your on-premise technology is moved to the cloud, what security challenges do you have, and what are you potentially exposing on the Internet that was previously secured on-premise behind firewalls, access control lists, and intrusion detection systems? More often than not, the answer to that question is simply unacceptable to the business.

Consider legacy applications that may contain end-of-life components or require strict change control schedules, just to apply security updates without accompanying downtime. When organizations begin to audit these risks, a conclusion to "redo" the application becomes more viable based on the quantity and severity of these challenges. The biggest drawback is time to market and cost to develop the application, but those can be offset if the mission is just not achievable with existing technology.

Starting from scratch or developing all new solutions to be cloud native, even if you self-host them in a private or hybrid cloud, will help ensure they are better enabled for the future. It is kind of like buying an electric car vs. a gas guzzler that has no benefits based on its design, features, or even performance. Therefore, evaluate these action items to determine whether to build or rebuild your applications as cloud native, rather than simply cloud washing your current solutions:

- If the application has a limited set of users, has a very predictable workflow and minimal risk surface, cloud washing is generally acceptable.

- If the application cannot scale to meet business needs when moved to the cloud, consider rewriting portions (hybrid) or all of it to be cloud native.

- Determine how much downtime is acceptable for the solution over a given time period due to maintenance or security updates. If the downtime is unacceptable to the end-user community, consider moving all, or portions of it, to a cloud-native architecture and codebase.

- Mission-critical functions for high availability, scalability, and disaster recovery have different architectures from on-premise to the cloud. If you cloud wash your application, can you maintain the same service-level agreements as before for all of these items? If not, a cloud-native approach may be required.

- If your application was previously virtualized using a definable set of containers or virtual machines, cloud washing may be acceptable as a simple lift and shift.

- Consider the runtime costs of cloud washing a solution vs. modernization of the same application. Development costs, in many cases, can be offset by the savings in monthly runtime paid to a cloud service provider.

- One of the hardest decisions in going cloud native is selecting technology stacks that will be supported in the future and, most importantly, for which your organization can find developers to support the platform. Choosing a cloud technology just because it is "the best" is not necessarily always optimal, if finding resources to maintain and develop it will cost more than utilizing a mainstream solution. Therefore, measure the usage of a technology and its road map so you do not get locked into a cloud-native solution that will ultimately not be supportable.

- A cloud-native solution will have different cloud attack vectors than a cloud-washed solution. Make sure your security basics – identity, vulnerability, patch, and privileged access management — are implemented to handle cloud-native technologies. This is one area where a lift and shift can leave significant gaps, if the appropriate investment is overlooked.

- Consider developing and testing using modern approaches, as well as using Agile, Swarm Intelligence, Chaos Engineering, Artificial Intelligence (covered earlier in the book), etc., to ensure the best possible security and resiliency for your cloud-native solution.

Cloud-native architectures represent the next generation of technology when moving to the cloud. However, a cloud-native architecture may not always be the right path, or even feasible. When innovation is needed and costs can be managed, there can be clear business advantages from a cloud-native approach. Many of the household names we associate with the cloud today embraced the starting over approach, but still suffer from the cloud attack vectors we have already discussed. Cloud-native does not always equate to security.

Hybrid

There is very little public discussion behind why a hybrid cloud architecture would be a good design to mitigate cloud attack vectors. Before we dig in, it is important to understand what is meant by a hybrid cloud implementation. First, it should not be confused with multicloud. Multicloud architectures utilize multiple cloud service providers to deliver a solution. Hybrid cloud architectures can be multicloud, but they have distinct components that are located on-premise in a traditional data center or colocation. The reasons to keep components on-premise include, but they certainly are not limited to:

- Securing sensitive or personally identifiable information in a specific data store or database that is unequivocally monitored and controlled.

- Supporting a legacy component that is not easy or cost effective to move to the cloud or virtualize.

- Security controls for an architectural component require special considerations that are not available in the cloud, including physical access.

- Support for availability on-premise and in the cloud without the dependencies of the Internet for local access.

- Components that use excessive bandwidth that would be cost prohibitive to move to the cloud based on a consumption pricing model.

Once an organization has established that some components (typically, a database or mainframe) will remain on-premise, then the focus of securing access to it becomes a textbook access control list implementation. Local connectivity comes from trusted workstations, users, and administrators; direct access is segmented or zoned to the cloud. Only specific middleware is authorized to communicate, and access control lists are applied to prevent lateral movement. This can include a CASB (Cloud Access Service Broker) to monitor and manage cloud network traffic, if needed. To help prevent an attack in the cloud, or on-premise, from navigating to additional components in either environment, no secrets should be shared between assets.

From a regulatory compliance and security perspective, a hybrid architecture can have significant benefits:

- Data mapping requirements for regulatory compliance can ensure sensitive and personally identifiable information is stored in a known electronic and physical location.

- For regional data privacy laws, the geolocation of critical information at rest can be positively identified, including any backups.

- Data and sensitive systems are under the organization's control for encryption and data loss prevention, as opposed to a third party, like the cloud service provider.

- Only authorized requests and data can egress the environment to the cloud-hosted application.

- Physical security for access to assets that house sensitive information remains in control of the organization, and not the cloud service provider.

Based on these security and regulatory compliance benefits, organizations may choose a hybrid cloud architecture simply to maintain compliance with geolocation privacy laws. Having possession of critical components for a solution like the primary database (on-premise) also allows for explicit control, even during a security breach. As an example, if data is actively being exfiltrated and the organization has lost control of the system that controls data flow in the cloud, then a breach cannot be easily stopped. On-premise, pulling a network cable is always an option.

Ephemeral Implementations

One of the largest challenges with solutions in the cloud is the persistent nature of secrets when linked to accounts, instances, and privileges. If the secret is static, then an attack can be leveraged against a cloud asset, just like knowing the credentials for single-factor authentication. One of the best strategies for solving this problem is to make the risk surface ephemeral. That is, make all the components time based and limit access based on duration, time of day, and simultaneous account usage based on both time and duration. This is more than just stating that access is limited by a unit of time, but rather, components needed for authentication and authorization may not even be created or enabled until the conditions, based on time, are met. This is a key design decision when architecting solutions in the cloud and a modern best practice that can significantly lower the risk surface. If ephemeral attributes occur at a rapid rate, consider real-time logging and monitoring to account for all changes, and determine if they are appropriate. If you do not, a threat actor may take advantage of these rapid changes and model their attack between monitoring windows and go undetected.

Secrets

As we previously have discussed, secrets can be anything from a password to a key. If the secret is not static and is not known, the risk surface can be significantly lowered. To achieve this goal, most organizations implement privileged access management (PAM) solutions. These solutions are capable of managing secrets by:

- Frequently changing secrets and ensuring the complexity is humanly difficult to read, write, and remember

- Ensuring secrets are only available in accordance with time-based policies for access by privileged users

- Randomizing secrets after any usage to limit the amount of time they are exposed

- Maintaining a history of secrets, just in case a backup of the asset is restored and access is needed

Dynamic (or ephemeral) secret management is only one component for architecting better security in the cloud. Next, consider how it can be linked to accounts.

Accounts

A secret is irrelevant unless a user or threat actor knows which account to apply it to. So, if we make the secrets ephemeral, why can't we make the account itself ephemeral, too? The simple answer is, yes you can, and the concept is typically referred to as "just in time." To make accounts ephemeral, the account itself should not be static nor enabled for authentication. This leads us to a few techniques that can make accounts ephemeral:

- The account itself is created only for the duration it is needed and then deleted.

- The account exists, but is disabled. It is enabled only for the duration it is needed and then is instantly disabled.

- The account exists and is dynamically moved into a logic group for access or privileges for the duration it is needed.

- A privileged access management solution is utilized on the endpoint to elevate privileges based on policy, enforcing ephemeral usage at runtime.

When the account and secret are ephemeral, a high degree of confidence can be applied to any form of user or machine account access request. Of course, users should not be allowed, at their own discretion, to follow this workflow without monitoring and without the implementation of a change control process that will document when an account has been utilized. In other words, only authorized users and machines can access ephemeral accounts, and when this occurs, a full audit trail should be available to prove usage was appropriate.

Instances

One of the architectural benefits of the cloud is the ability to start up and tear down assets rapidly for scalability and security. When instances are created from templates or dynamically built using DevOps pipelines, they can be destroyed and replaced, if any tampering or indicators of compromise are present. For many organizations with rapid development cycles, this makes instances ephemeral and, potentially, an architecture to embrace as mitigation against cloud attack vectors. Let's explore why and remember our discussions on lateral movement.

Successful penetration in any environment typically requires lateral movement through assets. A threat actor will establish a beachhead on a number of assets to probe and continue their penetration as a part of the attack chain. If the assets they compromise are refreshed, renamed, given new secrets, and patched on a frequent basis, the ability for a threat actor to maintain persistence is greatly diminished. This, in itself, hinders lateral movement, until the endpoints are exploited again (if that is even possible).

As an architectural best practice in the cloud, consider making your instances (assets) ephemeral. Allow them to be created, torn down, refreshed, and to have new secrets applied on a regular basis to mitigate threats. Any previous exploitation is simply erased, and the threat actor has to start over.

The biggest risk to this approach is if a threat actor has compromised your templates, source code libraries, or DevOps pipelines. Then, the threat actor's persistent presence is actually being created by you each time a new instance is deployed. This, unfortunately, has happened recently with SolarWinds and Kaseya, and the solutions they market were leveraged against their clients. This was discussed in detail when we covered third-party supply-chain attacks. While this attack vector is beyond the control of an end user, organizations that develop software should be mindful of these risks so that they do not provide a backdoor for attackers into their customers' environments.

Privileges

Managing privileges using ephemeral techniques is similar to just-in-time (JIT) account management. The primary goal is to eliminate persistent privileged access (also called, "standing privileges") wherever possible. Consider the following for managing privileges on an account using an ephemeral/just-in-time access approach:

- The desired task is executed with low privileges, and based on policy, the application is elevated using RunAs, Sudo, or a vendor proprietary technique.

- The application being executed is modified before execution to include a one-time privileged token that elevates the application in the kernel to a higher privilege. This is generally associated with patented technology from a privileged access management vendor.

- Based on the account and the specified task, privileges are added and removed only for the duration that is needed, by integrating into the application or operating system.

Managing privileges in accordance with a just-in-time access model is one of the best ways to enforce least privileged operations in a cloud environment. Under this model, no account has privileged access unless approved and a predefined workflow has been satisfied. If you combine this technique with ephemeral account management, a best-in-class strategy can be developed for any, and all, account-based authentication in the cloud. Finally, when coupled with multi-factor authentication, even if the workflow is compromised, the threats can be reduced due to the layers of security controls that have been designed to complement each other. Identity and privileged based attacks can be drastically diminished, and only vulnerabilities, exploits, misconfigurations, and poor hardening could allow an entry point for an attack.

CHAPTER 10

Swarm Intelligence

The motion of bees, ants, and other insects looking for food and protecting their colony from attacks involves complex peer-to-peer communications, with no centralized command and control. Insects use a variety of communication methods – from auditory sounds to chemicals to transmit messages to peers – to convey a message and spread information about a situation. Once the message is passed and acknowledged (in some form) by others in the "swarm," a decentralized mission is formed to manage the situation.

Based on the reaction of just one insect in the swarm and the passing of messages to others in a peer-to-peer fashion, an entire environment can react without the need of a central leader processing data and giving orders. This is a foreign concept to most people, who are accustomed to a hierarchical structure of authority. However, this swarm intelligence concept is crucial to understanding a potential modern approach to cybersecurity.

In the last few years, the world has embraced broad-scale digital transformation, with migration and deployments to the cloud as an engine for these advancements. This evolution has led to an explosion of Internet and cloud-enabled devices. The use cases for these IoT devices range from personal digital assistants to home appliances.

In 1989, the term swarm intelligence was coined by Gerardo Beni and Jing Wang applying basic artificial intelligence models to self-organized and decentralized systems. Then, in 2019, researchers at Glasgow

Caledonian University and COMSATS University in Pakistan[1] developed an innovative model that could potentially protect the Internet and cloud resources from cyberattacks. The attack method was presented at the IEEE's China Emerging Technologies Conference and is derived from an Artificial Bee Colony (ABC) and a Random Neural Network (RNN). Figure 10-1 represents the basics of this algorithm.

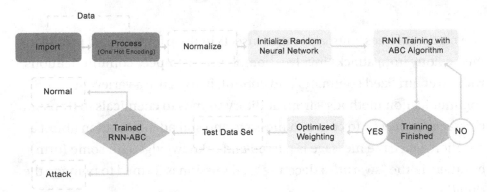

Figure 10-1. *Simplified Artificial Bee Colony and Random Neural Network processing algorithm*

To mitigate IoT cloud threats, an ABC algorithm is a swarm intelligence model that uses AI to simulate the searching behavior of honeybees and applies the concepts to solve real-world computational problems. To make this model work, an RNN is applied to the ABC model using machine learning that is based on the behavior of biological neural networks in the human brain.

"In this paper, an anomaly-based intrusion detection scheme is proposed that can protect sensitive information and detect novel cyber-attacks," the researchers authored in their paper. "The artificial bee colony (ABC) algorithm is used to train the random neural network (RNN) based system (RNN-ABC)."

---

[1] https://ieeexplore.ieee.org/abstract/document/8881840

The researchers trained their intrusion detection model based on ABC and RNN using a dataset that established algorithms to detect a cyberattack and contain a large quantity of Internet traffic data for training and analysis. After priming their RNN-ABC, the researchers carried out a sequence of assessments to measure its performance in identifying and quantifying cyberattacks. The research produced findings that classified new attacks with an astonishing accuracy of 91.65%. The researchers also concluded that the model's accuracy in classifying cyberattacks was greater when the "colony" size of its ABC swarm intelligence was larger. Therefore, the more "artificial bees" contributing to the model, the higher the overall confidence in the solution.

Today, IoT devices are proliferating and present on the Internet and connecting to the cloud. Can we realistically use these IoT devices as a part of the swarm to identify a potential threat and ultimately mitigate the risk?

First, and most importantly, swarm intelligence needs a large colony size to enable devices that can communicate information and process relevant data for the swarm, as opposed to just network traffic alone. With the increasing presence of IoT devices that have a simple behavioral model, this is possible. Second, we need a mesh-style Internet protocol that allows a reliable method for the devices to communicate and provide information to the ABC-RNN model and each other. At the time of the writing of this book, such a large-scale peer-to-peer protocol does not exist – yet. Third, the ABC and RNN model needs rules, policies, and output that can classify any findings into human-readable results.[2] TAXII (Trusted Automated Exchange of Intelligence Information) has begun to embrace and address this type of problem, but it falls short for peer-to-peer communications at scale (requirement number two). Finally, we need to consider cloud security for this model. The trust of data being processed in the model must be reliable and accurate or the entire system can be abused and undermined.

---

[2] www.oasis-open.org/2021/06/23/stix-v2-1-and-taxii-v2-1-oasis-standards-are-published/

The purpose of swarm intelligence is to create a new method for determining the risk of cyberattacks. This concept, using something new, innovative, and potentially highly reliable, is what today's increasingly complex cloud environments need for protection.

While you consider the protection you need for the cloud, sometimes you need to think outside the box. Swarm intelligence is just one potential method, and realistically, if you read this book ten years after publishing, this might be the de facto method for protecting the cloud and IoT devices.

CHAPTER 11

Chaos Engineering

If you are old enough to remember the television show *Get Smart*,[1] you may be familiar with the concept of applying chaos to provide order. While this spy show spoof mocked political stereotypes of the time for control vs. chaos, the slapstick humor was designed to highlight the differences between a world with and without order. In some cases, chaos definitely seemed like the better alternative. So, what does *Get Smart* have to do with chaos engineering? Sometimes, chaos is the key ingredient for us to put the world in perspective and to better understand and make key discoveries about how complex systems operate and how they are vulnerable.

Chaos engineering is the concept of experimenting on a resource with the goal of building confidence in the resource's capability to tolerate unpredictable circumstances during operations. It's sort of like a more sophisticated version of having a monkey throw a wrench into a complex machine and seeing what happens. In fact, Netflix, which popularized the concept of chaos engineering, monikered their chaos-making tool "Chaos Monkey."

The cloud, digital transformation, and the massive use and dependency on software have truly changed our lives. Businesses have developed millions of lines of code in a short period of time (ten years or so), and it begs the question of resiliency and security for the solutions we have put into production.

---

[1] https://en.wikipedia.org/wiki/Get_Smart

© Morey J. Haber, Brian Chappell, Christopher Hills 2022
M. J. Haber et al., *Cloud Attack Vectors*, https://doi.org/10.1007/978-1-4842-8236-6_11

Today, the number of applications deployed in the cloud is mind boggling. These applications were developed by many thousands of different vendors, the open source community, and in diverse locations. How can we ensure these applications and systems will operate correctly when other security, scalability, and environmental issues become unpredictable? After all, who knows what the next attack vector or cause of an outage will be?

Our world grows more digital by the day. From industrial IoT to wearables, every scrap of our reality is being digitized. As the Internet is built into almost anything and everything in our lives, real-world events (i.e., pandemics, natural disasters, etc.) and cybersecurity threats can have a significant impact on these production environments in ways humans cannot always easily anticipate. Even advanced simulation software is not great at predicting potential second- and third-order effects of unanticipated events. The resolutions to return stability may not always be well understood. After all, you cannot just reboot the cloud like your personal computer. The results for the cloud could be distributed in nature, affecting all the different components in unpredicted ways. Hence, chaos and not control.

To understand the problem across the entire environment, the risk surface itself must be understood and the potential outcomes established – from data corruption to denial of service. This encompasses everything from attack vectors to collateral outages that could cause a localized issue or a cascading failure, including the inability to access resources needed to ultimately resolve the issue. Once the potential outcomes are uncovered via testing and are understood, you can embark on the process of remediation. The weakest issues must be addressed first, especially for single points of failure, all the way through complex issues that have a likelihood of occurring that could impact service-level agreements, customer satisfaction, or other stated missions. The goal is ultimately to improve the stability of, and confidence in, cloud solutions.

Based on a potential empirical (albeit cynical) approach to cybersecurity, chaos engineering allows for testing of cloud resources based on a controlled environment, in production, while testing the system based on realistic conditions, including attacks, outages, and other forms of corruption (chaos). The outcome demonstrates what could really happen, and what will happen, when the control of a predictable cloud resource is stressed and jeopardy and chaos are introduced. This is in strong contrast to the controlled testing generally done by quality assurance.

Implemented with care and diligence, chaos engineering can be a powerful tool for facilitating experiments that uncover systemic weaknesses in a controlled production environment. Chaos engineering's potential to tackle the insecurity of distributed systems in the cloud at scale is unique and unparalleled.

These experiments typically can be broken into five steps:

1.   Start by defining "normal operations" as some measurable output of the environment that indicates proper and expected behavior. This will be your control group as opposed to your chaos engineering test group.

2.   Hypothesize that these "normal operations" will continue in both the control group and the chaos experimental group. These are your best educated guesses as to what will happen.

3.   Design the experiment to include individual tests, combinations of tests, and a mix of manual and automated steps. This will help you develop resolution plans when they occur in the real world.

4. Introduce attacks, changes, outages, hardware failures, virtual machine (VM) and instance failures, etc., that reflect real-world events to measure in the cloud. Collect the results.

5. Document the performance of the system and expected availability when comparing the control group vs. the chaos engineering test group. This will help you engineer remediation and apply the solution to avoid any future undesirable results.

The workflow in Figure 11-1 defines the steps for chaos engineering.

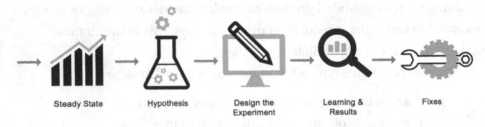

Steadyeady State   Hypothesis   Design the   Learning &   Fixes
                                          Experiment   Results

Figure 11-1. *Five steps to a successful chaos engineering implementation*

The primary goal is to make it very hard to deviate from the expected steady state of normal operations and to create predictable behavior from the system when chaotic events are introduced standalone or in conjunction with each other.

The following five recommendations provide the best practices for chaos engineering implementations. The recommendations correlate to the confidence of your testing and remediation plans to resolve any identified issues.

1. **Model Normal Operational Behavior:** Focus on the measurable output of the system, such as streaming video. Also, make sure to include internal

system metrics, such as CPU consumption, error rates, network latency, etc. All these metrics could model normal steady-state behavior. By focusing on systemic changes during experiments, chaos engineering verifies that the system is working as expected, as opposed to trying to validate how it works.

2. **Model Real Issues**: To provide value, chaos engineering requires the input of attacks, outages, and other issues that reflect real-world events – even if such events seem to have a low potential likelihood. It is very important to prioritize testing criteria by risk and other priorities relevant to the business. Even though you are testing in the cloud, consider events that correspond to an instance failure, VM outage, software failure, network outage, denial of service, malformed traffic, vulnerabilities, etc., that could occur. Any test capable of disrupting the normal operations is a potential candidate for a chaos engineering experiment.

3. **Experiments in Production**: Performing these experiments in production based on defined tests is critical to derive value from chaos engineering. Cloud resources will absolutely behave differently in development, test, quality assurance, and production environments. Since real-world operations can truly change at any time, the product environment is critical to the success of this method.

4. **Automation**: Running experiments manually is
   labor intensive and, eventually, unsustainable for
   a chaos engineering project. The best way to tackle
   chaos engineering is to automate experiments and
   bind combinations of tests together to measure the
   impact when unlikely combinations are applied.
   The results will help prove what can be remediated
   as well as indicate what events or combinations of
   events may lead to unmitigable catastrophe.

5. **Controlling Chaos**: Experimenting in production
   has the potential to cause myriad problems, ranging
   from outages, performance degradation, corruption
   of data, and more. Such impacts will ultimately anger
   clients and users. Thus, consider limiting chaos
   engineering experiments to certain regions, clients,
   tenants, applications, instances, etc., and conduct
   them only during well-thought-out periods of time. A
   well-designed failover should also be in place.

As systems become ever more complex and interdependent, chaos
engineering is a valuable tool for uncovering vulnerabilities and potential
points of failure that are otherwise exceedingly difficult, if not impossible,
for humans to anticipate.

Chaos engineering can be implemented to further uncover risks of cloud
threat vectors by leveraging many standardized techniques (penetration
testing) against your environment. While other tests will address scalability
and resiliency, chaos engineering helps to address uncertainty in distributed
systems, when real-world events are applied in combination. The results
will provide confidence in your cloud implementation and properly test
the controls in place from your cloud service provider to help mitigate any
long-term outages or other security concerns. The goal is to get smarter (pun
intended) when implementing cloud solutions.

CHAPTER 12

Imposter Syndrome

If you listen to security podcasts, webinars, and panels, you probably have
come across the term "imposter syndrome." If you are not familiar with
the term, it is defined as a psychological pattern in which an individual
distrusts their abilities or accomplishments and has a persistent mental
fear of being exposed as a "fraud." Despite evidence of their capabilities
and knowledge, individuals experiencing this condition remain
convinced that they are scams and should not receive accolades for
their accomplishments. Individuals with imposter syndrome incorrectly
attribute their success to being lucky, attest their success to being a con
artist with faux intelligence, or believe that they have perpetrated a ruse
over other individuals.

Imposter syndrome is very real in technology communities, and it has
come into focus in cybersecurity communities because it is impossible
for a single person to be a true expert in everything cybersecurity related.
Just like a medical doctor, a cybersecurity professional can have a broad
range of medical knowledge, but, in practice, they focus on one medical
discipline or another, like radiology or internal medicine.

You would not allow a general practitioner to perform open heart
surgery, just as you would not want a forensics expert performing the
network and operating system hardening of a new infrastructure. For
doctors, their skills and knowledge are monitored and tested at every step
along their medical journey. This creates reference points and a plan that
one must follow before becoming a physician of any type.

© Morey J. Haber, Brian Chappell, Christopher Hills 2022
M. J. Haber et al., *Cloud Attack Vectors*, https://doi.org/10.1007/978-1-4842-8236-6_12

For cybersecurity professionals, outside of a few industry standard certifications, there are no formal paths required to becoming a professional in the cybersecurity industry. In fact, many individuals excel at being experts without an ounce of formal training. They speak publicly, participate in panels, and have even written books without a single security certification or suffix attached to their name, like CISSP. This opens the question: when does someone become an expert in cybersecurity, and how do we overcome the self-doubt that leads to imposter syndrome?

We know a doctor is a doctor because they finished medical school and passed all the required exams to become accredited. How do we know someone is a cybersecurity professional and that they have proof to overcome the mental duress that causes imposter syndrome? From our perspective, a touch of self-doubt is healthy. It helps drive you harder to ensure you are an expert in your area of concentration and truly an expert to the best of your abilities. Depression, however, is a killer. If you are feeling low, uncertain, and have low self-esteem, the results can be devastating. When you exhibit signs of self-doubt and depression together, in our opinion, you have the traits necessary to exhibit imposter syndrome. In all the years I have worked in cybersecurity (20+ now), I have never met anyone suffering from imposter syndrome who was not also depressed.

Unfortunately, outside of a person's personal opinion about themselves, imposter syndrome has another, more modern effect on individuals. It is when others have branded you an "imposter." This syndrome is the personification of another person's prejudice or jealousy to label someone else as an imposter. It is the accuser's disbelief that the victim could actually achieve the results they obtained, and the accuser is labeling them a fraud, creating self-doubt, to undermine their work or mental well-being in lieu of celebrating their success. This is the most serious set of circumstances for someone who is susceptible to imposter syndrome. And, based on the recent discussions I have seen on panels, webinars, and chats, this practice occurs quite frequently to discredit the speaker (expert). When it does occur, the accuser is truly the one with esteem issues – not the speaker!

Imposter syndrome is an actual condition affecting cybersecurity professionals. One version is self-induced and the other instigated based on malicious intent.

Some cases of impostor syndrome can be effectively managed or cured with personal mental health improvement. However, in cases where an individual's credibility is being unduly and maliciously attacked or undermined, that's when it's important for the cybersecurity community to step up and provide support to others. While this may sound controversial, negative attacks should not be allowed to go unchecked, and actions could easily include deleting negative demeaning posts, blocking the user or even respectful constructive responses to the attack. Negative responses to an attack just play into the accuser's game and should always be avoided. Always take the high road when responding to an attacker, and remember, your results are your own. If you are honest with yourself, self-reflective, humble, and periodically seek out the counsel of your peers, you can avoid imposter syndrome, or at least recover from it.

So, what does this have to do with cloud security? If you consider how new the cloud is and how fast and broad innovation is happening, it is impossible to know everything about it. There truly is no one that is an expert regarding "everything" cloud. Choose your discipline in the cloud, become an expert for that component, and accept that if someone accuses you of being an imposter, or if you have guilt of your own, it more than certainly is unfounded.

And just for the record, the authors of this book are not experts in the cloud. However, we do have high confidence in our knowledge of cloud attack vectors and how to mitigate them. If you don't believe us, please start reading this book again. This is not "Yesterday's Enterprise" in *Star Trek: TNG*.

CHAPTER 13

Selecting a Cloud Service Provider

Digital transformation is more than just moving things to the cloud and externalizing assets and resources for more flexible consumption. Choosing your cloud service provider as a partner is almost like a marriage. The intent is to be in the relationship for the long haul, and they never should be selected as a one-byte (night) stand. The selection itself is crucial to your success. If you consider we only covered a few major players in the space and the attack vectors that plague all of them, the truth is that there are myriad differences, such as geolocations, financials, services, support, and legal terms, to name a few, that differ between them all and that apply to both small and larger providers.

Before you can successfully select a cloud service provider, you need to understand your business requirements. While this may be obvious to most people, discussing it with your team and documenting your needs, service-level agreements, and minimum expectations before searching for a provider are crucial to your success.

Accepting the CSP boilerplate of features and services typically leads to gaps in your success criteria, and this could be devastating to your business if the risks, roles, and responsibilities are not well understood upfront. Therefore, when assessing potential cloud service providers, create a gradable checklist that compares your requirements to their services and that compares one provider against another. A sample of a cloud service provider questionnaire is available in Appendix B.

© Morey J. Haber, Brian Chappell, Christopher Hills 2022
M. J. Haber et al., *Cloud Attack Vectors*, https://doi.org/10.1007/978-1-4842-8236-6_13

With this in mind, consider the following traits to help you select a cloud service provider:

- **Certifications and Standards**: CSPs that comply with industry standards for quality and security demonstrate an adherence to the latest established best practices. At a minimum, your selection should have similar certifications and should adhere to equivalent standards at your own organization – or else the provider could become a liability.

- **Technology and Strategic Road Map**: The technology stack underpinning your cloud service provider selection should be aligned with your strategic direction. For example, if they have chosen an RDS (relational database service) as the primary data store and your applications use another, verify they can provide the support and services you need. This is also true for operating systems used in virtual machines, as well as any orchestration and automation that you will be developing against. A strategic road map discussion will help you determine what they can provide today and what is planned for the future.

- **Data Security, Data Privacy, Data Protection, and Data Governance**: Data management is often considered one of the biggest risks in the cloud. And while security, privacy, protection, and governance are all different, they all apply to the well-being of data. As a part of the vetting process, it is important to determine how the cloud service provider manages data and what security controls they use as a model to ensure data integrity. This includes everything from unauthorized access detection, encryption, data loss prevention, malware mitigation (including ransomware), and so on. Similar to certifications, the cloud service provider should have controls that are equal to or more stringent than your internal controls.

- **Operational Dependencies**: When licensing a service, we often overlook the people and technologies that provide that service in the first place. This includes vendors, subcontractors, and other licensed solutions that are incorporated into their offering. If your business has strict requirements around employee citizenship, outsourcing of sensitive information, and export restrictions, please consider any service and operational dependencies as a part of your selection criteria.

- **Technology and Business Partnerships**: Cloud service providers are like CISOs – they tend to operate in herds. Cloud service providers tend to build technology and business relationships that differentiate themselves from other providers. In other words, one provider aligns with one vendor, and their competitor aligns with another. In rare cases, a third-party vendor aligns and services everyone. When selecting your cloud service provider, consider who they partner with for foundational technology in all major disciplines, like IAM, IGA, PAM, VM, PM, and SIEM, or if these stacks are native only to their offerings.

- **Contractual Terms and Pricing**: Most cloud service providers prefer to use their own paper (their boilerplate contract) for onboarding and servicing a new vendor. There is nothing wrong with this, but you must engage your legal team to review all the terms of the contract and ensure it meets your business requirements. If it does not, don't be afraid to mark it up with corrections and send it back. Simple changes will typically be accepted. On the other hand, without asking, you may be bound to services and reporting (especially around security) that are not acceptable to your business and your clients.

- **Service-Level Agreements (SLA)**: Cloud service providers will state a wide variety of SLAs in their marketing material and in their contracts. The truth is that they actually mean nothing unless there are credits or penalties associated with any violations. The SLA itself becomes just a metric or a goal with no accountability. Therefore, when reviewing any stated SLA, make sure there is some form of enforcement based on noncompliance and, most importantly, that the stated values are the minimum you are willing to provide your customers. For example, if the cloud service provider claims 99.9% availability, you cannot state to your own customers any higher. Unfortunately, this is a shell game that is rampant in the industry, when depending upon the cloud for your services.

- **Reliability and Performance**: All cloud service providers are different. Some have better infrastructure for auto-scaling, bursting, and adapting to performance requirements. Others are focused on providing services for virtual machines, hybrid environments, and workload migrations from on-premise. Only a few do both well and can provide reliability and performance across diverse geolocations. For example, can my services in the cloud perform the same in Europe and Asia, as in the North America? Understanding the fundamentals of your mission and how and where you plan to conduct business will help you build a model for the reliability and performance you will need.

- **Backup, Recovery, High Availability, and Disaster Recovery**: To achieve any realistic SLA for operations, the CSP must provide a robust platform to mitigate an outage from virtually any type of fault. It is in your best interest to ask questions around these services, as well as about the average time to recover based on a wide range of events, from accidental deletion all the way through a security breach. Do not assume just because you are in the cloud that these security disciplines don't matter anymore. The truth is they matter even more because the resources in the cloud are not yours. You are just licensing someone else's computers. Pulling a hard drive for data recovery is just not possible in the cloud.

- **Technology Stickiness (Vendor Lock In)**: One of the undocumented goals of every cloud service provider is to make their services and platform sticky. That is, to provide a technology stack and implementation that locks a buyer into their offerings, making it difficult, and potentially cost prohibitive, to change to another provider. While this may sound like a deceptive business practice, many times, it is marketed as a capability or feature only available within their cloud services. For example, if you choose Azure as your cloud service provider and develop an application using Microsoft Fabric Technology, you will not be able to easily migrate the application to another provider. This is true for any component, from a specialized RDS to an orchestration solution. When selecting a cloud service provider, consider how sticky your solution will become on that platform and what the effort and cost might be to migrate, or even host, on another cloud platform. Many organizations choose to build their solutions to be cloud-agnostic simply for this reason.

- **Business Viability**: What happens if your cloud service provider goes out of business? Unfortunately, this has happened in the past, and for many tier 2 and tier 3 providers with specialized services, this threat is real due to rising costs, competition, and even supply-chain challenges. If you choose a tier 2 or tier 3 provider based on specialty services, geolocation, etc., request an independent audit, and/or proof of viability, to ensure they will be able to continue providing you services. And consider a contingency plan just in case they do default. While this is never a pleasant conversation, selecting the right vendor does include reviewing the business viability, just as much as their technical capabilities.

- **Company and Cultural Match (Sales, Operations, and Technical Support)**: There is truth in that people who enjoy their jobs enjoy the people they are working with. Executive relationships and a culture match among rank-and-file employees is important to ensuring that all aspects of the business relationship are operating as one team with a common goal. As a part of any cloud service provider selection, consider a trial period where various team members get to

meet and work with their counterparts. Personality
conflicts will always happen, but verifying teams can
communicate and work together from the start will go a
long way for the success of your cloud projects.

Selecting a cloud service provider is much more than pricing, region,
and support. While the technical questions in Appendix B may help
determine compatibility with your security model, the business and
operational terms are equally important. An RFP (Request for Proposal)
or an RFI (Request for Information) may be helpful to vet out the right
provider, even if they are not in the top 5. If there is any doubt in the
selection, leading analyst firms have a wealth of information and empirical
feedback to help resolve any ambiguity in cloud service provider selection.
Finally, remember that many of the XaaS solutions that you license are
probably operating on someone else's cloud. Therefore, any criteria
from the hosting CSP will probably be reflected through to the vendor
themselves and it is nearly impossible for them to offer anything different.
A good example is availability. An XaaS vendor can rarely offer a better SLA
for availability than the hosting vendor themselves.

CHAPTER 14

Security Recommendations for Your Cloud Environment

The cloud will not solve all of your computing problems, enable all of your future business initiatives, nor will it always save your business money. In many use cases, the cloud may be more expensive and be a trade-off in staffing skills that would support a legacy solution if cloud washed. Regulations, compliance, and security best practices will dictate how to proceed in the cloud, but implementing an end-to-end solution will require a secure architecture along with many of the mitigating controls discussed in this book.

In order to achieve a secure cloud environment, several key takeaways must be instilled within the organization. Without them, your protection of the cloud could potentially fail.

Cloud attack vectors represent some of the lowest-hanging fruit for today's threat actors. While architecting and securing any environment can be relatively complex, the cloud adds further layers and planes of complexity because, after all, they are not your computers. And remember, the more things change, the more they stay the same.

© Morey J. Haber, Brian Chappell, Christopher Hills 2022
M. J. Haber et al., *Cloud Attack Vectors*, https://doi.org/10.1007/978-1-4842-8236-6_14

These recommendations are not strictly for the cloud; many of them have their roots (pun intended) in what we know best. And finally, some recommendations are very specific because of the attack vectors we have discussed, while others reflect general disciplines. The reason they are all included here is simple: all of these will significantly improve your cloud security posture and ability to mitigate cloud attack vectors. So, please consider the top recommendations that follow to help any organization achieve success in the cloud and minimize risks to the business.

Recommended Security Disciplines:

- **Password and Secrets Management**: Control, record, monitor, and audit requests for administrative, root, or other privileged accounts and the launching of sensitive sessions. This control includes implementing session monitoring and performing keystroke logging and screen recording via privileged access management (PAM). Also, consider implementing just-in-time access to ensure credentialed access is finite and only given when the proper context and triggers are met.

- **Endpoint Privileged Management**: Privileged access and privileged account usage on all endpoints, whether in an office, home, or in the cloud, should be managed for privileged activity using the concepts of least privilege to ensure all activity is appropriate.

- **Identity Management**: Every identity and its associated accounts in the cloud should be managed and monitored. Follow the best practices for joiner, mover, and leaver, and ensure no rogue identities and accounts exist at any time.

- **Asset Management**: Security Basics 101 teaches us that, without a good asset inventory, cybersecurity professionals have no way to classify (risk, sensitivity, importance, etc.) and effectively protect assets. Operating in the cloud is no different. Asset management needs to include all assets, identities, accounts, roles, risk, data mapping, workflows, etc., to be effective in the cloud.

- **Vulnerability Management**: Ensure you have a robust vulnerability assessment process to continuously monitor for risks in the cloud. This process should be as close to real time as possible and link to a larger vulnerability and risk management program. In the cloud, there are multiple ways to do vulnerability management. Protection of applications and workloads are fundamental to this process.

- **Configuration Management**: Configuration management (including asset hardening) ensures that vulnerable default settings are addressed and security best practices are applied to all assets to make them threat resilient in the cloud. This process should be incorporated at the beginning of an asset's life cycle and measured throughout its usage to ensure configurations have not drifted or been tampered with.

- **Patch Management**: There is a difference between mitigating a risk and remediating a risk. Mitigation entails a simple change, with no new code applied. A remediation truly fixes the vulnerability by applying a software patch. In many cases, mitigating a risk stops a threat, but does not make the application less vulnerable. Only a remediation does that, and this is why a robust patch management process in the cloud is needed for all assets.

- **Penetration Testing**: While vulnerability management assesses and addresses risks, penetration testing proves they can be exploited. This difference has crucial implications for your cloud protection strategy. Penetration testing can prove that a risk is real and identify how flaws can be linked together as a part of the attack chain to breach an environment the same way a threat actor would.

- **Regulatory Compliance**: Everyone involved in the cloud should be aware of the risks in and to the cloud. Businesses should never consider regulatory compliance as a checkbox. Always strive to understand the intent of a control. Understanding what the requirement is, and the best way to meet the mandates, can make every cloud resource more secure. And, just remember, being compliant alone does not make you secure. Making your cloud implementation secure generally makes you compliant.

- **Architecture**: Review the architecture of your cloud implementation, and ensure that all the technology is appropriate and properly segmented. It is one thing to operate in the cloud and another to correctly deploy it. Having up-to-date architectures to model your security program from will help provide coverage for all the other recommendations we have made.

- **Education**: Training, training, training. Educating every and all identities that interact with the cloud about security and the risks is not only a compliance requirement, but is also a powerful strategy to minimize risk. It all starts with your people. If they are aware of what could happen, how it would happen, and how to prevent it, you can reduce cloud attack vectors to your business. Again, training, training, and more training (at least twice a year and mandatory for all new hires).

Specific Recommendations:

- **Standard User Accounts**: Enforce that all identities with access to cloud-based resources have a standard user account. Any identity that has an associated administrator or privileged account across should never use that account for daily work or maintenance. Standard user accounts should always follow the model of least privilege.

- **Never Share Identities, Accounts, or Credentials**: Identities, accounts, credentials, and associated secrets should never be shared with peers, vendors, contractors, or auditors. Sharing these resources just elevates the risk of a secret being misused and potentially leaked to a threat actor.

- **Never Reuse Passwords/Secrets**: If one resource is compromised, then every other resource with the same shared secret is at risk, even if the identity, account, or username is different.

- **No Hardcoded Secrets**: Secrets should be kept secret. They should never be in plain sight, no matter how they are stored, even if they are using strong encryption. Thus, eliminate hardcoded passwords in service accounts and automation tools, such as those supporting DevOps.

- **Vulnerabilities**: While vulnerability management is a required discipline, ensuring that security patches and mitigations are applied in a timely manager is critical. Using service-level agreements (SLA) to document and track the application of patches is a security best practice.

- **Break Glass**: If secrets need to be documented, they should be in an encrypted file and placed on a secured file system or locked away in a physical safe, as required based on business requirements.

- **Logging**: The ability to make all activity traceable (and not obfuscated from hackers) is key to correlating user activity to a single identity.

- **Minimize the Creation and Usage of Cloud Administrative or Root Accounts**: The lower the number of identities associated with privileged or administrative (root) accounts, the better. This lowers the privileged risk surface and provides better auditing for privileged activity.

- **Rotate Secrets**: Secrets should be managed and rotated periodically on a regular schedule. This keeps them from becoming stale and less likely to be leaked over time. Dynamic secrets or one-time passwords should be used for highly privileged accounts.

- **Ensure Secrets Are Complex:** Secrets should not be easily humanly readable. This keeps them from being copied, transcribed, or verbally discussed. The complexity needed should be based on the sensitivity of the access/account and the risk to that account.

- **Require Multi-factor Authentication:** Implement multi-factor authentication for access to all cloud resources. Full stop. If the login interface is available to everyone, then single-factor authentication is just not acceptable for businesses operating in the cloud. When executing the most sensitive commands or accessing sensitive data, consider stepping up the security and triggering to reauthenticate with multi-factor to be certain the identity is who they claim to be.

- **Implement the Principle of Least Privilege:** If an identity does not need access to resources, applications, or data in the cloud, remove their entitlements, privileges, permissions, and rights. Excessive privileges are a prime target for threat actors in the cloud.

- **Implement Behavioral Monitoring:** Implement technology based on advanced analytics, machine learning, and/or artificial intelligence, including advanced threat detection, to more accurately and quickly detect compromised identities and potential abuse of resources in the cloud.

CHAPTER 15

Conclusion

One of my (Morey) favorite memes about the cloud is a quote stating, "The cloud is mostly Linux servers, mostly." Now, if you are a science fiction movie fan, and like the movie *Aliens* (not the original, but the sequel), there is a scene where Newt says, "They mostly come out at night, mostly." Now imagine that same meme with Newt saying, in her voice and childlike horror, "The cloud is mostly Linux servers, mostly" – I think you will giggle, but also be legitimately frightened, just like Newt, of the risks in the cloud and what can happen if no one is monitoring your assets and you do not have the appropriate security controls to keep everything protected. That's the point of this book.

Cloud attack vectors can occur at anytime, anyplace in the cloud, and if no one is watching, a breach can occur and potentially be a game-over event for your organization. This, of course, is true for on-premises well. The more things change, the more they stay the same, and our philosophy for security best practices on-premise just needs to be translated to the cloud to be effective. The fact that Linux powers the vast majority of the cloud is proof that things are the same, but different, and we just need to adapt our strategy.

Some may consider securing the cloud to be an insurmountable undertaking, akin to "boiling the ocean." Cloud security does seem out of reach, or out least a distant hope, when you consider the rate at which cloud growth continues and when you keep in mind the number of breaches and the attack vectors that have been exploited in those breaches.

© Morey J. Haber, Brian Chappell, Christopher Hills 2022
M. J. Haber et al., *Cloud Attack Vectors*, https://doi.org/10.1007/978-1-4842-8236-6_15

As security professionals, there is far too much to understand about securing the cloud. We need to make sure that we do our own part and also hold those responsible and accountable with good intention. As I (Chris) have said many times, it's not what you "know" about that poses the greatest risk to your organization, it's what you "*don't*" know about. Securing the cloud is no different. Trying to understand what and how to secure everything needs to be our collective responsibility. Together, we can reduce the threat landscape and eliminate attack vectors, making the cloud safer for everyone.

As Morey and Chris have said, securing the cloud is a big task and a vitally important one, but I, Brian, will close with what I consider to be the most important thing to take away from this book. Don't be afraid of the problem, whether it's securing the cloud or anything, in fact. I firmly believe that many problems persist in our environments because, when looked at as a whole, the problem seems insurmountable. It's just too scary to even begin to tackle. Some of that is the result of scare tactics from less scrupulous vendors, but probably more so from the various media outlets who jockey for "eyes" through sensationalism. And some is simply the seeming enormity of the problem.

It's here I trot out my approach, what I call my "Big Ball of String" approach – so called because it feels as though I'm looking at the biggest ball of string you can imagine, with loose ends everywhere. It's too easy to get caught up looking for the best thread to pull to get the best return, but that leads to analysis paralysis. In these situations, I reach for the nearest thread and pull on it. Then the next, and so on. Eventually, the problem becomes manageable, and I've made progress at every step. Each thread is simple and can't be scary. The solutions for each thread should also be simple. This isn't always easy, either, but keeping each step simple will result in the whole being greater than the sum of its parts. You might not see it at first, but believe me, it's there.

We hope this book empowers you with clearer insight into the problem of securing the cloud, and with this insight, you now also have the tools to address the problem within your organization and for the cloud vendors you license.

APPENDIX A

Sample Security Assessment Questionnaire (SAQ)

The following is a sample security questionnaire that covers the basic requirements needed by any organization looking to host solutions, of any type, in the cloud.

Control Number	Control Depth	Question	Response (Yes, No, N/A)	Reference Information
1. Cybersecurity Management and Personnel Security				
1	Organizational Security Controls	Is there a dedicated information security organization responsible for security functions, including managing the security program?		

(continued)

© Morey J. Haber, Brian Chappell, Christopher Hills 2022
M. J. Haber et al., *Cloud Attack Vectors*, https://doi.org/10.1007/978-1-4842-8236-6

Control Number	Control Depth	Question	Response (Yes, No, N/A)	Reference Information
2	Organizational Security Controls	Is there an information security program in place that has been approved by management and communicated to appropriate employees?		
2.1	Organizational Security Controls	Is the information security policy reviewed annually?		
3	Organizational Security Controls	Is a background screening performed prior to allowing constituent (employees and subcontractors) access to systems and data in scope? Please describe the scope (credit, criminal, education, employment, etc.).		
4	Organizational Security Controls	Has the organization established and documented a data governance classification scheme with multiple sensitivity tiers?		
4.1	Organizational Security Controls	Have handling procedures, including encryption, been established to support each classification scheme?		

Control Number	Control Depth	Question	Response (Yes, No, N/A)	Reference Information
5	Organizational Security Controls	Does the organization have acceptable use policy, outlining permissible use of computing equipment?		
6	Organizational Security Controls	Does the organization have a nondisclosure agreement (NDA) and/or confidentiality agreement, outlining permissible use of data including customer data?		
6.1	Organizational Security Controls	Are all employees and subcontractors required to sign an NDA/confidentiality agreement prior to being granted access to customer data?		
7	Organizational Security Controls	Does the organization perform self-assessments of its internal controls in the area of information security for purposes of verifying compliance with its information security program, as well as with any legal, regulatory, or industry requirements?		

(*continued*)

Control Number	Control Depth	Question	Response (Yes, No, N/A)	Reference Information
8	Organizational Security Controls	Are independent audits performed to ensure compliance with applicable regulatory requirements?		
9	Organizational Security Controls	Do you have an independent assessment of your information security controls performed annually? (This might include a SOC/SSAE-16 report, internal audit, security assessment, vulnerability, or penetration assessment conducted by an independent third party.)		

2. IT Network Security

Control Number	Control Depth	Question	Response (Yes, No, N/A)	Reference Information
1	Organizational Security Controls	Is there an asset management policy or program in place that includes both hardware and software?		
2	Organizational Security Controls	Does the organization have formally documented hardening guides for assets deployed within your organization (on-premise and cloud)?		

Control Number	Control Depth	Question	Response (Yes, No, N/A)	Reference Information
3	Organizational Security Controls	Are firewalls in use for all internal connections?		
4	Organizational Security Controls	Are firewalls in use for all external connections?		
5	Organizational Security Controls	Are firewalls used to segment internal networks?		
6	Organizational Security Controls	Does the organization have a web application firewall (WAF) in place?		
7	Organizational Security Controls	Is your network separated with DMZ segments for devices that initiate outbound traffic to the Internet?		
8	Organizational Security Controls	Does your network and production systems limit communications with known malicious IP addresses (block list) or limit access only to trusted sites (allow list)?		
9	Organizational Security Controls	Will customer-applicable systems and data traverse wireless networks?		

(continued)

Control Number	Control Depth	Question	Response (Yes, No, N/A)	Reference Information
10	Organizational Security Controls	Is remote access to systems and networks containing customer data permitted? If so, how?		
10.1	Organizational Security Controls	Is multi-factor authentication required for remote access? Describe the method.		
11	Organizational Security Controls	Has the organization implemented network monitoring or a network access control device (NAC) such that you can detect when an unauthorized machine connects to the network?		

3. Data Protection and Recovery

1	Organizational Security Controls	Has the organization implemented a data loss prevention solution to monitor and control the flow of data within the network containing customer data? Network or host based?		

Control Number	Control Depth	Question	Response (Yes, No, N/A)	Reference Information
2	Organizational Security Controls	Is scoped data sent or received electronically? Has this workflow been mapped out?		
3	Organizational Security Controls	Is scoped data sent or received via physical media or paper?		
4	Organizational Security Controls	Is the appropriate transport layer security in place for scoped data?		
5	Organizational Security Controls	Is data layer encryption in place for in scope data?		
6	Organizational Security Controls	Is customer data, including manipulated data, reports, or additional information obtained sent back to the customer securely?		
7	Organizational Security Controls	Does the organization allow customer data to be copied to endpoint devices (laptops, workstations)?		
8	Organizational Security Controls	Has the organization deployed approved hard drive encryption software to protect laptops?		

(continued)

Control Number	Control Depth	Question	Response (Yes, No, N/A)	Reference Information
9	Organizational Security Controls	Has the organization deployed approved hard drive encryption software to protect mobile devices?		
10	Organizational Security Controls	Does the organization allow customer data to be copied to mobile media (USB drives, CDs, DVDs, external drives, etc.)?		
11	Organizational Security Controls	Is there a documented policy for business continuity and disaster recovery that has been approved by management, communicated to appropriate constituents and an owner to maintain and review the policy?		
12	Organizational Security Controls	Are system backups of scoped systems and data performed?		
4. Physical Security				
1	Organizational Security Controls	Does the organization have a physical security policy covering scoped systems and data?		

Control Number	Control Depth	Question	Response (Yes, No, N/A)	Reference Information
2	Organizational Security Controls	Does the organization have a service organization controls (SOC) report that covers physical and environmental security controls of the data center where scoped systems and data reside?		

5. User Access and Authentication Management

1	Organizational Security Controls	Does the organization have a formally documented access control policy in place that covers adding, changing, and removing users from its network and systems?		
2	Organizational Security Controls	Are unique user IDs assigned to all employees, contracts, and machine-based identities used for access?		
3	Organizational Security Controls	Are user access rights reviewed at least annually?		

(continued)

Control Number	Control Depth	Question	Response (Yes, No, N/A)	Reference Information
4	Organizational Security Controls	Does the organization have a formally documented password policy controlling length, strength, history, and account lockout for its network and systems?		

6. Vulnerability Management

Control Number	Control Depth	Question	Response (Yes, No, N/A)	Reference Information
1	Organizational Security Controls	Are systems and applications patched appropriately? What are your patching service-level agreements with the business?		
2	Organizational Security Controls	Are vulnerability scans performed on scoped systems and data?		
3	Organizational Security Controls	Are external penetration tests performed at least annually covering scoped systems and data?		

Control Number	Control Depth	Question	Response (Yes, No, N/A)	Reference Information
4	Organizational Security Controls	Is there an operational change management/change control policy or program that has been approved by management, communicated to appropriate constituents and an owner to maintain and review the policy?		

7. IT Security Monitoring and Response

Control Number	Control Depth	Question	Response (Yes, No, N/A)	Reference Information
1	Organizational Security Controls	Have you established a program, standard, or strategy for logging and monitoring suspicious activity?		
2	Organizational Security Controls	Does the organization employ an intrusion detection (IDS) or intrusion prevention (IPS) system?		
3	Organizational Security Controls	Are security event logs captured for all applications and solutions provided to the customer (successful and failed logon, admin activities)?		

(continued)

Control Number	Control Depth	Question	Response (Yes, No, N/A)	Reference Information
4	Organizational Security Controls	Are all logs sent to a centralized logging or Security Information and Event Management (SIEM) solution?		
5	Organizational Security Controls	Is there an antivirus/malware policy or program (workstations, servers, mobile devices) that has been approved by management, communicated to appropriate constituents and an owner to maintain and review the policy?		
5.1	Organizational Security Controls	Is the interval between the availability of a new signature update and its deployment no longer than 24 hours?		
6	Organizational Security Controls	Is there a documented policy for incident management that has been approved by management, communicated to appropriate constituents and reviewed as part of the annual review process?		

Control Number	Control Depth	Question	Response (Yes, No, N/A)	Reference Information
8. Supplier Management				
1	Organizational Security Controls	Do subcontractors have access to systems within the scope and applicable data (backup vendors, service providers, equipment support maintenance, software maintenance vendors, data recovery vendors, etc.)?		
2	Organizational Security Controls	Are there contractual controls to ensure that personal information shared with third parties is limited to defined parameters for access, use, and disclosure? If yes, describe. If no, explain reason.		
3	Organizational Security Controls	Is there a documented vendor/subcontractor management process in place for the selection and oversight of third-party vendors?		

(continued)

Control Number	Control Depth	Question	Response (Yes, No, N/A)	Reference Information
9. IT Application Management				
1	Organizational Security Controls	Is there a formal Software Development Life Cycle (SDLC) process?		
2	Organizational Security Controls	Is source code reviewed to ensure adherence to the programming standards, checking of design/logic, removal of dead code, and checking of critical algorithms (code walkthroughs)?		
3	Organizational Security Controls	Does the organization allow the use of open source software?		
4	Organizational Security Controls	Is there an automated secure source code review for all code prior to promotion to production?		
5	Organizational Security Controls	Are mobile applications developed and used for the in-scope data?		
6	Organizational Security Controls	Does mobile application development follow the same secure coding procedures as software?		

Control Number	Control Depth	Question	Response (Yes, No, N/A)	Reference Information
10. Solution-Specific Controls				
1	Solution-Specific Controls	Are all customer users provisioned to systems in scope based on job function or role, including administrator access?		
2	Solution-Specific Controls	Does the organization have formally documented termination procedures in place that cover customer stakeholders?		
3	Solution-Specific Controls	Are access reviews performed periodically for the solution provided to the customer?		
4	Solution-Specific Controls	If your organization is responsible for access, do you, in collaboration with the customer, review user accounts?		
5	Solution-Specific Controls	Is Single Sign On (SSO) available for the application provided to the customer?		
5.1	Solution-Specific Controls	Has SSO been implemented for the customer, vendors, or third-party organizations?		

(continued)

449

Control Number	Control Depth	Question	Response (Yes, No, N/A)	Reference Information
6	Solution-Specific Controls	Do inactive sessions time out for solutions provided to the customer? What is that timeout period?		
7	Solution-Specific Controls	Do systems used by customer stakeholders have password policies that meet the following requirements?– Minimum 12 characters.– Three-character types required for complexity.– Previous 12 passwords cannot be reused.– Maximum age is 90 days.– Accounts lock after more than five attempts in 24 hours.		
8	Solution-Specific Controls	Is self-reset allowed for passwords that have been locked or forgotten?		
9	Solution-Specific Controls	Are passwords encrypted at rest for the solution?		

Control Number	Control Depth	Question	Response (Yes, No, N/A)	Reference Information
10	Solution-Specific Controls	Is multi-factor authentication an option or required for the solution provided to the customer?		
11	Solution-Specific Controls	Have you developed a mobile application that is or may be used by customer stakeholders?		
11.1	Solution-Specific Controls	Has the organization had a mobile application penetration test performed on the solutions in scope in the past 12 months?		
12	Organizational Security Controls	Are application penetration tests performed at least annually on any in-scope applications?		

11. Cyber Insurance

Control Number	Control Depth	Question	Response (Yes, No, N/A)	Reference Information
1	Organizational Security Controls	Does your organization have insurance coverage for a cyber-related incident?		
1.1	Organizational Security Controls	What is the total coverage for cyber insurance in US dollars?		

451

APPENDIX B

Cloud Service Provider Questionnaire

This sample cloud service provider questionnaire highlights some of the most important features that your provider should be able to deliver. These questions build a foundation for selecting a vendor and their basic security foundation. It is important to note: if a cloud service provider does not have capabilities to meet some of these criteria, it is not a showstopper. Rather, you may need to implement your own security controls to mitigate the risk or leverage a third-party solution to fill the gap. Finally, you may need to add your own requirements based on your industry vertical to ensure compliance with initiatives like HIPAA or geolocations to manage GDPR requirements.

© Morey J. Haber, Brian Chappell, Christopher Hills 2022
M. J. Haber et al., *Cloud Attack Vectors*, https://doi.org/10.1007/978-1-4842-8236-6

Questions	Verification	Comments
Is the cloud provider root or administrator account used for managing all other accounts and instances?	Access the administrative account for the service and verify access and visibility to all accounts and instances.	
Are different accounts required for different development stages? (Dev, staging, production)	Access the Management Console for the cloud service provider and determine if there are separate roles, by default, for different development stages.	
Is a dedicated account being used for security audit and logging functions?	Access the Management Console and navigate to the security section for logging and audit reports. Verify role-based access can be applied.	
Is a shared email alias/group being used for the root account for each instance?	Access the Management Console for the cloud service provider and navigate to the identity, account, and profile section. Verify that a common email can be applied to all root accounts for notifications and the other email accounts can be added to notify owners.	
Does each root account have multi-factor authentication (MFA) enabled?	In the Management Console for the cloud service provider, verify root and all other administrative accounts have MFA enabled.	
Has the root account been used in the last seven days?	In the Management Console, create an alert or execute a report to verify that root accounts are not being used for daily activity.	

Questions	Verification	Comments
Are encryption at rest features implemented for all data stores?	Verify encryption at rest is available for multiple data store types. Within the Management Console, verify that encryption is enabled and applied to all types using the standard applicable to at least the compliance regulation governing your business.	
Is volume encryption implemented for volumes and snapshots?	Verify the encryption status of each volume and snapshot in the management view adheres to your current policy. This will be shown as an attribute for each selection.	
Is SAML-based Single Sign On being used for identity and access management?	In the configuration for access to the services and Management Console, verify SSO is enabled via SAML and denied for direct access.	
Are any identities configured with console access?	By viewing role-based access of identities or executing a report, verify no users have unauthorized console access. This should be absolutely limited.	
Does any identity or account have access keys configured for programmatic access?	By viewing role-based access of identities, or executing a report, verify no users have API access. This should be absolutely limited to machine-to-machine identities only. For some platforms, this may need to be reported using a script.	

(continued)

455

Questions	Verification	Comments
Does any identity or account have access keys that have not been used in > 90 days? (Or never used)	In the Management Console, create an alert or execute a report to verify that no identities or accounts have been stale for longer than 90 days. Note this value may vary based on individual business requirements.	
Does any identity or account have access keys that have not been rotated in > 90 days?	In the Management Console, create an alert or execute a report to verify that no identities or accounts have access keys that are older than 90 days. Note, 90 days should be your maximum and keys may need to be rotated more frequently, based on your business requirements.	
Does any identity or account have a business or technology role that has not been used in > 90 days? (Or never used)	In the Management Console, create an alert or execute a report to verify that no identities or accounts stale role-based access greater than 90 days.	
Do all relational database services (RDS) instances use identity-based authentication for database access?	Verify in the Management Console for all cloud service provider databases that access is only allowed via identity-based accounts.	
Does the cloud service provider support native secret and credential storage?	Verify the provider has a secret and credential storage mechanism for automated processes.	

Questions	Verification	Comments
Does the cloud service provider support third-party secret and credential storage from a privileged access management vendor?	Verify the provider has a secret and credential storage mechanism that can be integrated with a third-party privileged access management vendor to secure privileged access.	
Do any security groups permit non-HTTP service access from the Internet?	Verify that all services for management, remote access, APIs, etc., are disabled from Internet access, and all private access is encrypted.	
Are private subnets being used for internal servers, databases, and other resources?	Verify that management and database access is private and locked down via VPC.	
Are all RDS instances in private subnets and not publicly accessible?	Verify in the Management Console that all relational database services are only bound to internal addresses.	
Are security groups for outbound network access implemented for each VPC?	In the Management Console, identify within VPC services that the networks are locked down for private and public access, especially around outbound communications.	
For AWS only, do any S3 buckets permit open access permissions or allow access to any authenticated AWS user? Are block public access settings enabled for all S3 buckets?	In the Management Console, select the Trusted Advisor service. Once the page is updated, it will show the Amazon S3 Bucket Permissions action, which will detail S3 buckets that permit open access.	

(continued)

Questions	Verification	Comments
Is the cloud service provider enabled in all active and applicable regions?	Verify that services are only available in desired regions and that future target regions are supported. Disable any region for which the business is not ready to service yet.	
Are activity logging, data events, and access/ authentication logs enabled for all instances and services?	Verify logging is enabled for all services to provide indicators of compromise and forensics for daily operations. All collected data should be centralized using a cloud-native tool or a SIEM.	
Is intrusion monitoring enabled in all active regions?	Ensure intrusion prevention and firewall logging are enabled in all regions. The results should be centralized and combined with activity and authentication logging.	
Has an incident response plan been created and tested?	Obtain confirmation that the cloud service provider has an incident response plan and it has been tested on a regular basis.	
Verify the backup procedures and recovery service–level agreements from the provider.	Obtain confirmation that a backup solution has been implemented and that it is tested to recovery service–level agreements for restoration.	
Are instances regularly patched using system manager or another solution?	Obtain confirmation that a patch management solution has been implemented for all instances.	

Questions	Verification	Comments
Are hosted servers and databases accessed through a secure remote access solution?	Obtain confirmation that internal servers and databases are accessed using a bastion host or other remote access solution. Default access via RDP, VNC, and SSH should never be publicly used.	

Index

A

ABC-RNN model, 405

Access control lists (ACL), 20, 224–226

Account
architectures, 399, 400
cloud definitions, 53, 54

Active Directory (AD), 45, 98

Agency authorization process, 371

Agency process, 369, 371

Agent technology, 236–238, 243

Alibaba Cloud, 39

Aliyun, 39, 42

Amazon Elastic Compute Cloud (Amazon EC2), 95

Amazon Web Services (AWS), 33–36, 48, 95

Analytics, 28, 83, 96, 125

Anti-malware software, 175, 341

API keys, 56

API scanning, 294, 296

API side scanning technology, 236, 237

Application, attack vectors, 122

Application programming interfaces (API), 154–156

Application security, 23, 135, 319, 327

Application-to-database (A2D) communications, 58

App-to-app (A2A), 58

Architectures, 375
accounts, 399, 400
cloud native, 392–395
ephemeral implementations, 398
hybrid, 395–397
instances, 400, 401
privileges, 401, 402
secrets, 398, 399
zero trust, 376–382, 387, 392

Artificial bee colony (ABC) algorithm, 404, 405

Artificial intelligence (AI), 30, 281–284

Asset management, 107–110, 427
cloud accounts, 113
domain administrator accounts, 111
embedded credentials, accounts with, 115, 116
management solutions, 112
nonhuman automation accounts, 111, 112
service accounts, 112, 113
specialty accounts, 114

© Morey J. Haber, Brian Chappell, Christopher Hills 2022
M. J. Haber et al., *Cloud Attack Vectors*, https://doi.org/10.1007/978-1-4842-8236-6

D

Printed in the United States
by Baker & Taylor Publisher Services

Printed in the United States
by Baker & Taylor Publisher Services